HARVARD ECONOMIC STUDIES

VOLUME CXVII

The studies in this series are published by the Department of Economics of Harvard University. The Department does not assume responsibility for the views expressed.

INVESTMENT

AND

PRODUCTION

A Study in the Theory
of the Capital-Using Enterprise

VERNON L. SMITH

1966

HARVARD UNIVERSITY PRESS

Cambridge, Massachusetts

To my wife, Joyce

Preface

This book owes its origin to my Ph.D. dissertation, "A Theoretical and Empirical Inquiry into the Economic Replacement of Capital Equipment" (Harvard, 1955). However, very little of the original thesis has survived the rapid obsolescence of my own thinking to find its way into the present volume. Only Chapters V and IX make any extensive use of material contained in the original thesis. My major concern almost from the beginning has been to develop a unified theory of production and investment including the problem of equipment "replacement." Much remains to be done in this direction, but I feel that the present state of this work is sufficiently advanced to warrant publication of a book. It is not a treatise on investment theory. I have written on certain aspects of the theory on which I think I have something to contribute, and which I have considered to be inadequately or incompletely explored in the literature.

I wish to thank the Purdue Research Foundation for a grant during the summer of 1958, the Ford Foundation for a Faculty Research Fellowship for 1958–59, and the Institute for Quantitative Research at Purdue for support during the academic year 1959–60. The generous support of these organizations has made this book possible.

I am indebted to Wassily Leontief for first inspiring my interest in capital theory and for first urging me in the directions which have culminated in the present work. I would also like to acknowledge the assistance of E. T. Weiler and R. L. Stucky in helping me to obtain research support and providing a constant source of encouragement and help in the preparation of the manuscript. I am also indebted to R. W. Clower and W. J. Baumol who read the manuscript before final revision and provided many valuable comments and suggestions which have improved the plan and exposition of the book.

Finally, it would be difficult to exaggerate the importance of the contribution of my valuable and efficient secretary, Marilyn Schweizer, who typed the manuscript, proofed it, standardized the footnotes, traced or drew the diagrams, and handled all correspondence.

Acknowledgment is made to the editors of the *International Economic Review*, and the *Quarterly Journal of Economics*, for permission to reproduce portions of previously published articles. Chapter XI borrows heavily from articles appearing in these two journals.

Of course, none of the above organizations or individuals bears any responsibility for the conclusions, opinions, or errors contained herein.

Vernon L. Smith

Lafayette, Indiana
August, 1960

Contents

Chapter I

The Problem of Capital Goods
in the Theory of Production

1. Introduction

Economic theorists generally assume that a major economic goal of the production transformation process is the maximization of some consistent concept of "long-run" profits. This includes, as a subgoal, the minimization of a similarly appropriate concept of "long-run" costs. In achieving such goals the large number of decisions required by the firm fall roughly into the following interdependent categories: (1) the selection of a most profitable product or product mix to be produced, (2) the selection of best short-run day-to-day operating procedures, including the consumption rates of current or operating inputs to the productive process, (3) the determination of the optimal structure and levels of physical investment in inventories and in durable plant and equipment goods, and (4) the timing of "replacements" or reinvestments in inventories and in durable capital goods, taking into account the effect of such factors as deterioration, maintenance, and obsolescence.

There exists a great deal of theoretical and problem-oriented applied literature covering short-run operating and inventory decision rules. The Walras-Wicksteed marginal productivity theory of production is primarily a theory of short-run operating technique, though the inclusion of capital "service" inputs in some versions of the theory constitutes a clear attempt to recognize the necessity of making capital equipment decisions. However, the marginal productivity theory is distinctly vague concerning the relationship between decisions involving the "services" of capital and decisions involving the quantity and timing of the purchase of individual durable instruments of production. Similarly, the more recent development of linear programming is almost exclusively concerned with short-run operating problems in which non-inventory investment levels are fixed and form a major class of constraints under which optimal decisions are obtained.[1,2]

The body of thinking on investment theory is contained very largely in the literature of equipment analysis [3] and in the work of Friedrich and Vera Lutz.[4] Equipment analysis, as it is found in the work of Terborgh and others, is concerned with the economic replacement of particular machine and facility items. This literature has developed independently of the neoclassical Walras-Wicksteed theory of production, and modern activity analysis. Similarly, the theory of investment as found in the writings of the Lutzes is quite independent of the general body of production theory. For example, the Lutzes argue that the moment durable goods are introduced, the usual production function analysis can no longer be employed unless "time" is intro-

[1] See the collection of papers on applied linear programming in Part I of E. H. Bowman and R. B. Fetter, *Analyses of Industrial Operations* (Chicago, Richard D. Irwin, 1959).

[2] There are some important exceptions to this statement such as Alan Manne, *Scheduling of Petroleum Refining Operations* (Cambridge: Harvard University Press, 1956), and Bowman and Fetter, Chap. 4.

[3] See George Terborgh, *Dynamic Equipment Policy* (New York: McGraw-Hill, 1949).

[4] Friedrich and Vera Lutz, *The Theory of Investment of the Firm* (Princeton: Princeton University Press, 1951).

duced as an independent variable, but their analysis makes only slight use of such a concept of the production function.[5] Since the literature of investment and replacement theory is not explicit concerning the role of the production function, or other such technological constraints, there remains the important question of the relationship between the theory of investment and the theory of production of the firm. It would not appear to be likely that the firm's investment decisions are separable from the problem of choosing the optimal short-run production technique, with marginal productivity considerations applying to the latter but not to the former. Casual observation would seem to suggest that the theorist should at least be prepared for the possibility that the typical firm or productive process is confronted with a variety of substitutable inputs, including flow inputs whose consumption is contemporaneous with current production, inputs of intermediate durability requiring regular maintenance and replacement, and highly durable inputs such as pipelines and structures. The major characteristics of many, if not most, durable capital inputs are that (1) their presence is required if production is to occur, (2) there is no significantly discernible "consumption" of such inputs that can be associated with the production transformation process, and (3) such inputs can often be considered to be freely variable in amount (size) prior to installation, but, once installed, can only be reduced in physical amount by abandonment (or temporary idling). These important characteristics — particularly the phenomenon of "irreversibility" — will form the core of our analysis of the capital goods problem in production planning.

The central purpose of this study, then, is to explore the empirical and theoretical nature of the interdependence between "short-run" current account production decisions and "long-run" investment planning, with special reference to

[5] Indeed, they seem to deny the possibility (or at least the probability) of substitution between capital goods and flow inputs such as labor. See Lutz, *Theory of Investment of the Firm*, p. 7, n. 10.

the effect of technological considerations upon this relationship. This will involve the development of a stock-flow theory of cost and production which has imbedded within it the problem of optimal capital replacement policy.

2. *Summary of the Analysis*

Most of our analysis rests upon the hypothesis that many processes of production exhibit a production function defined over a class of imperfectly substitutable inputs. In general, these inputs include both current inputs and the physical stocks of certain capital inputs of varying degrees of durability or life. Such a production function, relating the rate of output to the consumption rates of current inputs and the stock levels of capital inputs, provides a crucial connecting link between "short-" and "long-run" decisions over the firm's planning horizon. We begin therefore, in Chapter II, with an empirical investigation of the production function in several simple, but real, production processes. The emphasis is upon revealing certain fundamental mechanisms of substitution that can be expected to prevail in a wide variety of production processes, rather than upon the complete specification of all input-output possibilities for any particular commercial operating process. By studying a few actual processes it is also possible to determine the manner in which capital goods can be expected to enter the production function and how such goods can most usefully be measured. Much of the literature of economics treats "capital" in production in such an abstract way that it is difficult, if not impossible, to relate such concepts to observable experience. The concepts of "capital services" and "the period of production" are excellent examples.

In Chapter II a study is made of various "engineering" processes such as the production and transmission of electricity, the transmission of gas, a multiple-pass regeneration process typical of the chemical and food industries, and a typical batch reactor process in the chemical industry. In each case substitution possibilities arise among one or more current and capital inputs. The mechanisms of substitution are such that the capital goods must be measured in terms of some appropriate size variable such as pipe or cable cross-sectional area, reactor volume capacity, boiler heating surface area, and so forth. Thus, in the case of an electrical transmission cable, using "more" capital means using a larger cable. The larger the cable, the less energy loss in the line and, therefore, the less energy input required to deliver any specified level of output.

The fundamental hypothesis growing out of this empirical examination is that of the stock-flow production function. If there is one current output, y, one current input, x_1, and two capital inputs of "size" X_2 and X_3, this function can be written

$$y = f(x_1, X_2, X_3).$$

Furthermore, the capital inputs are freely variable in considering hypothetical alternative production design plans, but once such stock inputs are installed, they can no longer be varied except by installing parallel facilities or by replacement. If X_3 is pipe size, then once this "capacity" of the transmission line is installed, an increase can be effected only by installing a parallel line or by replacing with a larger line.

In some processes there exist substitution possibilities between current and capital inputs in which a capital input is best measured by simply counting the number of units of a standard size that are employed. As an example, a simple truck maintenance queuing process is studied in Chapter II in which the number of trucks, X_2, is a substitute for x_1, the man-hour rate of consumption of repair labor.

An important characteristic of all the long-run production functions that are studied is the absence of decreasing returns to scale; they all show increasing or constant returns to scale.

Chapters III, IV, and VI are concerned with a reformulation of the theory of production and the theory of competitive markets based upon the stock-flow production function growing out of the empirical studies in Chapter II. Chapter III develops the theory of production and of competitive markets for capital goods of infinite durability. Chapter IV develops the analysis for capital goods whose life is fixed technologically, while Chapter VI is concerned with capital goods subject to deterioration and obsolescence, and whose life is an economic decision. The tools of comparative statics are employed throughout these chapters.

Since capital goods normally cannot be continuously expanded or contracted once they are installed, an important part of firm decision-making is to determine (1) the conditions under which a given installation is to be augmented by a parallel unit or replaced by a larger unit, and (2) the size of the parallel or replacement unit. Using the Kuhn-Tucker conditions for optimality, this problem is explored in some detail in Chapter III for capital goods that are of infinite physical life. These technological considerations affect the pricing of durable goods in the input market and the supply responses of an industry in the output markets. The existing stock-flow theory [6] of the pricing of durable goods has application here provided that the appropriate adjustments are made for the "lumpiness" of capital investment decisions.

The fact that capital goods, once installed, are not continuously expansible is an important consideration in the supply responses of an industry. For the polar case of infinitely durable goods, the analysis of Chapter III shows how such phenomena introduce path-dependent "hysteresis" effects in an industry's supply behavior. The conditions of supply at any time are shown to depend upon the whole history of demand changes in that industry, since each increase in demand above a previous "long-run" equilibrium point causes new facilities to be constructed in parallel with existing facilities. As long as the existing facilities have any positive value productivity they will be priced at a level at which it pays the industry to hold the entire stock. The resulting product supply conditions at any time are there-

---

[6] See R. W. Clower, "An Investigation into the Dynamics of Investment," *American Economic Review*, XLIV (March 1954), 64–81.

fore different from what they would be if the existing demand had prevailed since the industry began. In the latter case, if we have increasing returns to scale, each firm would have found it profitable to build a single large facility.[7]

Chapter IV considers the case of capital goods with a fixed life. As soon as the possibilities of replacement are introduced, the irreversibility effects analyzed in Chapter III become less severe. Eventually, through replacement, it is possible for the firms in an industry to reinvest in capital facilities whose size is compatible with any level of demand. In this case it is possible to derive from micro-economic decision theory both the asset demand and the replacement flow demand of an industry for a durable input. The stock-flow theory of the pricing of durable goods is thereby integrated with the theory of the firm. This stock-flow market model is also extended to consider simultaneously the market for both used and new equipment. The result is an explicit stock-flow competitive theory of the pricing of used as well as new durable assets.

Chapter V is concerned with economic replacement policy. The main objective here is to prepare the way for the integration of replacement and production theories that is attempted in Chapter VI. This requires some modifications in received replacement theory. Heretofore, replacement theory has been concerned very largely with determining the life of a machine that will maximize its net revenue. The procedure of allocating various age-variable revenue and cost components to a "machine" unit obscures the relationship between the replacement decision on the one side and demand considerations and the theory of production on the other. For example, suppose it is argued that a machine should be replaced because a new one can produce twice the output of the old and can therefore earn twice the revenue. It is not correct to burden the old machine with the "earnings" of the new one if they both produce qualitatively the same product. If, in fact, it pays to double the

---

[7] It is assumed that the size of the individual firm is limited by capital rationing, legal or risk considerations which are given.

scale of production, this should be done at lowest cost, which in turn may require the purchase of a second old machine or perhaps a new one of equal capacity. The problem of expansion is a question of scale which cannot be solved without introducing demand considerations, and has nothing to do per se with replacement. In Chapter V it is argued that pure replacement decisions are fundamentally concerned with minimizing the cost of producing any given level of output. Replacement, like choice of input-output technique is concerned with obtaining the lowest possible total cost function. Certainly the process of buying new equipment and discarding old equipment may change the scale of output, but if it pays to buy the new equipment it is because that is the cheapest way to produce the new output level. There may be many ways of increasing the scale of output other than by replacing the old equipment with new equipment.

A great deal is made of this simple — perhaps obvious — point because (1) the literature of replacement theory is not clear regarding the assumptions that are being made concerning demand or output, and (2) it is necessary to be clear on this point before it becomes apparent how replacement theory can be integrated with production theory. The general view of replacement policy in Chapters V and VI is that replacement is part of the problem of minimizing the cost of producing a given output. In the case of equipment whose deterioration and obsolescence can be measured in terms of maintenance and servicing costs the replacement decision becomes a problem of determining the lowest rental or flow cost of capital to the process. In this special case replacement policy becomes independent of input policy, but input policy is not independent of replacement policy since the latter determines the "price" of the capital input. By "input policy" we refer to the class of substitutable inputs appearing in the production function. Maintenance inputs in this case constitute part of the "logistics" support given the stock of capital and therefore part of its rental cost.

There is at least one important circumstance under which

the problem of cost minimization cannot be separated from profit maximization with respect to the replacement decision. This is the case in which equipment is subject to cost-reducing technical improvements *and* the firm regularly adjusts its price-output policy at the same point in time that old equipment is replaced by new. Cost minimization can be separated from profit maximization, as in the conventional theory of the firm, if price-output decisions are timed independently of equipment replacement decisions.

Chapter VI derives simultaneous conditions on the consumption level of current input, the stock of capital, and the economic life of capital, such that the discounted current account cost of producing a given flow of output is minimized. Chapter VI also explores the "short-" and "long-run" responses of the firm to once-for-all increases in output under cost minimization, and once-for-all increases in demand under profit maximization. One of the decision variables is the life of the incumbent capital equipment. This variable tells us how long is the "short-run." The result is an explicit theoretical analysis of the Marshallian concepts of short- and long-run decisions.

Also in Chapter VI the market for a durable input with variable life is investigated. The analysis parallels that of Chapter IV for durable goods with fixed life.

All the analyses of Chapters IV–VI are predicated upon the assumption that equipment life is not directly a parameter in the production function. Appendix 6A develops a simple process in which the life of equipment, L, appears in the production function along with the consumption of a current input, and the number of equipment units, X_2, that is, $y = f(x_1, X_2, L)$. The example is obtained from a modification of the truck-queuing process discussed in Chapter II. In this case the economic life of equipment is inseparably bound up with the problem of least-cost choice of technique. Appendix 6 briefly generalizes the formal conditions for optimality, contained in Chapters III–VI, for the case of $n + m$ substitutable inputs of which n are current and m are capital stock inputs.

Chapter VII qualifies the decision theory of Chapters III, IV, and VI by introducing explicitly the phenomenon of capital rationing. Both the firm's working capital to meet book credit requirements and its fixed capital needs are recognized in a simple static model. The analysis provides a conceptual means of integrating asset and balance sheet considerations with the theory of investment and production of the firm. The firm's problem is now viewed as one of minimizing cost or maximizing profit under a constraint on the total money capital available. Part of the problem of choosing a best input mix becomes one of obtaining an optimal allocation of money capital between fixed and working capital uses. By including book credit in the analysis, the possibility of negative as well as positive working capital requirements is introduced. This case has some intellectual novelty in that working capital becomes a source of funds to meet long-term capital needs. The Kuhn-Tucker conditions continue to provide the main tool of analysis.

An important body of applied production planning problems arises in the engineering literature, usually under the title of "engineering economy." This literature has developed outside the framework of the Walras-Wicksteed theory of production. Generally, the study of engineering economy has been highly case-oriented and the methods of solution have not made use of such concepts as the production function and marginal productivity. Such concepts, however, are implicit in engineering economy problems. The purpose of Chapter VIII is to derive the relationship between the "economic balance" theory of production planning used by the engineer and the modified (in the sense of being explicit about capital goods) marginal productivity theory of Chapters III–VI. Two very simple classical engineering economy decision problems are discussed in detail — the problems of conductor size and insulation thickness — and numerous additional examples are cited. Many of the processes for which production functions were derived in Chapter II have been analyzed in the engineering economy literature. In all these cases the "economic balance" methods of the engineer yield solutions equivalent to our marginal productivity analysis. These provide strong direct evidence in favor of the hypothesis that (at least some) firms follow optimal policies in the choice of production-investment technique. Often these problems of engineering economy production design involve only a single stage and a relatively small part of the over-all production planning problem in a complicated process. For example, a typical process involves the operation of several subprocesses in series. It is shown in Chapter VIII that if marginal cost or internal efficiency pricing is used to value all intermediate inputs (outputs), the engineer will obtain an over-all optimum by solving a sequence of partial "economic balance" problems, one for each production stage or subprocess. However, the required efficiency prices, even in the simple case considered, can only be obtained by designing all stages simultaneously.

The best-known decision rule in business practice for the global allocation of capital among alternative investment projects is the pay-off requirement. In Chapter IX a rational theory of capital allocation is developed and interpreted in terms of two concepts of the pay-off period — the net profit pay-off and the cash flow pay-off. The cash flow pay-off is the most common concept in business practice.

By translating a set of Kuhn-Tucker marginal profitability rules for optimal capital allocation into a set of marginal cash flow pay-off rules for optimal capital allocation, it is shown that the pay-off rules of business practice have the form and structure of optimal rules. Since the optimal rules contain certain parameters, and since the rules of business practice vary with different firms and conditions, the question arises whether the variation in business practice can be qualitatively related to variations in the parameters of the optimality conditions. For example, it is shown that the equilibrium pay-off criterion is shorter, the greater the rate of obsolescence of an investment project and the smaller the amount of money capital available to the firm. Now, if in practice it is found that businesses set shorter pay-off criteria for equipment subject to relatively rapid obsolescence, this is consistent with the hypothesis that firms follow optimal (in the sense of our model) investment policies. It is also consistent with optimality if firms are observed to set shorter pay-off criteria in those periods when less capital funds are available.

No attempt is undertaken to make an exhaustive test of this hypothesis. However, several relevant quotations from the trade literature, concerning pay-off criteria in practice, are presented. These quotations tend to show that the reported practice is consistent with our conditions for optimality. There is, at the very least, some business practice which is consistent with these optimal investment conditions. I am of the opinion that a great deal of business investment practice is consistent with the requirements of optimality. This view is not common in the literature. The more common view is that the pay-off criteria of business practice lead to excessive conservatism, with a great deal of plant and equipment retained in service longer than economy requires.

Chapter X returns to the main stream of the static theoretical analysis with the major purpose of developing more fully the multiple-unit production implications of the earlier analysis. The analysis serves to rationalize the observed fact that firms typically meet output requirements from multi-facility production complexes operated in parallel, even though the typical production process exhibits increasing returns to scale. Multifacility production is a rational consequence of the firm's growth and adaptation to changing conditions, given the irreversible sunk cost characteristics of durable capital goods.

Chapter X generalizes the theory of the multiplant firm in the economics literature into a theory of multifacility production. The conditions for optimal short-run facility loading, given the operating cost functions of each facility, are developed using the Kuhn-Tucker conditions. The analysis is illustrated in detail using an iso-cost analysis of two facilities. The iso-cost analysis conveniently replaces the cumbersome marginal cost graphical analysis contained in the multiplant firm literature. The two-facility production problem serves admirably to contrast and compare the necessary, interior, boundary, locally sufficient, and total conditions for optimization.

Some empirical engineering literature on the loading of parallel facilities is also discussed in Chapter X. This literature has a much longer history than the multiplant firm literature in economics. Indeed, the so-called "incremental rate" loading rule seems to have been first published in the engineering literature in 1923. The problem of loading parallel facilities arises most dramatically in power-plant systems in which parallel production units appear at each stage of the production and distribution process. The total electric power load on a transmission network must be allocated among various plants serving the network. Then within each plant the electrical power load must be distributed among alternative turbine-generator units, and the resulting steam load must be distributed among alternative boiler units.

This empirical example suggests a general problem of multistage-multifacility production with parallel production facilities employed at each stage in a process. Such a generalization is formulated, using the power-plant example as a guide.

In the case of a single-stage multifacility allocation problem, necessary conditions for optimal loading are that all operating facilities produce at levels that equate their marginal costs. No facility is held idle if its marginal cost at zero output is less than the marginal cost of the operating facilities. The corresponding conditions in the multistage-multifacility problem require all production "routes" through the system to be operated at levels that equate their marginal cost. A "route" is a sequence of production facilities — one in each production stage — by which a unit of primary input may be transformed via intermediate outputs into final output. In general, the multistage-multifacility problem cannot be solved by treating each stage as an independent multifacility allocation problem. This procedure could be used if it were known in advance what the efficiency prices for each intermediate output would be, but these implicit valuations can only be obtained in the general case by solving for all stages simultaneously. In power plant operating practice the engineer typically loads the units of each stage independently. However, in this application it is approximately true that the only variable input to each stage is the output of the previous stage. Under such special conditions over-all optimization can be obtained by independent suboptimization on each stage. The final output requirements are distributed among the facilities in the last stage so as to equate their marginal physical productivities. The resulting final-stage input requirements are then distributed so as to equate the marginal physical productivities of the next stage, and so on. This provides an optimal loading structure for the system.

The final task of this book is to develop a decision theory of production-investment planning over time. The main technical features of the capital investment decision, that is, the phenomenon of substitution, the asymmetry of expansion and contraction, and production with multiple parallel facilities, also characterize the dynamic models of Chapter XI. Under a cost minimization criterion, with a given time path of production requirements to be met, decision rules are derived for determining when to add new facilities, how much to invest in added facilities, when to discard an old facility, and how to load and utilize parallel production facilities in the operating intervals between investment and/or discard points. "How to load" involves choosing the time paths of current input consumption for each installed facility. In the simplest models, which abstract from inventory considerations and assume no capital maintenance cost, these time paths can be chosen by ordinary scalar calculus methods. However, even the simpler models are formulated as calculus of variations problems to bring out the essential unity of method throughout the analysis. The calculus of variations is of course essential when capital maintenance costs and inventory considerations are introduced, since the cost integrals for such models contain the time derivatives of the extremals to be chosen. The essential result of all this is a formal dynamic synthesis of short- and long-run decision rules in production planning.

One of the conclusions of this analysis is that optimal investment planning may lead to a kind of "overcapacity" which is entirely due to the dynamics of the problem. This is illustrated by an example in which the criterion is to minimize cumulative cost over a finite horizon. In the example, optimal investment in capital goods is greater when the output requirements path, $y(t)$, is a sine function of time than when it is a constant equal to the average value of $y(t)$ over the planning interval. Also, the cost of current inputs in the dynamic case exceeds that in the corresponding static problem. Owing to diminishing returns, upswings in output requirements lead to more than proportional increases in the consumption of current inputs, while downswings lead to less than proportional decreases in current input consumption. This asymmetry leads to an increase in the average cost of current inputs and induces substitution of capital goods. Under such conditions, if society wishes to consume a given total amount of product in a sine-wave cycle over time rather than at a constant steady rate, it will be necessary to employ more capital and current input resources. The economic consequences of underutilized "capacity" cannot be made up by a corresponding overutilization. These results are obtained when the criterion is undiscounted cumulative cost. Under a discounted cost criterion the results do not follow unambiguously. It is possible that less capital and current inputs would be required if production begins on the downsweep of a cycle, and if the rate of interest is sufficiently high or the cycle length sufficiently long. This is because the effect of discounting is to attach greater weight to the costs incurred in the depressed earlier years of the planning period.

By introducing the possibility of producing for inventory, our model is able simultaneously to develop conditions for optimal dynamic inventory policy and durable goods investment planning. The problem of inventory planning over time, as it has been treated recently in the literature, has abstracted from the problem of choice of technique including long-run investment programming. Investment in inventories of product and investment in capital facilities in this model are viewed as alternative ways of smoothing the dynamic impact of sales requirements on the short-run operating cost structure of a productive process. This is quite obvious after one understands it, but I doubt that investments in product inventories and in durable equipment have been considered to be "substitutes" (albeit imperfect substitutes) in quite this sense.

Brief examination is made of a dynamic model of profit maximization in which price policy, instead of being continuously variable with time, is to be fixed at a constant level over the planning interval. In this respect both price and investment policies are viewed as "long-run" decisions, while current input-output policy is a "short-run" decision. Under such conditions cost minimization and profit maximization are separable as in conventional static theory.

Finally, a simple continuous model of production and investment, including replacement, is explored in part for the purpose of deriving the individual firm's optimal "Keynesian" investment demand function. This microeconomic investment demand function includes the rate of interest, the rate of change of output, *and* the level of output. This demonstrates the inseparability of "marginal efficiency" and "accelerator" theories of investment behavior. Of special interest is the fact that, in general, both the level of output and its time rate of change appear as parameters in this function. By using a Cobb-Douglas production function it is shown that investment is a decreasing or increasing function of the level of output according to whether the process shows increasing or decreasing returns to scale. Under constant returns to scale investment is independent of the level of output. These results are not intuitively obvious; if they are correct, and if increasing returns to scale prevails in industrial processes, then investment functions should be decreasing functions of output — a fact which is surely not generally believed.

Chapter II

Empirical Analysis of "Long-Run" Production Functions: Their Derivation, Form, and Properties

1. Introduction

The extent and importance of input substitution in industrial production processes are subjects which have not been adequately exposed to a rigorous empirical examination. Most economists would argue, in line with classical production theory, that substitution is a significant characteristic of the typical production process. They would most likely agree with Samuelson, "Go into any machine plant, pick up any engineering catalogue, study the books of physics and the histories of industrial processes, and you will see the variety of different ways of doing anything." [1] Yet there are few examples of input substitution beyond the class-

---

[1] P. A. Samuelson, "Wages and Interest: A Modern Dissection of Marxian Economic Models," *American Economic Review*, XLVII (December 1957), 907.

room, shop-worn, labor-land-capital illustration, with its vague intuitive appeal to crowding conditions and reorganization possibilities.

Since considerable use will be made of the production-function concept in our later construction of a general theory of production, investment, and replacement, it is of some importance that we first subject the nature and form of the production function to an analytical-empirical examination. This will be accomplished through the derivation and discussion of several production functions arising in diverse engineering and other processes. Special emphasis will be placed upon the technical mechanisms, scientific principles, and empirical engineering laws which generate the observed substitution possibilities in each case. Also, in such processes, we shall be concerned particularly with the characteristic properties of capital inputs and their appropriate measurement.

The pioneering papers by Hollis Chenery [2] and other associates [3] of Wassily Leontief at the Harvard Economic Research Project deserve credit for having first introduced economists to the potentialities of the use of engineering data and principles in the economic analysis of production problems. Prior to these papers, the area of direct empirical production function research seems to have been exclusively the concern of certain investigators in agricultural economics.

[2] See Hollis B. Chenery, "Engineering Production Functions," *Quarterly Journal of Economics*, LXIII (November 1949), 507–531, for the detailed derivation of the production function for gas transmission. For a discussion of the general methodology and a theory of engineering production functions, see Chenery's Chapter 2, "Process and Production Functions from Engineering Data," in Wassily Leontief, *et al.*, *Studies in the Structure of the American Economy* (New York: Oxford University Press, 1953). The best-known paper of Chenery's is probably his "Overcapacity and the Acceleration Principle," *Econometrica*, XX (January 1952), 1–28, in which the investment implications of the earlier gas transmission analysis are explored.

[3] Other analytical-empirical analyses of production processes using engineering materials are to be found in the chapters by Mathilda Holzman, Anne P. Gross, and Allen R. Ferguson in Leontief, *Studies in the Structure of the American Economy*, pp. 326–447. Also, see Vernon L. Smith, "Engineering Data and Statistical Techniques in the Analysis of Production and Technological Change: Fuel Requirements of the Trucking Industry," *Econometrica*, XXV (April 1957), 281–301, and Alan Manne, *Scheduling of Petroleum Refinery Operations* (Cambridge: Harvard University Press, 1956).

In the determination of agricultural production functions, the method of experimentation has been a principal means of analysis.[4] The great variability and uncontrollability of many of the factors influencing agriculture output would seem to render impractical any attempt to synthesize agricultural production functions from the underlying primitive biological principles. In most engineering processes, on the other hand, the variability of these factors is relatively small, and in some cases the technical principles involved are sufficiently simple to permit their manageable analytical representation. In such processes much can be said in favor of methods that derive the production function directly from these principles. Even where the processes deviate in commercial operating practice from that predicted from engineering theory, production functions based upon that theory can be enormously useful in focusing heuristic attention on the input-output possibilities that one can expect in an actual process design problem. By deepening understanding, such production functions hold forth the possibility of sharpening rule-of-thumb field practices.

2. Tree Production; A Familiar Example

As a means of illustrating the general methodological technique in deriving production functions from technological information, it is perhaps appropriate to begin with a somewhat hypothetical example of tree production. This is a familiar process to capital theorists, and has been used as a concrete guide in theory making since at least the days of Ricardo. It is especially appropriate for our initial consideration, not only because of its familiarity and time-honored position in the history of economic theory, but because it is an excellent example of a well-known process whose implicit production function exhibits substitution possibilities that do not seem to have been recognized.

---

[4] See Earl O. Heady, "An Econometric Investigation of the Technology of Agricultural Production Functions," *Econometrica*, XXV (April 1957), 249–268.

In the simplest typical tree investment problem [5] a revenue function or a physical growth function, $F(t)$ is postulated. For our purposes we will assume that $F(t)$ is a growth function, giving the number of cubic feet or board feet in a tree as a function of its age t in years. This function represents the basic technological data of the process and comes from the principles of biology and arboreal ecology, assumed to be beyond the realm of economic analysis. It will be assumed in the simplest case that production is for a continuous market, and that an even-age distribution of trees is maintained under a static production plan in which each year's output is obtained by cutting the mature trees and replacing them with an equal number of saplings.

Under the assumptions of such a static synchronized process, if y is the output of timber per year, and x_1, the number of saplings planted per year, then

$$y = x_1 F(t), \qquad (2.2.1)$$

where any given batch, x_1, of saplings yields y units of timber t years later. However, from an economic point of view, the process may be viewed as a black box with a uniform current input, a uniform output, and a certain volume of "goods-in-process." The expression (2.2.1) is analogous to an "engineering production function."

In the complete production function we also have land requirements, X_2. If we measure X_2 in tree units, that is, the amount of land required to grow a single tree (assumed fixed), then

$$X_2 = x_1 t, \qquad (2.2.2)$$

since $x_1 t$ is the total planting over any t-year period. By eliminating the parameter t from (2.2.1) and (2.2.2) we get the production function

$$y = x_1 F(X_2/x_1) = f(x_1, X_2). \qquad (2.2.3)$$

If $F(t) = t^\alpha = x_1^{-\alpha} X_2^\alpha$, $0 < \alpha < 1$, then

$$y = x_1^{1-\alpha} X_2^\alpha, \qquad (2.2.4)$$

[5] See Lutz and Lutz, *Theory of Investment of the Firm*, pp. 27, 33.

resulting in a Cobb-Douglas function with constant returns to scale.[6]

Notice in this process that substitution between the current input, saplings, and the capital input land, occurs because of the possibility of varying the growth period of trees. A given level of output can be produced with less land if the growth period is shortened and the input of saplings increased, and vice versa. Shortening the maturity time causes cutting to take place at the terminus of a more productive range of the growth curve, that is, where the absolute growth rate is higher, while lengthening the maturity period pushes the cutting point to a less productive range of the growth curve. Observe that the production function (2.2.4) presents a set of long-range "process" design alternatives and is relevant for the initial planning of a synchronized timber cutting-replacement program. *It is not relevant for dynamic production planning decisions*, since it organizes technological data on the hypothesis of static conditions. This will be true as a general principle for processes whose static production function has an internal organizational decision structure. That structure will be inappropriate for dynamic analysis. Indeed, an explicit formulation of the dynamic process will generate a structure of its own.

Equation (2.2.4) is not the end of the story in the static problem, for it does not exhaust the economic implications of the process technology. In addition to a current cost associated with x_1 consumption, and an investment cost associated with the use of X_2 units of land, there is an investment in goods-in-process. In order to produce the synchronized state of the process, t years of planting x_1 saplings per year are necessary. The inventory of wood in the form of partially grown trees at any time t is then

$$Y(t) = \int_0^t x_1 F(x) \, dx \qquad (2.2.5)$$

[6] The inputs x_1 and X_2 must, of course, be nonnegative. In the remainder of this chapter all inputs will be understood to be subject to nonnegativity restrictions.

or if $F(t) = t^\alpha$,

$$Y = \frac{x_1 t^{\alpha+1}}{\alpha+1} = \frac{x_1^{-\alpha} X_2^{\alpha+1}}{\alpha+1} \qquad (2.2.6)$$

gives goods-in-process as a function of x_1 and X_2.

3. *Engineering Efficiency and Production Functions in Energy Transformation*

An important class of production functions arises in a very large number of engineering processes in connection with energy transformation equipment such as boilers, compressors, engines, turbines, motors, generators, and so forth. Such equipment varies in importance with respect to production planning from those concerned with incidental and auxiliary functions in the firm — fan motors, for example — to those which constitute the heart of the entire firm's productive activity, say, turbine-generator units in utility plants.

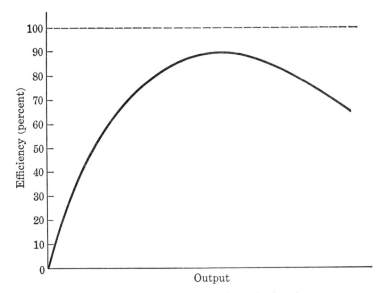

Fig. 2-1. Typical efficiency curve for unit of equipment.

To the engineer, one of the most important performance characteristics of such equipment is usually expressed in the form of an efficiency curve. Because of the fundamental equivalence of all forms of energy, both the output and input

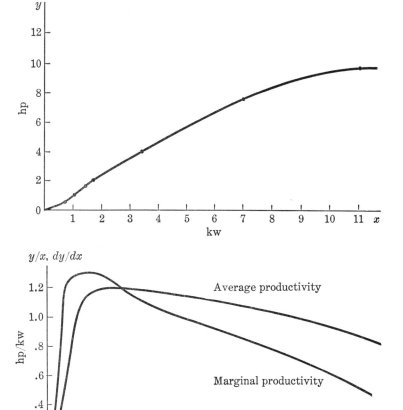

Fig. 2–2. Production function for electric motor (upper figure). Average and marginal productivity curves for electric motor (lower figure).

of energy transformation equipment can be measured in terms of the same units, for example, British thermal units per hour, kilowatt hours, horsepower, foot pounds per minute, etc. All of these energy measures differ by a scale factor only. Therefore, the engineer's concept of efficiency, defined as the ratio of output to input, is always expressible as a dimensionless number. Owing to internal energy losses, input always exceeds output so that efficiency becomes a fraction never exceeding unity. The efficiency of a unit of equipment is typically plotted as a function of output by the engineer, as shown in Fig. 2–1.

The engineer's concept of efficiency, defined as the ratio of output to input, corresponds to the economists's concept of average productivity, and, given an efficiency function for a boiler, motor, turbine, transformer, etc., we also have an average productivity function for that equipment. Since the two-variable production function is completely determined by the average productivity function, we can always obtain an input-output function from the efficiency curve for an item of equipment.

The production function for an electric motor is shown in Fig. 2–2 together with the corresponding marginal and average productivity curves.

4. Energy and Material Transportation Processes

The transportation of energy in the form of heat or electricity and of material in the form of natural gas, petroleum, and petroleum products, water, and so on, represents a set of processes which generates another important class of closely related production functions.

ELECTRICAL TRANSMISSION

In its most elementary form, the transportation of electrical energy gives rise to a classical problem in the literature of engineering economy, usually described as the problem of determining the most economical size of electrical conductor.[7] The problem goes back to the work of Lord Kelvin,[8] but it is never stated in production function terms, which we shall find of interest to do.

Assume that electrical energy in the form of alternating current is to be transported via a power line from a single generation source, such as a hydroelectric dam, to a consumption outlet such as a city. By restricting the analysis to one source and one sink, we abstract from the extraneous problem of distributing several loads among several generating plants in a power-line network.[9] Attention will be concentrated on two major substitutable inputs to the transmission process, electrical energy (at the power plant source) and transmission cable. It is thus assumed, for the sake of simplicity, that such inputs as land right-of-way and cable supports cannot be substituted for either cable or electrical energy. We shall also abstract from the possibility of using transformers to raise the transmission voltage and lower line losses. The process, therefore, is stripped to one involving one current or flow input (electrical energy) and one capital or stock input (transmission cable).

If the distance over which electrical energy is to be transported is fixed, then variation in the quantity of cable input can only occur because of the possibility of choosing among different wire sizes. Hence, the input "cable" could be measured in terms of its cross-sectional area, weight, or volume. The natural units in which to measure the electrical

[7] See C. E. Bullinger, *Engineering Economic Analysis* (New York: McGraw-Hill, 1942), pp. 152–153.

[8] It is most interesting to read Lord Kelvin's (Sir William Thomson's) original paper in which he set forth the principle later known as Kelvin's Law. His paper, "On the Economy of Metal in Conductors of Electricity," *Report of the British Association for the Advancement of Science*, Sec. A, September 2, 1881, pp. 526–528, states and proves that the most economical size of conductor for the transmission of electricity is determined by the condition that the value of the energy lost annually in heat generated in the conductor be equal to the annual interest on the investment in the conductor. I am indebted to my colleague, Charles Howe, for an ingenious search of the literature which produced the Lord Kelvin paper.

[9] See Fred Westfield, "Marginal Analysis, Multi-Plant Firms, and Business Practice: An Example," *Quarterly Journal of Economics*, LXIX (May 1955), 253–268.

energy input to the transmission line is in kilowatt-hours, and similarly for the electrical energy output at the load end of the line. It will be argued that energy input and cable input are substitutes in this process.

It is a well-known engineering phenomenon that the resistance of a wire to the flow of electricity is greater, the smaller the cross-sectional area and therefore weight of the wire. But, the greater the resistance of the wire, the greater the energy loss from heat generated in the wire. Therefore, the smaller the wire the greater must be the input of electrical energy to meet any required level of electrical energy output. Or, the greater the cable input, the less is the energy loss in transmission, and therefore the smaller is the input of electrical energy required to meet any output level. The mechanism of substitution here is the possibility of controlling energy loss through the choice of cable size.

The exact form of the production function for this process can be derived from four empirical laws of physical science — the law of energy conservation, the law of heat dissipation in electrical circuits, Ohm's law governing electricity flow in a circuit, and an empirical law concerning the conductive and resistive properties of materials.

If P_0 is the power output requirement of the transmission line, P_i is the power input at the generating source, and P_L is the power loss in the line due to resistance, then the law of the conservation of energy for this system requires that

$$P_0 = P_i - P_L. \tag{2.4.1}$$

The energy lost in the form of heat in a conductor of electricity is equal to the square of the electrical current flowing through the conductor times the electrical resistance of the conductor. This simple law gives us

$$P_L = I^2 R \tag{2.4.2}$$

where I = current flow, and R = resistance in ohms of the line. If E_0 is the (effective or "root-mean-square") voltage at which customers require energy to be delivered to them, and cos ϕ is the power factor of the consumer's load,[10] then from Ohm's Law

$$P_0 = E_0 I \cos \phi, \quad \text{or} \quad I = P_0/(E_0 \cos \phi). \quad (2.4.3)$$

Finally, the resistance R of a transmission cable is related to the cross-sectional area of the cable, A, the round-trip length of the power line, which is $2L$ for a line L feet long, and the so-called "coefficient of resistivity" of the wire, ρ, as follows:

$$R = 2L\rho/A. \quad (2.4.4)$$

L is, of course, determined by the distance between the power source and the consumption load, while ρ is a property of the cable material, being extremely low for such "conductor" metals as copper, silver, and aluminum, and relatively high for such "insulating" materials as plastics, rubber, and glass. Of course, what is used as a conductor or an insulator in commercial practice is as much a question of economics as one of physics.

Substituting from equations (2.4.2) and (2.4.3) into the fundamental relationship (2.4.1) gives

$$P_0 = P_i - \left(\frac{P_0}{E_0 \cos \phi}\right)^2 \frac{2L\rho}{A}. \quad (2.4.5)$$

The remaining task is to transform the engineering variables of equation (2.4.5) into economic variables, that is, variables with which prices can be associated. We have output $y = P_0$, while input No. 1, electrical energy, is $x_1 = P_i$. If A is the cross-sectional area of the cable in square feet, and the density of the conductive material of the cable is d pounds per cubic foot, then input No. 2 cable, in pounds, is given by $X_2 = 2dLA$.

---

[10] The angle ϕ represents the lag between voltage and current variation in an alternating-current circuit. For our purposes it is sufficient to note that the nearer cos ϕ is to unity, the more nearly is all the energy generated made available in a usable manner. Cos ϕ is a characteristic of the types of equipment which consume the electricity.

Hence (2.4.5) can be written as the production function

$$F(y,x_1,X_2) = X_2(x_1 - y) - \frac{4L^2 y^2 \rho d}{E_0{}^2 \cos^2 \phi}$$

$$= X_2(x_1 - y) - Ky^2 = 0 \qquad (2.4.6)$$

where $K = 4L^2 \rho d / (E_0{}^2 \cos^2 \phi)$. Observe that, *ceteris paribus*, for any given output requirement, the input of electrical energy is smaller, the larger is the cable input, the shorter the line, the smaller the resistivity of the cable, the higher the voltage at which energy is delivered, and the greater the power factor of the consumer's load.

An isoproduct contour map for the production function (2.4.6) is shown in Fig. 2–3. In this example it is assumed that the cable is made of copper; thus, $\rho dL = 873.75$ (ohms resistance per pound-mile of cable).[11] Also, it is assumed that $L = 100$ miles, $E_0 = 50,000$ volts, and $\cos \phi = 0.80$. With these parametric values $K = 218.44 \times 10^{-6}$.

It should be noted in passing that the production function (2.4.6) is incomplete in two respects. In the first place it cannot be assumed without proof that it is possible to design a power line independently of the design of the power-generating source. P_i, the power input to the transmission line, is the power output of the generating station. Using procedures analogous to those used above we could express the output of the generating station as a function of the number (or capacity) of turbine-generators employed and the consumption of fuel (in the case of a steam generating station). Hence, in a complete process $x_1 = P_i$ is an intermediate output, and in the corresponding production function would be replaced by its appropriate relation to fuel and equipment inputs to the generating process. A more complete analysis of a power generation transmission system is discussed below in section 5. Secondly, there are certain bounds and supplementary technological restrictions on the input-output combinations specified in (2.4.6) which, in some

---

[11] See Archer E. Knowlton, Editor-in-Chief, *Standard Handbook for Electrical Engineers*, 8th ed. (New York: McGraw-Hill, 1949), p. 230.

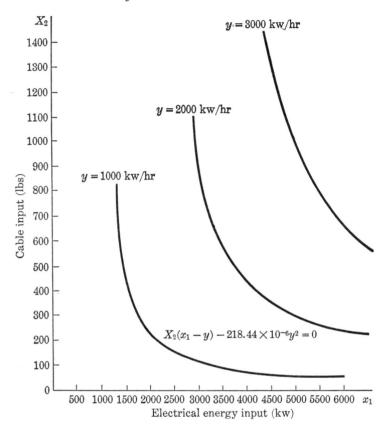

Fig. 2–3. Isoproduct map for the transmission of electrical energy.

applications, are important. For example, a minimum cost design based upon (2.4.6) may yield a cable size which will produce overheating or, in the case of high voltage systems, there may be power losses due to the "corona" [12] effect in addition to line resistance. In commenting upon these considerations Lovell states:

There are four general factors affecting conductor design: (1) economic, (2) thermal, (3) regulation (voltage), (4) structural. If our

---

[12] "Corona" refers to the ionization of air in the vicinity of a high-voltage line which converts the air into a conductor and provides additional power loss.

economic design is adequate, it will usually be found that the line can carry its load without overheating or excessive voltage drop, except for secondary distribution in small towns, and that it is structurally strong. In certain special cases, however, other criteria than the economic may govern. For example, the economic current for a No. 00 23,000-volt underground cable may be 200 amp, but owing to the type of duct construction used and the radiating facilities to dissipate heat, the current may have to be limited to 100 amp to prevent damage to the cable insulation by overheating. Again, in the case of the conductor for a series incandescent lighting circuit carrying, say, 4.4 amp, the economic section may be a No. 11 wire. Obviously, no conductor less than No. 8 or No. 6 would be structurally strong enough to string on a pole line.[13]

HEAT TRANSMISSION

Another classical problem of engineering economy is concerned with the most economical amount of insulation to use on a heat-using or transporting device.[14] It has application to the insulation of buildings, furnaces, boilers, steam pipes, and so forth. Basically, the problem involves substitution between a capital input, insulation, and a current input, heat or fuel.

Consider the problem of heat transmission by pipe, say in the form of steam, from a boiler to a heat-consuming unit. If the heat output of the pipe (heat required by the consuming unit) is H_0, while H_i is the heat input from the boiler, and H_L the heat lost in transmission, then from the conservation of energy we have

$$H_0 = H_i - H_L, \qquad (2.4.7)$$

precisely as in (2.4.1) for the power-line problem. In this case the heat loss from the pipe, due to conduction through

---

[13] Alfred H. Lovell, *Generating Stations* (New York: McGraw-Hill, 1951), p. 215. See below, Chapter III, section 3, for a nonlinear programming discussion of how these additional constraints can be handled in a decision problem.

[14] See H. E. Schweyer, *Process Engineering Economics* (New York: McGraw-Hill, 1955), pp. 211–213.

the pipe walls, can be reduced by "lagging" (insulating) the pipe. The relationship between H_L and the thickness, t, of insulation used is given approximately by an empirical formula of the form

$$H_L = \frac{T_0 - T_i}{K + t/kS},$$
(2.4.8)

where T_0 is the air temperature (average) outside the pipe, T_i is the temperature of the steam in the pipe, and K is a constant depending upon the thickness and thermal conductivity properties of the pipe, the steam film just inside the pipe, and the air film layer immediately outside the pipe. The constant k is the thermal conductivity of the insulating material of thickness, t, and S is the surface area of the pipe.

Combining (2.4.7) and (2.4.8) gives

$$H_0 = H_i - \frac{T_0 - T_i}{K + t/kS}.$$
(2.4.9)

If we let output be $y = H_0$, heat input be $x_1 = H_i$ and insulation input by volume be $X_2 \cong St$, then (2.4.9) becomes the production function

$$y = f(x_1, X_2) = x_1 - \frac{T_0 - T_i}{K + X_2/kS^2}.$$
(2.4.10)

For example, if the pipe is carrying saturated steam at 360° F, the outside room temperature is 80° F, $K = 0.01381$, $k = 0.042$ British Thermal Units per hour per square foot per inch, and $S = 200$ sq ft, then the production function is [15]

$$y = x_1 - \frac{280}{.01381 + 0.000595 X_2}.$$

[15] The numerical example is adapted from W. H. Walker, W. K. Lewis, W. H. McAdams, and E. R. Gilliland, *Principles of Chemical Engineering*. 3rd ed. (New York: McGraw-Hill, 1937), pp. 161–162.

The iso-product contours for this function are shown graphed in Fig. 2–4.

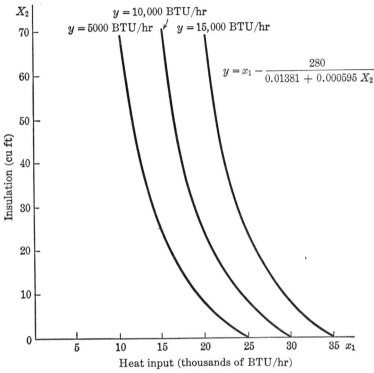

Fig. 2–4. Isoproduct map for the transmission of heat.

For this process the mechanism of substitution between the current and capital input is the same as in the transmission of electrical energy. For any specified output rate, an increase in the quantity of the capital good, insulation, reduces energy loss and therefore saves on the current input, heat.

CHENERY'S GAS TRANSMISSION PRODUCTION FUNCTION

A production function for the process of gas transmission has been derived by Hollis Chenery,[16] drawing upon an im-

[16] Chenery, "Engineering Production Functions," and "Process and Production Functions from Engineering Data."

portant paper by H. C. Lehn [17] in the engineering economy literature. In Chenery's reformulation of the Lehn problem along neoclassical production function lines, attention was centered on the two basic capital inputs to the process, pipe and compressors. A simplified flow diagram of the process is shown in Fig. 2–5. Compressors are employed to raise the

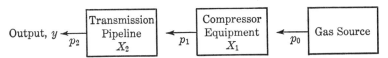

Output, y ← p_2 | Transmission Pipeline X_2 | ← p_1 | Compressor Equipment X_1 | ← p_0 | Gas Source

Fig. 2–5. Flow diagram of gas transmission process.

pressure of the gas from p_0, its pressure at the source (for example, a natural gas field), to p_1, its pressure as it leaves the compressor equipment and enters the pipe. The higher inlet pressure of the pipe causes the gas to be transported through the pipe, and the energy loss in the pipe due to friction causes the pressure to drop to p_2, the outlet pressure.

Chenery writes two equations for the system. The first represents an engineering relationship governing the flow of gas in a pipe: [18]

$$Y = KD^{\frac{8}{3}}(p_1{}^2 - p_2{}^2)^{\frac{1}{2}} = KD^{\frac{8}{3}}p_1[1 - (p_2/p_1)^2]^{\frac{1}{2}} \quad (2.4.11)$$

where p_1 is the inlet pressure and p_2 the outlet pressure in the pipe, D is the inside diameter of the pipe, Y is capacity output, and K is a parameter depending upon the temperature and specific gravity of the gas, the length of the pipe, and the roughness of the interior surface of the pipe.

The second relationship concerns the process of compression,[19] and can be written approximately in the form

$$H = [k_1(p_1/p_0) - k_2]Y(k_1 = 28.75, k_2 = 13.9), \quad (2.4.12)$$

where p_0 is the inlet pressure to the compressor, H is compressor horsepower requirements, and k_1 and k_2 are parame-

[17] H. C. Lehn, "An Analysis of Gas Pipeline Economics," *American Society of Mechanical Engineers Transactions*, July 1943, pp. 445–460.

[18] See Chenery, "Engineering Production Functions," p. 515.

[19] *Ibid.*, p. 516.

ters depending upon the type and efficiency of compressor equipment employed.

If it is assumed that the inlet pressure to the compressor process is equal to the outlet pressure of the pipe, then $p_0 = p_2$, and $R = (p_1/p_2) = (p_1/p_0)$ represents the relative pressure rise during compression as well as the relative pressure drop in transmission.[20] This assumes that gas is delivered at the same pressure (or approximately at the same pressure) that it is received by the compression-transmission system.

An auxiliary relationship exists between the inlet (the highest) pressure in the pipe, the dimensions of the pipe, and its allowable working stress, which in turn depends upon the construction material of the pipe; that is

$$p_1 = 2ST/D \qquad (S = 15{,}000 \text{ lb/in.}^2), \qquad (2.4.13)$$

where S is the working stress and T is the pipe thickness. A production function for gas transmission is contained in (2.4.11)–(2.4.13). We could eliminate p_1 from (2.4.11)–(2.4.13), retaining p_0 and p_2 as exogenous variables, since p_2 will depend upon customer loads and requirements, and p_0 will depend upon the characteristics of the gas field. Chenery, by assuming that $p_2 = p_0$ and hence $R = (p_1/p_0) = (p_1/p_2)$, is able to write (2.4.11) in the form

$$Y = KD^{\frac{8}{3}}p_1(1 - 1/R^2)^{\frac{1}{2}} = K_1 D^{\frac{5}{3}}T(1 - 1/R^2)^{\frac{1}{2}}, \quad (2.4.14)$$

and (2.4.12) in the form

$$H = (k_1 R - k_2)Y. \qquad (2.4.15)$$

If we eliminate R between (2.4.14) and (2.4.15) and let $X_1 = H$ be the measure of compressor input and $X_2 = D$ be the measure of pipe input (given T), then the production function can be written:

$$F(Y,X_1,X_2) = \frac{X_1}{k_1} + \frac{k_2}{k_1}Y - K_1 X_2^{\frac{5}{3}}T\left[\left(\frac{X_1}{k_1 Y} + \frac{k_2}{K_1}\right)^2 - 1\right]^{\frac{1}{2}} = 0.$$
$$(2.4.16)$$

[20] Chenery (*ibid.*) does not seem to make this assumption explicitly, but it is contained implicitly in his equations (12) and (14).

A graph of this function is shown in Fig. 2–6.

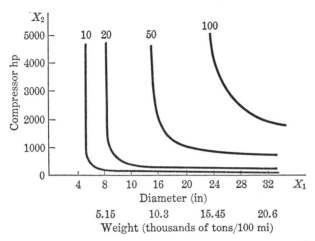

Fig. 2–6. *Isoproduct contours for gas transmission.* (Source: Hollis B. Chenery, "Engineering Production Functions," *Quarterly Journal of Economics,* 63: 524, November 1949.)

Though the derivation of this production function has seemed to involve principles different from those employed in previous sections, the underlying principles are the same. Indeed, the principles governing the pipeline problem are entirely analogous to those governing the transmission-line problem. In the pipeline problem, energy is required to transmit the gas. Compressors are a type of industrial equipment that will transfer mechanical energy from a motor or other prime mover to the gas to be transported. Since there is energy loss in the pipe due to friction in transmission, and this loss is a decreasing function of pipe size, it follows that the greater the pipe diameter, the smaller the required compressor capacity to pump any given amount of gas a specified distance. Fundamentally, then, the mechanism of substitution between pipes and compressors is the inevitability of energy loss in engineering processes, and the effect of equipment size (investment) in reducing this loss.

It should be noted that Chenery's production function derived in (2.4.16) is a capacity function and in this sense is quite different from the corresponding function for electrical power transmission. The production function for power transmission was incomplete in the sense that it abstracted entirely from the generation process and concentrated upon the transmission process in isolation. Chenery's pipeline production function is incomplete in that it does not include an explicit analysis of the energy input to the compressor process. This energy is typically supplied by the natural gas itself so that the complete production function would be of the form $F(y,x_1,X_2,X_3) = 0$, where x_1 is gas consumed as fuel, X_2 is compressor capacity, X_3 is pipeline capacity, and y is the actual volume of gas pumped per unit of time. An extension of Chenery's analysis to embrace this important current input to the process as well as the two major capital inputs requires an analysis similar to that in the next section in which the principles discussed in this section are extended to the analysis of a complete "plant."

It is perhaps appropriate at this juncture to point out an important characteristic of the production functions that we have been considering. They provide a catalogue of input-output possibilities within a certain limited set of planning objectives. In particular, there may be some kinds of dynamic production planning problems in which the technological horizon should be broadened when deriving the appropriate technological constraints on the decision problem. For example, in designing a gas transmission system to meet dynamic variations in output requirements, the problem presents an additional dimension in the form of inventories of gas that can be stored in special tanks or at high pressure in the pipeline itself. Using the pipeline as a storage tank in periods of low demand requires a larger pipe than under static load conditions and/or a thicker pipe, where the peak pressure in the pipe is increased. Hence, in any dynamic formulation of the problem in which pipeline inventory considerations are to be entertained, the technological horizon must be broadened beyond that underlying equations (2.4.11)–(2.4.16). The principles and methodology used in deriving the appropriate input-output possibility function will remain the same, however.

5. Plant and Process Production Functions: The Production and Transmission of Electrical Energy

Having derived and discussed in detail the production functions for several specific industrial processes, with a special emphasis on the substitution mechanism in energy transmitting processes, it is perhaps in order to turn briefly to a consideration of the relation between process production functions and plant production functions before broadening our empirical investigation to totally different types of processes.

The typical plant is obviously composed of a collection of processes which are quite distinct in the engineering sense. Sometimes the individual processes are operated in parallel and exhibit very little in the way of input interdependence beyond using the same building facilities, a common source of energy, and sharing time on certain kinds of general-purpose machines, such as presses and mills. This condition is prevalent in plants which fabricate a variety of products that are related because of certain kinds of materials or skills or marketing economies that are common to the members of the product mix. A full-scale input-output analysis of such plants by direct techniques would be a difficult task.

In many instances the individual processes comprising a "plant" are operated essentially in series, the output of each process being an input (along with other inputs) to another (the "next") process. In such plants an exhaustive analysis can still be a difficult task, especially if there are several products involved. Examples abound in the oil and chemical industries. A somewhat less formidable problem of analysis is presented by facilities which are composed of several processes operated in series in the production of a single, more or less homogeneous, product. Examples include the electrolytic reduction of certain metals, electrical power production and transmission, and the production of some of the standard chemicals.

We shall find it most advantageous to center attention on the steam production and transmission of electrical energy as a "plant." This case lends itself exceedingly well to a concentration upon principles and provides a maximum of continuity with the analysis of sections 3 and 4.

A steam-generating plant is composed of four distinct engineering processes operated in series; a boiler process which converts the source of energy (coal or natural gas, for example) into heat in the form of superheated steam, a turbine process which converts the intermediate product "superheated steam" into mechanical energy, a generator process which converts mechanical energy into electrical energy, and, finally, a transmission process (including transformer equipment) which transmits electrical energy from the producing to the consuming source. An energy flow diagram for such a system is shown in Fig. 2–7. The inputs and outputs of the various processes are:

x_1, power input to boiler process and to system,
x_6, power output of boiler process (input to turbine),
x_7, power output of turbine process (input to generator),
x_8, power output of generator process (input to transmission),
y,   power output of transmission process and of system,

all measured in the same energy flow units (that is, kilowatt hours per year, or British Thermal Units per hour, etc.).

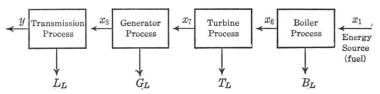

Fig. 2–7. Flow diagram of electrical energy production and transmission.

Each process will experience energy losses as follows:

B_L, boiler losses,
T_L, turbine losses,
G_L, generator losses,
L_L, line losses.

From the law of the conservation of energy, four energy balance equations — one for each process — can be written.

$$x_6 = x_1 - B_L, \tag{2.5.1}$$
$$x_7 = x_6 - T_L, \tag{2.5.2}$$
$$x_8 = x_7 - G_L, \tag{2.5.3}$$
$$y = x_8 - L_L. \tag{2.5.4}$$

It will be recalled that in our derivation of the production function for a simple transmission process the power losses in the process were an increasing function of the process load (output) and a decreasing function of the process capacity (wire size). In that particular example such losses were proportional to the product of the square of output and the reciprocal of wire size. Though the exact manner in which energy losses vary with output and process capacity varies considerably in different types of energy transformation equipment, the same general relationship holds in boilers, compressors, motors, generators, conductors, turbines, etc. Energy losses are an increasing function of output and a decreasing function of capacity.

This general relationship is revealed most often in the engineering literature in the indirect form of efficiency curves. There are frequent references in this literature to the fact that the efficiency of an energy-transforming machine increases with the machine's capacity.[21] For example, with regard to electrical generators:

The purchase price and installed cost per kilowatt of a generator decrease and the efficiency increases as the size of the unit in-

---

[21] To show that when the loss function decreases with capacity, efficiency increases with capacity, let y = output, x_1 = energy input, X_2 = capacity of an energy converting machine. Then if $g(y,X_2)$ is the loss function, $y = x_1 - g(y,X_2)$, and

$$\text{efficiency } e = y/x_1 = 1 - \frac{g(y,X_2)}{x_1} = \frac{y}{y + g(y,X_2)}.$$

Hence,

$$\frac{\partial e}{\partial X_2} = \frac{-y(\partial g/\partial X_2)}{[y + g(y,X_2)]^2} \text{ and } \frac{\partial e}{\partial X_2} > 0$$

unambiguously, if $\partial g/\partial X_2 < 0$, and conversely.

creases within normal limits of design of the particular type of generator and prime mover, although gains in cost and efficiency decrease with increased size.[22]

Having established the general relationship between losses, output, and capacity, we can write

$$B_L = g_1(x_6, X_2), \qquad (2.5.5)$$
$$T_L = g_2(x_7, X_3), \qquad (2.5.6)$$
$$G_L = g_3(x_8, X_4), \qquad (2.5.7)$$
$$L_L = g_4(y, X_5), \qquad (2.5.8)$$

where X_2 is the boiler capacity, X_3 is the turbine capacity, X_4 is the generator capacity, and X_5 is the transmission-line capacity, all measured in appropriate physical units. The energy balance equations (2.5.1)–(2.5.4) can now be converted into the following functions for each process:

$$x_6 = x_1 - g_1(x_6, X_2), \qquad (2.5.9)$$
$$x_7 = x_6 - g_2(x_7, X_3), \qquad (2.5.10)$$
$$x_8 = x_7 - g_3(x_8, X_4), \qquad (2.5.11)$$
$$y \ = x_8 - g_4(y, X_5). \qquad (2.5.12)$$

By repeated substitution the three intermediate outputs, x_6, x_7, and x_8 can be eliminated to give the production function for the entire production-transmission system; thus,

$$F(y, x_1, X_2, X_3, X_4, X_5) = 0. \qquad (2.5.13)$$

As an illustration, let us suppose

$$g_1 = \frac{k_1 x_6}{X_2}, \quad g_2 = \frac{k_2 x_7}{X_3}, \quad g_3 = \frac{k_3 x_8}{X_4}, \quad g_4 = \frac{k_4 y}{X_5},$$

where the k's are constants. Then (2.5.13) has the simple form

$$y = \frac{x_1 X_2 X_3 X_4 X_5}{(k_1 + X_2)(k_2 + X_3)(k_3 + X_4)(k_4 + X_5)}. \qquad (2.5.14)$$

[22] Knowlton, *Standard Handbook*, p. 1059. For similar information on steam turbines, see R. T. Kent, *Kent's Mechanical Engineers' Handbook*, 11th ed. (New York: John Wiley, 1936), pp. 8–63.

Equations (2.5.9)–(2.5.12) and the illustrative example (2.5.14) represent "complete" descriptions of plant input-output possibilities.[23] Such functions clearly exist and, in principle, can be derived. The present example will provide a demonstration of one method of deriving such a function (or set of functions) as well as an indication of some of the inherent difficulties involved in more complex processes.

It will be evident that a similar type of production function can be derived for the gas transmission process relating the actual flow of output (rather than capacity output) to the consumption of energy and the physical stocks of pipe and compressor equipment.

6. Multiple-Pass Regeneration Processes

An important class of processes that appear in the chemical, petroleum, and metallurgical industries is characterized by the use of some form of material substance which is not consumed in production, but must be in contact with the raw materials of the processes for production to occur. The productive "efficiency" of the substance declines with contact. Sometimes a portion of the efficiency of the substance may be restored by regeneration — by cleaning, heating, or other form of treatment. Filtration processes such as the use of clay for decolorizing and deodorizing mineral oils is an example.[24] Another example is a chemical wash solution that is recycled and its cleansing action reduced at each pass, as in the caustic treating of gasoline, pickling operations in

[23] Obviously the possibilities are not exhausted in several respects. For example, not all inputs have been analyzed. There will be another capital good in the form of the plant building or buildings, but this input, X_6 (measured, say, in square feet), can be supposed a function of the capacity stocks of boilers, turbines, and generators, that is, $X_6 = X_6(X_2, X_3, X_4)$. Also, certain auxiliary equipment and labor inputs will be involved, but usually such incidental inputs are related in some fixed way to the key inputs or the output appearing in the production function.

[24] For a discussion and engineering analysis of such a process, see W. H. McAdams in C. Tyler, *Chemical Engineering Economics*, 3rd ed. (New York: McGraw-Hill, 1948), pp. 128–129. Also, see Schweyer, *Process Engineering Economics*, pp. 271–273.

metal processing, and the solvent cleaning of textiles.[25] In this class of processes the reagent is usually not regenerated after each pass, whereas in the filter processes the efficiency of the adsorbent can be partially restored by treatment. Still another example is in some catalytic reactor processes in which the mixture of reactants is passed over a bed composed of a catalytic substance. At each pass the efficiency of the catalyst is reduced, and part of this efficiency is restored by regeneration before the next pass.[26]

The multiple-pass declining efficiency characteristic of these processes generates substitution possibilities between the clay, or other yield agent, and process equipment capacity. This substitution mechanism will be illustrated for the process of decolorizing and deodorizing mineral and vegetable oils in which the oil is passed through fuller's earth (clay).[27]

In this process the filtering operation saturates the clay adsorbent, but it can be regenerated by washing and burning in a furnace. The regenerated adsorbent can then be reused, but its adsorbing capacity decreases with each regeneration. It will be assumed that the adsorbent capacity declines by a constant percentage with each regeneration. After repeated adsorption operations, the adsorbent eventually declines in efficiency to the point where it pays to begin the operation with a new adsorbent charge. We shall call each filtering and regenerating operation a pass, and the total number of passes run with a given charge of adsorbent a cycle.

Suppose the output of filtered oil in the initial pass of each cycle, when the adsorbent charge is new, is y_0 pounds. If it is assumed that the capacity of the adsorbent after each regeneration is r times its capacity before regeneration, where $r < 1$, then the output of the first pass is y_0, the output of the second pass is ry_0, the third is r^2y_0, and so forth. Output per cycle, after $u + 1$ passes, is therefore $y_0(1 + r + r^2 + \cdots + r^u)$. Consequently, if there are N cycles run per year, total out-

[25] See Schweyer, p. 274.
[26] *Ibid.*, pp. 315–317.
[27] Tyler, pp. 128–129.

put per year, y, will be

$$y = y_0(1 + r + r^2 + \cdots + r^u)N = \frac{y_0 N}{1 - r}(1 - r^{u+1}); \quad (2.6.1)$$

that is, output per year is the product of output per cycle and the number of cycles per year.

If the filtering operation requires θ_f hours per pass, then the filtering time per cycle is $\theta_f(u + 1)$, while if regeneration time is θ_r per pass, then it is $\theta_r u$ per cycle. Hence, if the process is operated H hours per year, the number of cycles that can be run per year is

$$N = H/[\theta_f(u + 1) + \theta_r u]. \quad (2.6.2)$$

If it is assumed that the output of the initial pass of each cycle is proportional to the initial size of the adsorbent charge, x_{10}, then

$$y_0 = \alpha x_{10}, \quad (2.6.3)$$

where α is a constant. Since the input of adsorbent per year, x_1, is the product of input per cycle and the number of cycles per year, we have the identity

$$x_1 \equiv N x_{10}, \quad (2.6.4)$$

and (2.6.1) can be written

$$y = \frac{\alpha x_1}{1 - r}(1 - r^{u+1}). \quad (2.6.5)$$

Since the amount of adsorbent tower capacity and the capacity of regeneration facilities are directly affected by the volume of adsorbent charge handled, it is assumed that the capacity of adsorbent tower and regeneration facilities X_2, is proportional to the initial adsorbent charge of each cycle:

$$X_2 = \beta x_{10}, \quad (2.6.6)$$

where β = constant. From (2.6.2), (2.6.4), and (2.6.6) we can eliminate x_{10} and N, and solve for u,

$$u = \frac{H X_2}{\beta x_1(\theta_f + \theta_r)} - \frac{\theta_f}{\theta_f + \theta_r}. \quad (2.6.7)$$

Equation (2.6.7) relates the engineering variable u to the economic inputs x_1 and X_2. It tells us that for a given filtering equipment capacity, X_2, the adsorbent input per year to the process can be reduced only by increasing the number of passes per cycle, and thus using the clay to a lower degree of efficiency.

Substituting for u from (2.6.7) into (2.6.5) yields the constant-returns-to-scale production function

$$y = Ax_1[1 - Br^{\gamma X_2/x_1}], \quad A = \frac{\alpha}{1-r}, \quad B = r^{1-(\theta_f/\theta_f+\theta_r)},$$

$$\gamma = \frac{H}{\beta(\theta_f + \theta_r)}. \tag{2.6.8}$$

Two isoproduct contours for this function are shown in Fig. 2–8. The hypothetical numerical values for the parame-

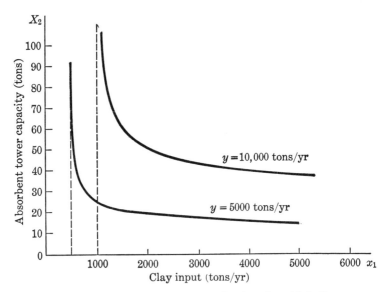

Fig. 2–8. Isoproduct map for production of purified oils.

ters used in this diagram are $\alpha = \beta = 1$, $\theta_f = 6$, $\theta_r = 2$, $H = 2000$, and $r = 0.9$. For given y it is seen that the adsorbent clay input per year can be substituted for filtering equipment capacity. The substitution is possible via variation in the number of passes per cycle, that is, the number of times the clay is regenerated and reused before it is finally discarded and a new charge employed. A given output can be produced with less clay adsorbent consumption per year provided we increase the size of the adsorbent charge for each cycle, and consequently the capacity of the filtering equipment, at the same time increasing the number of times a given adsorbent charge is reused and thereby decreasing the number of cycles per year.

7. Batch Reactor Chemical Processes

Our survey of the basis in natural science for input substitution in a selection of engineering processes would be far from adequate without some discussion of the design of chemical process operations. Such processes typically present very complex multiple-input substitution possibilities. Our main purpose in this section will be to show how certain fundamental principles operating in various industrial chemical processes provide a widespread basis for the existence of input substitution in the chemical process industries. These nonlinear input-output possibilities have their roots so firmly established in the equilibrium and kinetic principles of physical chemistry that it is difficult indeed to exaggerate the extent of substitution phenomena in individual chemical processes. Our attention, therefore, will be directed first to the Guldberg-Waage law of mass action and the general subject of reaction kinetics in physical chemistry,[28] following which the production function will be derived for a simple version of a recycling batch process for esterification reactions.

---

[28] The textbooks and journals of chemistry and chemical engineering are filled with chapters and articles on these subjects. Specific references will be given in the context of the discussion to follow. Two general references are Samuel Glasstone, *The Elements of Physical Chemistry* (New York: D. Van Nostrand, 1946), chaps. x, xviii, *passim*, and F. H. Getman and F. Daniels, *Outlines of Physical Chemistry*, 7th ed. (New York: John Wiley, 1943), chaps. xii and xiv.

In chemical processes the typical product or products are produced by charging two or more chemical reactants [29] (the raw materials of the process) into a reactor vessel and allowing the chemical reaction to proceed, or possibly aiding the reaction either by the application of heat or the use of catalytic reagents.[30] After the reaction has been allowed to proceed for a certain period — called the residence time of the reaction — the product or products having commercial value are separated from those which do not and from the unreacted residue of the original reactant materials. The vessel is then recharged with materials for a new batch run. Sometimes the process is continuous (or semicontinuous) with reactants continuously being supplied and products continuously being withdrawn from the reactor vessel.

To illustrate the law of mass action and show its relevance to production theory, consider an ideal reversible reaction of the form

$$A + B \rightleftarrows C + D,$$

that is, 1 mole [31] of A combines with 1 mole of B to produce 1 mole each of the products C and D in the "forward" reaction, and vice versa in the reverse reaction. In general, the

[29] Sometimes only a single reactant is converted into product by application of heat or other treatment.

[30] A catalyst is any substance the presence of which accelerates the rate of chemical reaction, but which itself remains unchanged chemically in the process. Since catalysts do not change chemically as a result of the process, many can be used indefinitely. Where there is a decline in "efficiency" it is due usually to some kind of physical alteration, such as the breaking up of crystals, abrasion, or roughening.

[31] A mole is a physical measure of the quantity of a compound defined by the chemist as the molecular weight of the compound in grams. Thus oxygen, by convention, has a molecular weight of 16. Therefore, one mole of oxygen is 16 grams of the compound. Carbon dioxide is made up of one carbon atom with weight 12.01 and two oxygen atoms of total weight 32. Because of the law of the conservation of mass (this is not the same as the law of mass action to be discussed shortly) in chemical reactions, carbon dioxide will have a molecular weight of 44.01. Therefore, one mole of carbon dioxide is 44.01 grams of the compound.

two opposing reactions tend to occur simultaneously, with existing A and B tending to transform into C and D, while at the same time C and D tend to decompose or transform into A and B, until eventually a chemical equilibrium is established between the opposing transformations.

Now, according to the law of mass action, due to C. M. Guldberg and P. Waage in 1864, the rate of a chemical reaction is proportional to the molar concentrations of the reacting substances. Thus, if the rate of forward reaction is dF/dt, and the molar concentrations of A and B are c_A and c_B, then we have

$$dF/dt = k_1 c_A c_B, \qquad (2.7.1)$$

while if the rate of reverse reaction is dR/dt, and the molar concentrations of C and D are c_C and c_D, then we have [32]

$$dR/dt = k_2 c_C c_D. \qquad (2.7.2)$$

When a state of chemical equilibrium is reached, the rates of the forward and reverse reactions must be equal, that is, $dR/dt = dF/dt$ so that

$$K = k_1/k_2 = c_C c_D / c_A c_B. \qquad (2.7.3)$$

The constant K is called the equilibrium constant of the reaction.

One of the best-known examples of a reversible reaction in a liquid system is that occurring between acetic acid (A) and alcohol (B) to form the ester, ethyl acetate (C), and the by-product, water (D). If we let a and b represent the number of moles of acetic acid and alcohol present initially in the system, and c represent the number of moles of ethyl acetate (and also water) produced in equilibrium, then in equilibrium there will remain $a - c$ moles of acid and $b - c$ moles of alcohol. Hence, in equilibrium the mole concentrations are $c_C = c_D = c/q$, $c_A = (a - c)/q$, $c_B = (b - c)/q$, where q is the total quantity by volume of the initial mixture, and, for the esterification reaction, equation (2.7.3) becomes

$$K = \frac{c^2}{(a - c)(b - c)} \qquad (2.7.4)$$

[32] See Glasstone, *Elements of Physical Chemistry*, pp. 291–293.

The constant K for this reaction has been found to be 4.[33]

Superficially, (2.7.4) appears to be an example of the economists' production function, since c is an "output," while a and b are "inputs." However, this is a production function only from the view of a simple point-input point-output process, that is, a single batch-run of the reaction. To express the production technology under stationary state conditions we need to specify how it is that the process is employed over time. Suppose we assume production takes place in a sequence of batch operations (as in fact it typically does in practice). We begin with charges of a moles of acetic acid and b moles of alcohol. The reaction proceeds (ideally) to equilibrium generating a mixture of c moles of ethyl acetate, $(a - c)$ moles of acetic acid, and $(b - c)$ moles of alcohol. The unreacted residue is then separated from the product, recharged into the reactor along with c moles of fresh acid and c moles of alcohol, providing again a total charge of a moles of acid and b moles of alcohol for the second batch.

If a constant number N of such batches is run per year then the output of acetic acid (the by-product water having no commercial value) per year will be

$$y \equiv Nc. \tag{2.7.5}$$

Since c moles of acetic acid and of alcohol are converted per batch, it follows that the annual consumption of acetic acid is

$$x_1 \equiv Nc \tag{2.7.6}$$

and of alcohol is

$$x_2 \equiv Nc. \tag{2.7.7}$$

However, the process requires a continuous inventory of goods-in-process. Since each batch-run begins with a moles of acetic acid and b moles of alcohol, and ends with $a - c$ moles of acetic acid and $b - c$ moles of alcohol, the average inventory of A is $a - c + (c/2) = a - (c/2)$ and of B is

---

[33] Glasstone, p. 310

$b - (c/2)$. (We assume that the unreacted residue of each batch can be separated from product at zero cost. At the other extreme, if it is prohibitively expensive to separate and recycle the reactant residue, then a of acetic acid and b of alcohol are *consumed* per batch with the result that $x_1 = Na$, $x_2 = Nb$, where x_1 and x_2 are the consumption rates of A and B.) Hence, the stock input of acetic acid required by the process is

$$X_1 = a - (c/2),$$
(2.7.8)

and that of alcohol is

$$X_2 = b - (c/2).$$
(2.7.9)

Substituting from (2.7.8), (2.7.9), and (2.7.5) into (2.7.4) gives the technology of our process as follows [34]

$$\left. \begin{aligned} K &= \frac{4y^2}{(2NX_1 - y)(2NX_2 - y)} \\ x_1 &= x_2 = y \end{aligned} \right\}.$$
(2.7.10)

The production of y moles of ethyl acetate per year requires flows of x_1 and x_2 moles each of acid and alcohol per year, and the continuous presence of stocks of X_1 and X_2 moles of acid and alcohol. The latter substitutive requirements grow out of the basic dependence of the reaction rates upon the physical bulks of the reactants. Observe that (2.7.10) exhibits constant returns to scale.

In this process we find substitution possibilities between raw material stocks in contrast with the derivations of the previous sections in which substitution was always between current flows and stocks of producer's durables. Note in particular that *the necessity for holding raw material inventories is entirely a technological phenomenon in the strict engineering sense and is not dependent in any way upon risk or dynamic considerations*. This is precisely the situation in many processes in the chemical, biochemical, and petroleum

---

[34] If the unreacted residue of A and B is not recycled after each batch, then we substitute from $x_1 = Na$, $x_2 = Nb$, and $y = Nc$ into (2.7.4) and get $F(y,x_1,x_2) = y^2/(x_1 - y)(x_2 - y) = K$.

industries. It arises not only because of the influence of quantity on reaction rates, but also in catalytic processes. Attention has already been called to the significance for input substitution of production processes in which a catalyst of declining efficiency is employed. However, in many catalytic processes the catalyst does not decline in efficiency, and is required only to be present in order to speed up the reaction. Generally the rate of catalytic action is considered to be proportional either to the concentration of the catalyst or to the exposed area of the catalyst surface.[35] Under these conditions, as will be demonstrated shortly, catalyst inventory can be substituted against reactant inventory, since increasing either of these variables increases the reaction speed.

PRODUCTION FUNCTIONS AND REACTION KINETICS

In making use of the law of mass action to derive equation (2.7.3), and thus express the relationship among the reactant and product concentrations in a chemical reaction, it was assumed that the reaction was allowed to proceed to completion. This equilibrium state may be impossible to attain in practice, and even if approximately attainable in practice may not be economical. Our purpose was to show the physical possibility of substitution between reactant inventories even under ideal yield conditions. The typical commercial chemical reaction is likely to be terminated and the products removed before that reaction reaches a stationary chemical equilibrium. As it turns out, this fact generates additional input-output possibilities of interest in applied production theory. These possibilities are broadened still further in the typical commercial chemical process because of the use of catalytic materials and heat to speed the rate of chemical reaction. Such considerations are the subject matter of the very complex field of reaction kinetics.

In a reaction in which 1 mole each of A and B form 1 mole each of C and D as in the esterification process discussed

[35] Glasstone, p. 620.

before, we know from equation (2.7.1) that the rate of forward reaction at time t is $k_1(a - c)(b - c)$, where a and b are the initial moles of A and B and c is the total moles of C (equal to total moles of D) formed up to time t. Similarly, from equation (2.7.2) the rate of reverse reaction (decomposition of C and D into A and B) at time t is $k_2(c)(c) = k_2c^2$. Hence, the net rate of formation of C, dc/dt is given by [36]

$$dc/dt = k_1(a - c)(b - c) - k_2c^2. \qquad (2.7.11)$$

Integrating (2.7.11), and setting $c = 0$ when $t = 0$ (the reaction begins in a solution containing none of the products C and D), gives

$$t = K_1 \log \left\{ \frac{c - K_2 - K_3}{c - K_2 + K_3} \right\} = g(a,b,c), \qquad (2.7.12)$$

where $K_1 = \dfrac{1}{[k_1^2(a + b)^2 - 4k_1ab(k_1 - k_2)]^{\frac{1}{2}}}, \quad K_2 = \dfrac{k_1(a + b)}{2(k_1 - k_2)}$

and $K_3 = \dfrac{1}{2(k_1 - k_2)K_1}.$

In (2.7.12), t is an increasing function of c and a decreasing function of a and of b.

Equation (2.7.11) and (2.7.12) were derived with the assumptions that no catalyst is used and the reaction takes place at a constant temperature. However, by supplying heat to the process and raising the reaction temperature, it is possible to increase the reaction rate. As pointed out by Glasstone, "Increase of temperature almost invariably increases the rate of a chemical reaction to a marked extent; for homogeneous processes the specific rate is usually increased by a factor of about 2 or 3 for every 10° rise of temperature." [37]

---

[36] See *Encylopedia of Chemical Technology* (New York: Interscience Publishers, 1947), V, 781. Also, see Glasstone, pp. 600–602, for a discussion of opposing reactions.

[37] Glasstone, p. 606.

Similarly, as indicated earlier, the rate of a chemical reaction may be increased by the presence of a material catalyst. Typically, the rate of reaction is roughly proportional to the concentration of catalyst. Hence, the constant k_1 in equation (2.7.11) will normally be an increasing function of the concentration of catalyst present and the temperature maintained in the reaction chamber.[38]

A Wicksellian engineering relationship of the form illustrated by equation (2.7.12) will be at the heart of the production function for many chemical processes.[39] The process of esterification of butanol (*n*-butyl alcohol) and acetic acid has been studied with the object of obtaining a more complete analytical-empirical specification of the form of the function (2.7.12).[40] Leyes and Othmer found that equation (2.7.11) and (2.7.12), based entirely upon theoretical considerations of a reversible reaction, did not apply in the range up to 75–85 percent conversion of the reactants. Only in the range above 75–85 percent conversion did the results approach those given by the general reversible reaction represented by equation (2.7.11). Up to 75–85 percent conversion the differential equation best fitting the experimental data was

$$dc/dt = k(a - c)^2, \qquad (2.7.13)$$

---

[38] Heat and catalytic materials are assumed to increase only the rate of forward reaction, since such agents would not be used if they increased the rate of reverse reaction. Catalysts which increase the rate of reverse reaction can be rejected on engineering grounds, that is, any given output can be produced using less of one or more inputs.

[39] This is not to suggest that such a function can be easily obtained in practice. Indeed, there are few commercial chemical processes for which the subject of reaction kinetics has been thoroughly explored by analytical methods. Commercial designs still lean very heavily upon empirical methods.

Note that the general technical relationship $t = g(a,b,c)$ underlying all such chemical processes, of which (2.7.12) is an example, is simply an alternative form of the point-input point-output "production function" employed by K. Wicksell, *Lectures on Political Economy* (London: Routledge and Kegan Paul, 1934), I, 181. Also, see Lutz and Lutz, pp. 77–79. The Wicksell hypothesis was that $c = f(a,b,t)$, where t is the period of production or investment.

[40] Charles E. Leyes and D. F. Othmer, "Esterification of Butanol and Acetic Acid," *Industrial and Engineering Chemistry*, October 1958, pp. 968–977.

giving

$$t = \frac{c}{ka(a - c)}. \qquad (2.7.14)$$

That is, the reaction rate was proportional to the square of the concentration of acid.[41] The reaction rate constant k, however, is related to temperature, the concentration of catalyst, and the ratio of butanol to acid initially present.

Using (2.7.14) as a basis, Leyes and Othmer obtained the following equation for the predicted reaction rate constant, k_T,

$$k_T = \left(\alpha_1 + \alpha_2 K + \alpha_3 K \frac{b}{a}\right) \frac{10^{(\beta_1 + \beta_2/T)}}{\alpha_4}, \qquad (2.7.15)$$

where $\alpha_1 = 0.000618$, $\alpha_2 = -0.376724$, $\alpha_3 = 0.180917$, $\alpha_4 = 1.745$, $\beta_1 = 9.140142$, $\beta_2 = -3320.0564$, K = sulfuric acid catalyst by percent weight, a = initial acetic acid in moles, b = initial butanol in moles, and T = temperature in degrees Kelvin. From (2.7.14) and (2.7.15) we obtain

$$t = \frac{\alpha_4 c}{a(a - c)\left(\alpha_1 + \alpha_2 K + \alpha_3 K \dfrac{b}{a}\right) 10^{(\beta_1 + \beta_2/T)}}$$

$$= g(a,b,c,K,T). \qquad (2.7.16)$$

Hence, for the esterification of butanol and acetic acid, we find that residence time is a decreasing function of the quantities of the reactants charged, a and b, the concentration of sulfuric acid catalyst, K, and the reaction temperature, T, and an increasing function of the quantity of ester formed, c.[42]

---

[41] *Ibid.*, p. 971.

[42] Equation (2.7.16) still does not exhaust the engineering analysis of the process as employed commercially. In commercial esterification processes alcohol, acetic acid, and sulfuric acid are fed into a distilling column and the ester product is continuously removed. A complete analysis of such a continuous process requires analytical distillation considerations as well as kinetic analysis. See Charles E. Leyes and D. F. Othmer, "Continuous Esteri-

Equation (2.7.12) represents a theoretical example while (2.7.16) represents an empirical example of "engineering" production functions of the kind likely to prevail in individual chemical processes. To convert such a function into a stock-flow production function requires us to relate the inputs and outputs of a batch reaction to the stock-flow inputs and outputs of production theory. The simpler equation (2.7.12) will be used to illustrate the general method of deriving such a production function.

Residence time per batch, t, and the number of batches run per year, N, are related as follows:

$$N = H/(t + h), \qquad (2.7.17)$$

where H = hours of operation per year (assumed constant), and h = hours down time per batch — that is, time spent in preparing and recharging the reactor vessel between batches (assumed constant). The goods-in-process inventory of acid is

$$X_1 = a - (c/2). \qquad (2.7.18)$$

For alcohol it is given by

$$X_2 = b - (c/2). \qquad (2.7.19)$$

It will be assumed that reactor capacity, X_3, is proportional to output per batch, that is,

$$X_3 = \alpha c. \qquad (2.7.20)$$

This is an approximation that simplifies the derivation. A more realistic assumption is that X_3 is a linear function of a and b, since the reactor vessel must be large enough to hold the combined physical bulks of the input charges. The annual molar consumption of acid and alcohol, and the

fication of Butanol and Acetic Acid, Kinetic and Distillation Considerations," *Transaction of the American Institute of Chemical Engineers*, XLI, (1945), 157–196, for an extension of the analysis to include distillation considerations. The complete analysis requires simultaneous considerations of the law of mass action, the law of kinetics, and the distillation laws.

annual production of ester is given by equations (2.7.5)–(2.7.7) written above, that is, $x_1 = x_2 = y = Nc$.

If we eliminate the engineering variables a, b, c, and t from (2.7.12), (2.7.17)–(2.7.20), and (2.7.5)–(2.7.7), we get the production technology given by

$$y = f(X_1, X_2, X_3) = \frac{HX_3}{\alpha g\left(X_1 + \dfrac{X_3}{2\alpha}, \ X_2 + \dfrac{X_3}{2\alpha}, \ \dfrac{X_3}{\alpha}\right) + \alpha h} \qquad (2.7.21)$$

and

$$x_1 = x_2 = y. \qquad (2.7.22)$$

A similar production function can be derived from (2.7.16) by employing the appropriate transformations to convert the engineering variables K and T into stock or flow economic inputs. Thus, fuel or some other source of heat is required to operate the reaction at the temperature T.

8. *Input Substitution and the Theory of Queues*

The previous sections have emphasized the analysis of engineering production processes in which the input-output relationships are deterministic in character and based upon more-or-less "exact" physical principles. The principles of stock-flow production theory are not limited in application to such processes. There are many processes in which the production alternatives are subject to probabilistic analytical formulation and which involve reorganizations of man-machine systems. A wide class of these processes falls within the range of queuing or waiting-line theory.

According to Churchman, Ackoff, and Arnoff, "Waiting-line theory dates back to the work of Erlang in 1909. In Erlang's and subsequent work up to approximately 1945, applications were restricted in the main to operation of telephone systems. Since then the theory has been extended and applied to a wide variety of phenomena." [43]

[43] C. W. Churchman, R. L. Ackoff, and E. L. Arnoff, *Introduction to Operations Research* (New York: John Wiley, 1957), p. 389.

The extension and application of queuing theory to a wide variety of decision problems have been due to the research of numerous workers in the fields of probability theory and operations research.[44] Our purpose in this section is to show how the principles of queuing theory generate resource substitution in a typical application to a production decision problem.

Suppose we consider an important problem faced by any trucking firm, or, for that matter, any firm employing capital equipment subject to wear and breakdown, as, for instance, the problem of maintaining such equipment in operating order. Imagine, in the simplest case, that a trucking firm repairs leased vehicles and has only enough equipment and mechanics to work on one truck at a time. This assumption limits us to a so-called single-station queuing model. The production responsibilities of the firm are executed by sending trucks to pick up loads of freight commodities from shipping customers, and delivering such merchandise to the consignees. In performing such hauls, trucks develop a wide variety of malfunctions which require them to be withdrawn from service, sent to the repair shop, and undergo repairs before they can be returned to service. If a truck is sent to the repair station, one of two alternatives is possible: either the station is not occupied, in which case the truck is moved into the station and the repair process started, or the station is already occupied, in which case the truck enters a repair waiting-line or queue. Hence, trucks can and do lose hauling time because of time spent in repairs and time spent awaiting repairs. The time a truck spends awaiting repairs will, of course, depend upon the length of the waiting-line, which in turn may at times grow very large, depending upon the magnitude of the malfunction rate relative to the repair rate.

We will assume that truck malfunctions occur at random,

[44] A perusal of issues of the *Journal of the Royal Statistical Society*, the *Operations Research Quarterly*, and the *Journal of the Operations Research Society of America* will reveal a large number of papers on queuing theory and its applications. For a bibliography of some of these papers see Churchman *et al.*, pp. 415–416.

that is, the entry of trucks to the repair station is random, and that the exit of repaired vehicles from the repair station is random. It will also be assumed that the repair rate is independent of the number of units in the queue (no speed-up takes place when the line is long), and that the trucks in the line are repaired in order of their appearance in the line, with no moving forward of units requiring short repairs.

For a single-station queuing process such as that just described, it is possible to derive mixed difference-differential equations that express implicitly the relationship between waiting time, repair time, the number of units in the line, and the probability of there being n units in the line at some time t. If λ is the mean rate (trucks per unit time) at which trucks arrive at the station to be repaired, μ is the mean repair rate (repaired trucks per unit time), n is the number of units in the line (including the one being serviced) at time t, and $P_n(t)$ is the probability of n units in the queue at time t, then [45]

$$\frac{dP_n(t)}{dt} = \begin{cases} \lambda P_{n-1}(t) + \mu P_{n+1}(t) - (\lambda + \mu)P_n(t), & n > 0, \\ -\lambda P_0(t) + \mu P_1(t), & n = 0. \end{cases} \quad (2.8.1)$$

Solutions to (2.8.1) can be very difficult if $P_n(t)$ is complex. In the simple case in which $P_n(t) = P_n$, that is, the probability that there are n units in the line is constant over time, (2.8.1) becomes

$$0 = \begin{cases} \lambda P_{n-1} + \mu P_{n+1} - (\lambda + \mu)P_n, & n > 0, \\ -\lambda P_0 + \mu P_1, & n = 0, \end{cases} \quad (2.8.2)$$

with solution

$$P_n = (\lambda/\mu)^n P_0. \quad (2.8.3)$$

Since $\sum_{i=0}^{\infty} P_i = 1$, it follows that $P_0 = 1 - \lambda/\mu$. One can also obtain an expression for the mean length of the waiting line $\bar{n}$.

$$\bar{n} = \sum_{n=0}^{\infty} nP_n = \frac{\lambda/\mu}{1 - (\lambda/\mu)}, \quad \frac{\lambda}{\mu} < 1. \quad (2.8.4)$$

[45] Churchman *et al.*, p. 395.

From the "technical" restriction (2.8.4) it is now possible to demonstrate the possibility of substitution between the current input, repair labor, and the capital input, trucks. Suppose the malfunction rate, λ, of trucks is proportional to total firm output, y, measured, say, in truck-miles per year, that is,

$$\lambda = \alpha y. \qquad (2.8.5)$$

Since λ is truck malfunctions per year, α is malfunctions per mile. Also, suppose that the mean repair rate of trucks, μ, is proportional to the man-hours of repair labor employed per year, x_1, that is,

$$\mu = \beta x_1. \qquad (2.8.6)$$

Since μ is repaired trucks per year, β is repaired trucks per man-hour.

We can now write an expression for the expected stock, X_2, of leased trucks required to meet any given level of output. This stock will be composed of two parts — the mean or expected number of units in the waiting line, $\bar{n}$, and the mean number of units, $\bar{N}$, required in service during the year to produce the given output level. Hence

$$X_2 = \bar{n} + \bar{N}. \qquad (2.8.7)$$

$\bar{n}$ is given by (2.8.4). If we let m be the annual mileage that a vehicle would be driven if it required no repairs and was used continuously, then

$$y = m\bar{N}. \qquad (2.8.8)$$

The constant m can be obtained in practice by multiplying the average speed of vehicles in service by total firm operating hours per year. Note that we cannot assume with consistency that average annual truck mileage is an independent constant, since this will depend upon truck utilization which, in turn, depends upon truck time lost awaiting repairs and being repaired. The primitive datum on intensity of utilization is m, which measures this intensity in use only.

From (2.8.5) and (2.8.6), $\bar{n}$ in equation (2.8.4) and (2.8.7) can be written in terms of output and labor input by eliminating λ and μ, while (2.8.8) can be used to express $\overline{N}$ in terms of output. Making these substitutions permits (2.8.7) to be written in the production function form,

$$F(y,x_1,X_2) = y\left(\frac{\alpha m}{\beta x_1 - \alpha y} + 1\right) - mX_2 = 0. \quad (2.8.9)$$

This function shows decreasing returns because it is really a "short-run" production function. We have fixed the input "repair station capacity" at the unit level in deriving (2.8.9).

A graph of two isoproduct contours for this function is shown in Fig. 2–9. For an output of y vehicle-miles per year, there is a lower limit, y/m, on the stock of trucks that can be employed. If the repair labor input is increased beyond bound, the expected length of the waiting-line and the time spent waiting and being repaired approach zero. Hence, the expected stock of trucks required approaches the "ideal" level, that is, $X_2 = \overline{N} = y/m$. Similarly, there is a lower bound, $\alpha y/\beta$, on the input of repair labor required, since if $\lambda = \alpha y \geq \beta x_1 = \mu$ (the input to the repair station exceeds or equals the output), the waiting-line will eventually grow beyond bound requiring an infinite investment in trucks. Between these two limits there is a wide range of substitution between trucks and repair labor. By using more repair labor it is possible to speed repairs, reduce truck time awaiting repairs, increase truck utilization, and thus produce the same level of output with a smaller stock of trucks. The mechanism of substitution here is the waiting-line. The expected length of the waiting-line — an intermediate "engineering" variable — is expanded or contracted in the substitution process.

The model can be readily extended to account for multi-station repair facilities.[46] It can also be extended in other directions — for example, where a fixed stock of trucks is owned by the firm and the waiting-line is bounded by this stock. In terms of applications, however, the most im-

---

[46] See Churchman *et al.*, pp. 404–407, for a discussion of multistation queuing models.

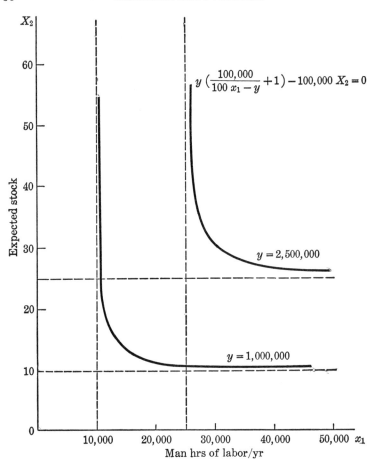

Fig. 2–9. Isoproduct map for trucking process.

portant extension has been the use of Monte Carlo techniques in queuing processes.[47] By this technique one simulates the actual queuing process on an electronic computer. For example, the computer might be programmed to select imaginary trucks at random to fill incoming orders which might be the actual orders received by a firm. The computer could also be programmed to draw from an empirical malfunction

[47] Churchman *et al.*, pp. 407–411.

distribution to generate a probabilistic sequence of truck malfunctions. The computer would also draw from an empirical distribution of repair times to determine the length of time each hypothetical truck will be in the repair station. This simulation process generates queues of the kind analyzed above, and one can "experiment" with different amounts of truck and repair labor inputs. This technique has the advantage of not having to depend upon the simplifying assumptions of analytical solutions. Monte Carlo techniques have been applied to extremely complicated queuing processes such as the flying, maintenance, and supply system of a USAF airplane base.[48]

[48] See R. A. Levine and R. B. Rainey, "Random Variations and Sampling Models in Production Economics," *Journal of Political Economy*, LXVIII, (June 1960), 219.

Chapter III

The Theory of Production and Investment: Indestructible Capital Goods

1. The Stock-Flow Production Function

The empirical investigation of the preceding chapter would seem to supply a considerable amount of evidence in favor of the hypothesis that the generalized firm or process production function should express output (or outputs) as a convex function of both the current inputs to current production and the stocks of durable equipment and inventories of inputs and goods-in-process employed in production. If there are n current inputs and m capital inputs used in the production of a single homogeneous product, then in explicit form our hypothesis is that

$$y = f(x_1, x_2, \cdots, x_n; X_{n+1}, X_{n+2}, \cdots, X_{n+m}). \quad (3.1.1)$$

In the case of a firm engaged in the steam production and transmission of electricity, y might be kilowatts per hour of electricity. The major current input might be natural gas, x_1, measured in energy units or cubic feet per hour. X_2, X_3, X_4, and X_5 would be the physical stocks of boiler, turbine, generator, and cable inputs respectively. The production function would be written

$$y = f(x_1, X_2, X_3, X_4, X_5) \qquad (3.1.2)$$

for this process. The function (3.1.2) and its generalization in (3.1.1) may be considered typical of the pattern of technological input-output interdependence, especially in engineering processes. Observe that this interdependence, even in the simplified power plant example, embraces an input which is consumed continuously and contemporaneously with the production of output (x_1), three inputs requiring periodic replacement (X_2, X_3, and X_4), and an input of almost infinite physical durability with use (X_5).

In any unified theory of production and investment (including replacement), one imagines the typical firm confronted with a variety of substitutable inputs, ranging all the way from inputs whose consumption is immediately and directly associated with current production, through replaceable and/or maintainable durable inputs whose "consumption" embraces many production periods, to highly durable capital goods such as pipelines, transmission cables, and buildings. The production function relating these various classes of inputs must necessarily be at the technological core of the theory of investment. The theory of investment must ultimately be able to describe the reaction of the firm to changes in output demand, input supply, and technological parameters, under production function constraints of the type suggested in (3.1.1) and (3.1.2). Our major concern in this chapter is to explore such a development.

Whether or not insistence on a production function of the general form (3.1.1) represents a major departure from current practice is difficult to say. I tend to the view that it is not, because I think much of the literary analyses of Marshallian short- and long-run production responses are based upon an implicit hypothesis such as that in (3.1.1). That the hypothesis has not been made explicit and its implications explored is evident. The literature of neoclassical production theory is not clear on the interpretation of the inputs appearing in this function. In their treatments of cost and production theory such writers as Paul Samuelson [1] and R. G. D. Allen [2] refer to the arguments of the production function as "inputs" without providing any interpretation at all. This is reasonable in view of the fact that both authors are concerned with the purely formal properties of the theory. Sune Carlson,[3] on the other hand, carefully interprets "inputs" as productive services which are classed as either variable or fixed. Direct labor is given as an example of variable services, while machine services and factory building services are given as examples of "fixed" services. The difficulty here is that only the physical stocks (compressors and pipe, for instance) are "fixed" in the short run. The intensity of utilization (machine hours), which would seem to be the proper measure of machine services, is not in fact fixed even in the short run. The direct objects of adjustment or action parameters of the firm are (1) the current inputs to current production, and (2) the physical stocks of the various kinds of capital goods employed. The distinguishing characteristic of capital goods is simply that their *presence*, in the form of physical stocks, is required if production is to take place. Only in special cases can we obtain any kind of a measure of capital services in the form, say, of machine hours. How does one measure the "services" of pipelines, power lines, and highways? By the number of units of output they produce? If so, then one does not have a meaningful *independent* measure of such inputs. The significance of such inputs is to be found in the fact that so many tons of pipe, or tons of cable, or cubic feet of concrete, arranged in a certain way, *must be present if output is to be produced.* Furthermore, the

---

[1] P. A. Samuelson, *Foundations of Economic Analysis* (Cambridge: Harvard University Press, 1948), pp. 57–58.

[2] R. G. D. Allen, *Mathematical Economics* (London: Macmillan, 1956), pp. 332–337.

[3] Sune Carlson, *A Study on the Pure Theory of Production* (New York: Kelly and Millman, 1956), pp. 12–16.

level of output that can be produced varies directly with the physical quantities of such inputs that are present when production takes place. Such inputs are not "consumed" in any sense similar to the consumption of raw materials or energy.[4] Thus, in the production function for electrical energy, (3.1.2), we would say that y kilowatts per hour of electrical energy can be delivered to consumers whenever x_1 units per hour of natural gas are burned in the presence of X_2 boiler units, X_3 turbine units, X_4 generator units, and the energy delivered through X_5 units of transmission cable.

It might be argued that *both* the stocks of capital and their intensities of current utilization (where appropriate) are among the direct objects of control in the firm.[5] However, it is difficult to imagine any production situation in which such utilization rates can be varied independently of one or more of the current inputs. Increases in machine utilization must necessarily increase energy consumption and perhaps raw materials and/or labor.[6] Therefore, the inclusion of all current inputs in the production function permits one to account for the economizing consequences of variations in equipment utilization through the impact of these variations upon the consumption of current inputs.

A stock-flow form of the production function very similar

[4] The same considerations apply to labor, except in this case it is the man-hours of labor activity which are bought and sold in the producers' market, whereas stock inputs are typically purchased, not rented, by firms.

[5] Such an argument is presented along with some empirical analysis in a multilithographed paper by the author, Vernon L. Smith, "Investment Theory and the Theory of Cost and Production: A Synthesis with Applications" (Lafayette, Indiana: Purdue University, May 1956).

[6] See the appendix to chap. 20 of R. K. Davidson, V. L. Smith, and J. Wiley, *Economics: An Analytical Approach* (Chicago: Richard D. Irwin, 1958), for the derivation of a production function from engineering equations for a simple machining process. The function exhibits substitution between machines and cutting tools. In this case the mechanism of substitution is the possibility of variation in machine speed. Output is shown to be an increasing function of the stock of machines and the speed with which machines are operated. But from an empirical engineering law, cutting tool consumption (due to wear and breakage) is an increasing function of machine speed. Therefore, machine speed can be eliminated as an intermediate "engineering" variable, and a relationship established between output, the consumption of cutting tools (a "current" input), and the stock of machines.

in appearance to that suggested in (3.1.1) has been employed by Dorfman, Samuelson, and Solow to study the nature of interest and certain intertemporal conditions for economic efficiency.[7] Since their interest settles on interindustry analysis and a generalization of the Leontief [8] dynamic model, they hypothesize a stock-flow production function for the output of each industry. For the two-industry case they assume smooth, continuous, convex, neoclassical functions,

$$\left.\begin{array}{l} X_1 = F^1(X_{11},X_{21},S_{11},S_{21}) \\ X_2 = F^2(X_{12},X_{22},S_{12},S_{22}) \end{array}\right\}, \qquad (3.1.3)$$

where X_1 and X_2 are the outputs of industries 1 and 2, X_{ij} is the output of industry i consumed on current account by industry j, and S_{ij} is the stock of the product of industry i whose presence is maintained by industry j. Hence, Dorfman, Samuelson, and Solow assume in general that a given item may be purchased on both current and capital account and that the two classes of inputs are substitutes and are continuously expansible and contractible. In our empirical study in the previous chapter, we found numerous examples of substitution between current inputs, substitution between capital inputs, and substitution between current inputs of one kind and capital inputs of another kind. There appears to be no empirical evidence to suggest that, at the level of individual processes, current and capital inputs of the same type may be substitutive, that the stock of lathes, for example, is a substitute over some range for the "current" consumption (replacement) of lathes. In the absence of such evidence an hypothesis such as (3.1.3) would seem to be unnecessarily general.[9]

[7] R. Dorfman, P. Samuelson, and R. Solow, *Linear Programming and Economic Analysis* (New York: McGraw-Hill, 1958), pp. 281–300, 305–335.

[8] Leontief, *Studies in the Structure of the American Economy*, pp. 55–58.

[9] It is not suggested that the Dorfman-Samuelson-Solow results are in any way dependent upon these considerations. Their conclusions are not affected if we omit some of the S_{ij} and X_{ij} in (3.1.3). On the other hand, potentially much more powerful theorems may be deducible if one delimits the generality of the hypothesis in (3.1.3).

The distinguishing characteristic of our stock-flow production function (3.1.1) is the fact that the stock inputs are continuously variable only in considering alternative long-run production plans. Once the X_i have been determined and the capital facilities installed they can only be varied by replacement, or by installing parallel units. A primary concern of this chapter is to develop the implications of such phenomena where capital goods are assumed to be of infinite durability.

2. The Criterion of Choice

The question as to what is the proper discount criterion for optimization in investment decision problems faced by the firm has received considerable attention in the literature.[10] The present study has nothing to add to this discussion except to assert the opinion that it is ultimately an empirical question roughly of the form, "What behavior criterion provides the most satisfactory analytical representation of the objectives which firm decision makers appear to be trying to achieve?"

In this study it will be assumed that in the choice of technique (the current input–capital input mix) to meet a given output target, the objective is to minimize "cost on current account" or simply "current" cost. Where output is also a decision variable to be adjusted in accordance with both cost and revenue considerations, it will be assumed that the objective is to maximize "current" profit. By *current cost* is meant the constant outlay stream that has a present value equal to that of all future cost outlays over the firm's

[10] See Lutz and Lutz, *Theory of Investment of the Firm*, pp. 16–55, for a summary of the pre-1951 literature on criteria and a comprehensive discussion of the matter by the Lutzes. In a more recent paper, J. Hirshleifer, "On the Theory of Optimal Investment Decision," *Journal of Political Economy*, LXVI (August 1958), 329–352, has criticized the use of internal rate of return criteria and provided some support for the maximization of present value. For arguments in favor of maximizing the ratio of profit to total investment (or the rate of return on ordinary shares), see André Gabor and I. F. Pearce, "The Place of Money Capital in the Theory of Production," *Quarterly Journal of Economics*, LXXII (November 1958), 537–557.

planning horizon.[11] By *current profit* is meant the constant income stream whose present value is equal to the difference between the present value of all future revenues and the present value of all future costs over the firm's planning horizon.[12]

3. The Theory of the Firm Using Infinitely Durable Capital Goods

CHOICE OF TECHNIQUE — NEOCLASSICAL ANALYSIS

In the interest of clarity we shall develop our analysis assuming that there are only two inputs — one current input and one capital input. The extension of the analysis to the general case of n current and m capital inputs is largely routine, and would inhibit the discussion of fundamentals that is so important at this formative stage. It will be assumed in this section that the capital input requires no maintenance, is of infinite physical durability, and is continuously variable in its initial installation, but once installed cannot be contracted in physical quantity except by replacement, though it can be expanded by adding parallel facilities of any desired size. For example, the capital good might be a power line or a pipeline. The production function, assumed to be continuous and differentiable, can be written

$$y = f(x_1, X_2), \qquad (3.3.1)$$

[11] This criterion is also used by George Terborgh in *Dynamic Equipment Policy*. Compare, for example, his concept of the uniform annual equivalent, p. 47.

[12] Perhaps some rational for my use of current cost and current profit as criteria is to be found in the concern which businesses show for depreciation accounting. Firms are continually concerned with how to allocate investment costs to current operating periods. Rarely does a firm cumulate current costs to express them on capital (present value) account. This concern for expressing costs on a current basis seems to reflect the greater intuitive significance of such information to the decision maker. Also, be it noted that engineers are trained to employ uniform annuity discounting in engineering economy decision problems. See the standard textbook in this area, E. L. Grant, *Principles of Engineering Economy*, 3rd ed. (New York: Ronald Press, 1938), Chaps. 4 and 7.

where y is the continuous steady-state flow of output, x_1 is the continuous consumption of the current input Number 1, and X_2 is the physical stock of the infinitely durable capital good Number 2. While y and x_1 are measured in physical units per unit time (say per year), X_2 is measured in physical units only.

If we assume an indefinitely long planning horizon, and let w_1 be the price of the current input, then the annual outlay for the current input is $w_1 x_1$ dollars per year. If we let W_2 be the price of the capital input, then $W_2 X_2$ is the investment in durable goods in the process. Using continuous discounting at an instantaneous rate r, the cost on current account of an initial investment outlay $W_2 X_2$ is $r W_2 X_2$. Therefore the expression for total current cost, C, is

$$C = w_1 x_1 + r W_2 X_2. \tag{3.3.2}$$

If we mean by the term "depreciation" (a term with so many meanings that it is almost useless for scientific purposes) the dollar amount of capital costs allocated to current operating periods, the second term in (3.3.2) is the depreciation on the investment $W_2 X_2$. If we imagine the firm selling perpetuities in the bond market at a price $1/r$ to finance the investment $W_2 X_2$, then $r W_2 X_2$ is the annual payment to bondholders of record. In a very real economic sense we can think of $r W_2 X_2$ as the cost per year of "maintaining" the "presence" of a unit of the capital good in production.

If the objective is to minimize (3.3.2) subject to (3.3.1) with y a parameter, then an equivalent problem is to minimize

$$\phi = w_1 x_1 + r W_2 X_2 - \lambda [f(x_1, X_2) - y] \tag{3.3.3}$$

where λ is the Lagrange multiplier. Minimizing ϕ with respect to x_1 and X_2 gives the familiar J. B. Clark (discounted) marginal productivity conditions

$$w_1 - \lambda f_1 = 0, \tag{3.3.4}$$
$$r W_2 - \lambda f_2 = 0, \tag{3.3.5}$$

where $f_1 = \partial f / \partial x_1$, and $f_2 = \partial f / \partial X_2$.

Solving (3.3.1), (3.3.4), and (3.3.5) simultaneously for x_1, X_2, and λ, determines the combined "short-" and "long-run" input equilibrium of the firm under steady-state conditions; thus,

$$x_1^0 = d_1(w_1, rW_2, y), \qquad\qquad (3.3.6)$$
$$X_2^0 = D_2(w_1, rW_2, y), \qquad\qquad (3.3.7)$$
$$\lambda^0 = \lambda(w_1, rW_2, y). \qquad\qquad (3.3.8)$$

Equations (3.3.6) and (3.3.7) are analogous to the well-known input demand functions of the received theory of cost and production.[13] The Lagrange multiplier in this context can be interpreted as marginal cost, that is, $\lambda^0 = \partial C/\partial y$.[14] The functions are all "virtual" relationships, however, that is, they express hypothetical relationships for planning purpose *prior* to the actual installation of X_2^0 units of capital. Once the investment is effected, these functions become meaningless for planning purposes, and in this sense differ from the analogous functions in received production theory.

The input equilibrium is displayed graphically in Fig. 3–1 in terms of the familiar isoproduct contour diagram. Conditions (3.3.1), (3.3.4), and (3.3.5) define the equilibrium point P. The "mix" of the firm's operations as between current and capital account depends upon output, the relative prices of the current and capital inputs and the discount rate or the parameters y, w_1, W_2, and r. The qualitative effect on the optimal employments x_1^0 and X_2^0, of changes in several of these parameters can be determined unambiguously from the convexity properties of the production function.[15] Thus, *ceteris paribus*, the greater is the price of input

[13] See P. A. Samuelson, *Foundations of Economic Analysis*, p. 59. Equation (3.3.6) is a neoclassical flow demand function while (3.3.7) is a stock demand function or a demand for durable goods to hold rather than consume.

[14] See Vernon L. Smith, "The Theory of Investment and Production," *Quarterly Journal of Economics*, LXXIII (February 1959), pp. 68–69, 1, for a derivation of the equality between Lagrange multipliers and the corresponding "shadow price" valuations placed upon parameters of constraint, such as y, at the margin.

[15] This can be done rigorously by writing total differentials of the equilibrium conditions and imposing the secondary conditions for a relative mini-

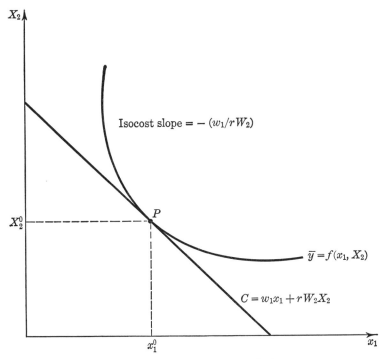

Fig. 3–1. Neoclassical choice of technique.

Number 1, the smaller is x_1^0, the larger is X_2^0, and therefore the greater will be the firm's "fixed" investment or its cost on capital account. Similarly, *ceteris paribus*, the lower is the unit investment cost, W_2, or the lower is the rate of discount, r, the smaller is x_1^0 and the larger is X_2^0.[16]

mum of current cost. See Samuelson, *Foundations* . . ., pp. 61–69, for an elegant parallel treatment of the classical theory of cost and production. All of Samuelson's theorems apply to the case under analysis here if we pretend that the "price" of the capital input is rW_2. The operational interpretation, however, is somewhat different, depending upon whether we are considering hypothetical alternative initial conditions or changes in conditions where the firm has a sunk investment, as is discussed below.

[16] Furthermore, total investment $K = W_2X_2^0$ is greater the lower is the interest rate. Changes in W_2 may either enlarge or contract total investment depending upon the elasticity of the capital stock demand function. To show

If we assume a finite planning horizon of T years then the expression for cost on current account becomes

$$C = w_1 x_1 + \frac{r W_2 X_2}{1 - e^{-rT}}, \qquad (3.3.9)$$

to be minimized subject to (3.3.1). The marginal productivity conditions can be written

$$\frac{w_1}{f_1} = \frac{r W_2}{(1 - e^{-rT}) f_2}. \qquad (3.3.10)$$

The slope of an isocost line in Fig. 3–1 for this case is $-\left[w_1(1 - e^{-rT})/r W_2\right]$. All the above qualitative statements concerning the effect of parametric changes applies to the finite horizon case with the added statement that the shorter is the horizon T, the larger is x_1^0 and the smaller is X_2^0 and $W_2 X_2^0$. Short planning horizons, as expected, favor a relatively smaller operation on capital account. To the extent that one can attribute short horizons to uncertainty, it might be argued that the greater the uncertainty of all the firm's data estimates, and, indeed, of the firm's very existence, the shorter is the planning horizon and therefore the smaller the firm's investment in long-term durable goods. Optimal investment-current account programming under uncertainty dictates the flexibility of relatively greater operations on current account.

---

this, write

$$\frac{dK}{dW_2} = W_2 \frac{dX_2^0}{dW_2} + X_2^0, \text{ where } \frac{dX_2^0}{dW_2} < 0.$$

Hence $dK/dW_2 \gtrless 0$, according as $W_2(dX_2^0/dW_2) + X_2^0 \gtrless 0$. In terms of elasticities we can write

$$e_K = \frac{W_2}{K} \frac{dK}{dW_2} = \frac{W_2}{X_2^0} \frac{dX_2^0}{dW_2} + 1 = e_2 + 1,$$

that is, the elasticity of demand for money capital, e_K, is 1 plus the elasticity of demand for physical capital, e_2. Hence, if $-\infty < e_2 < -1$, then $-\infty < e_K < 0$, while if $-1 < e_2 < 0$, then $0 < e_K < 1$. Note that K is the total money value of the stock of capital and not the flow of investment expenditures.

CHOICE OF TECHNIQUE — NONLINEAR PROGRAMMING
ANALYSIS

In neoclassical analysis, the point set of technologically achievable input-output combinations is contained in an area bounded on the southwest by an isoproduct contour such as that in Fig. 3–1, on the south by the x_1 axis (or the contour, whichever is higher) and on the west by the X_2 axis (or the contour, whichever is higher). That is, all possible combinations are in the positive quadrant of the input space above the appropriate isoproduct contour. This lower bound on the set of permissible input-output possibilities is not usually, in strict accuracy, representable by a single smooth neoclassical production function such as (3.3.1). There are typically other kinds of technological, institutional, and even legal, constraints on the minimum cost choice of technique. Optimization under several constraints, some of which may involve inequalities, is a natural for the Kuhn-Tucker [17] conditions for the solution of nonlinear programming problems.

As an illustration, consider the simple power-line process design problem of section 4 in Chapter II. The (implicit) production function form was $X_2(x_1 - y) - Ky^2 = 0$. Suppose we impose the condition that not less than $\bar{y}$ units are to be produced (a slight generalization of the requirement that we produce just $\bar{y}$ units), that is, $y \geq \bar{y} \geq 0$. Hence, one of our constraints is $- X_2(x_1 - \bar{y}) + K\bar{y}^2 \leq 0$.

An important physical feature of the electrical transmission process is the existence of maximum and minimum amounts (sizes) of cable that can be used. Maximum cable size may be limited by mechanical considerations — for example, too large a cable cannot be supported with safety — or by commercial availability, that is, cable beyond a certain size simply may not be produced. Hence, there will be a constraint of the form, $X_2 \leq M$, where M is the upper size

[17] H. W. Kuhn and A. W. Tucker, "Nonlinear Programming," in U. Neyman (ed.), *Proceedings of the Second Berkeley Symposium on Mathematical Statistics and Probability* (Berkeley: University of California Press, 1951), pp. 481–492.

limit on conductor cable. Minimum conductor size may also be determined by mechanical consideration, where, for example, too small a cable may not support wind loads; or by heat dissipation problems, where a small cable may cause so much energy loss in the form of heat as to melt the conductor, creating a safety hazard. Hence, we assume some lower limit, m, on conductor size, giving a constraint of the form, $X_2 \geq m$.

Adding the nonnegativity conditions on the inputs provides the convex technology set defined by the following conditions

$$\left.\begin{array}{ll} g_1(x_1,X_2) = X_2(x_1 - \bar{y}) - K\bar{y}^2 \geq 0, \\ g_2(x_1,X_2) = -X_2 + M \qquad\qquad \geq 0, \\ g_3(x_1,X_2) = X_2 - m \qquad\qquad \geq 0, \\ \qquad\qquad\qquad\qquad x_1,\ X_2 \geq 0. \end{array}\right\} \qquad (3.3.11)$$

This set is represented geometrically by the shaded area in Fig. 3–2. The nonlinear programming problem is to minimize $C = w_1x_1 + rW_2X_2$ subject to (3.3.11).

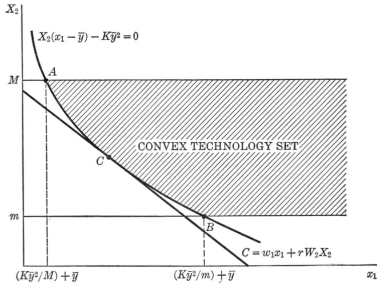

Fig. 3–2. The Kuhn-Tucker conditions and choice of technique.

Now, if (x_1^0, X_2^0) minimizes current cost subject to (3.3.11), then there must exist a set of three nonnegative Lagrange multipliers, λ_1, λ_2, λ_3 which impute values to the first three constraints in (3.3.11), such that the following conditions are satisfied: [18]

1) The solution must be feasible; in other words, it must satisfy the inequalities in (3.3.11). Furthermore, if

$$X_2^0(x_1^0 - \bar{y}) - K\bar{y}^2 > 0, \quad \text{then} \quad \lambda_1 = 0,$$
$$- X_2^0 + M > 0, \quad \text{then} \quad \lambda_2 = 0,$$
$$X_2^0 - m > 0, \quad \text{then} \quad \lambda_3 = 0,$$

that is, if any constraint is satisfied with a surplus, then the imputed value of reducing that constraint is zero.

2) The marginal imputed cost of each input must not exceed its unit cost ("market" price) on current account. That is,

$$w_1 - \sum_{i=1}^{3} \lambda_i \frac{\partial g_i}{\partial x_1} \geq 0 \quad \text{and} \quad rW_2 - \sum_{i=1}^{3} \lambda_i \frac{\partial g_i}{\partial X_2} \geq 0.$$

Furthermore, if

$$w_1 - \lambda_1(X_2^0) - \lambda_2(0) - \lambda_3(0) > 0, \ x_1^0 = \frac{K\bar{y}^2}{M} + \bar{y},$$
$$rW_2 - \lambda_1(x_1^0 - \bar{y}) - \lambda_2(-1) - \lambda_3(1) > 0, \ X_2^0 = m;$$

that is, if the unit cost on current account of any input exceeds its marginal imputed cost, that input is employed at its technologically minimum level.

Hence, we get a Walras-Pareto neoclassical interior solution such as C somewhere on the arc AB in Fig. 3–2 if

$$X_2^0(x_1^0 - \bar{y}) - K\bar{y}^2 = 0, \quad \lambda_1 \geq 0,$$
$$X_2^0 \leq M, \quad \lambda_2 = 0,$$
$$X_2^0 \geq m, \quad \lambda_3 = 0,$$
$$w_1 - \lambda_1 X_2^0 = 0,$$
$$rW_2 - \lambda_1(x_1^0 - \bar{y}) = 0.$$

[18] See Kuhn and Tucker, pp. 481–492. Also, see Dorfman, Samuelson, and Solow, *Linear Programming*, pp. 199–201, for an exposition of the Kuhn-Tucker conditions.

We get a Samuelson-Kuhn-Tucker boundary solution at A in Fig. 3–2 if

$$X_2^0(x_1^0 - \bar{y}) - K\bar{y}^2 = 0, \quad \lambda_1 \geq 0,$$
$$X_2^0 = M, \quad \lambda_2 \geq 0,$$
$$X_2^0 > m, \quad \lambda_3 = 0,$$
$$w_1 - \lambda_1 X_2^0 > 0, \quad x_1^0 = \frac{K\bar{y}^2}{M} + \bar{y},$$
$$rW_2 - \lambda_1(x_1^0 - \bar{y}) - \lambda_2 (-1) = 0.$$

Note that $w_1 > \lambda_1 X_2^0$ and $rW_2 = \lambda_1(x_1^0 - \bar{y}) - \lambda_2$ implies that $-(w_1/rW_2) < -(X_2^0/x_1^0 - \bar{y})$ is the slope of the isoproduct contour at A, that is, the solution is always at A if the slope of the isocost contour at A is algebraically smaller than (or equal to) the slope of the isoproduct contour at A. Similarly, we get a boundary solution at B if

$$X_2^0(x_1^0 - \bar{y}) - K\bar{y}^2 = 0, \quad \lambda_1 \geq 0,$$
$$X_2^0 < M, \quad \lambda_2 = 0,$$
$$X_2^0 = m, \quad \lambda_3 \geq 0,$$
$$w_1 - \lambda_1 X_2^0 = 0,$$
$$rW_2 - \lambda_1(x_1^0 - \bar{y}) - \lambda_3 > 0, \quad X_2^0 = m.$$

The technological (and economically competitive) alternatives are even more numerous in practice than those contained in the set defined by (3.3.11). To mention only one example, aluminum conductor is closely competitive with copper conductor, and the choice of which metal is to be used for power transmission work is, in fact, quite sensitive to the relative prices of the two metals. The production function using aluminum cable is the same as that using copper except for the parameter K. If we let K_c be the appropriate constant for copper, then the production function is $X_2(x_1 - \bar{y}) - K_c\bar{y}^2 = 0$. If K_a is the corresponding constant for aluminum, then the production function is $X_3(x_1 - \bar{y}) - K_a\bar{y}^2 = 0$, where X_3 is the quantity of aluminum conductor used. We can now impose upper bounds on the sizes of the two kinds of cable, that is, $X_2 \leq M_2$ and $X_3 \leq M_3$, as well as the lower bounds $X_2 \geq m_2$ and $X_3 \geq m_3$. The problem of power-line design is now one of choosing nonnegative values of x_1, X_2, and X_3 such that $C = w_1 x_1 + r(W_2 X_2 + W_3 X_3)$, where W_2 is the price of aluminum cable, is minimized subject to

$$X_2(x_1 - \bar{y}) - K_c \bar{y}^2 \geq 0,$$
$$X_3(x_1 - \bar{y}) - K_a \bar{y}^2 \geq 0,$$
$$- X_2 + M_2 \geq 0,$$
$$- X_3 + M_3 \geq 0,$$
$$X_2 - m_2 \geq 0,$$
$$X_3 - m_3 \geq 0.$$

An application of the Kuhn-Tucker conditions to the solution of this problem permits a determination of which of the two cable materials is optimal as well as the optimal quantity to install.

THE FIRM'S OUTPUT EQUILIBRIUM

If, in addition to producing the continuous flow of output, y, the firm also sells the product continuously, so that gross receipts $R(y)$ represent a continuous inflow of payments over time, then maximization of current profit $R(y) - C$ requires in addition to (3.3.1), (3.3.4), and (3.3.5), the condition

$$dR/dy = \lambda^0, \qquad (3.3.12)$$

that is, marginal current revenue and marginal current cost must be equal. These conditions define marginal revenue productivity demand functions for the current and capital inputs that are analogous to (3.3.6) and (3.3.7) except that y is no longer a parameter. That is,

$$x_1{}^0 = d_1(w_1, rW_2), \qquad (3.3.13)$$
$$X_2{}^0 = D_2(w_1, rW_2). \qquad (3.3.14)$$

In terms of the Marshallian analysis, $\lambda^0 = w_1/f_1 = rW_2/f_2$ is "long-run" marginal cost. The function $\lambda^0(y, w_1, rW_2)$ generates the incremental costs of hypothetical variations in y produced by an *initial* minimum cost mix of investment in the durable good and expenditure on the current input. Once the investment $X_2{}^0$ is made, this long-run marginal cost function is meaningless. It cannot represent the effect of balanced decreases in physical investment because decreases are impossible short of complete replacement of the capital facility. Similarly, by hypothesis, the function cannot portray the effect of minimum cost increases in investment because the investment once made cannot be augmented except by replacement or by installing parallel facilities. Once the initial long-run equilibrium stock of capital, $X_2{}^0$, is given, then $w_1/f_1(x_1,X_2{}^0)$ together with the short-run production function $y = f(x_1,X_2{}^0)$, provides the Marshallian "short-run" marginal cost curve along which output is adjusted by altering the volume of consumption of the current input only.

For the firm employing an infinitely durable producer's good, the output response to increases in the demand on its facilities is shown in Fig. 3–3. Initially, marginal revenue is given by MR, and the long-run marginal cost curve for optimal possible combinations of the two inputs is given by LMC_1. We imagine the firm installing that quantity of the

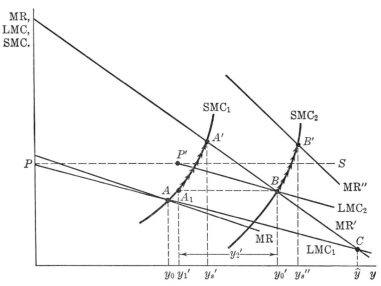

Fig. 3–3. The output response to an increase in demand.

capital good which enables it to operate with the minimum cost technique at point A, thereby producing y_0 units of output. Once this capital is installed, the short-run marginal cost curve SMC_1 is defined. At some time later an increase in demand occurs, such that marginal revenue rises to MR'. This increase in demand was not anticipated when the initial investment was made (we thus confine ourselves strictly to the analysis of comparative stationary states). With its existing stock of capital, the firm finds it more profitable to expand its consumption of the current input until the point A' is reached where $SMC_1 = MR'$. This leads to diminishing returns and high operating costs on current account since at A' we have $SMC_1 > LMC_1$. Some of these costs may be avoided by building a parallel facility of the appropriate capacity. Actually there are three possible optimal responses. If the increase in output requirements is not large, the best policy may be to produce the new requirements in the existing facility by increasing the consumption of current input(s). Alternatively, it may pay to install a parallel facility, and divide total requirements between the two facilities. Finally, if output requirements rise by a sufficiently large margin, it may pay to install a new larger facility and discard the old facility. We shall formulate the decision problem in such a way as to permit the Kuhn-Tucker conditions to generate any of these possible solutions.

In considering the size of a parallel facility, it is necessary to consider the resulting parallel long-run production function. If we let y_1 be the output, and x_1^1 the current input consumed in the old facility, then the production function for that facility is $y_1 = f(x_1^1, X_2^0)$. If y_2 is the output, and x_1^2 and X_2' are the variable current and capital inputs to the new facility, then the production function for the new facility is $y_2 = f(x_1^2, X_2')$. Total output for the dual facilities is then

$$y' = y_1 + y_2 = f(x_1^1, X_2^0) + f(x_1^2, X_2'). \qquad (3.3.15)$$

The rational firm will base its decision to expand investment on the cost function

$$C = w_1(x_1^1 + x_1^2) + rW_2(X_2' + X_2^0). \qquad (3.3.16)$$

The component $rW_2X_2^0$ represents a fixed burden in the new decision situation. The investment in the old facility cannot be varied and we assume that (perpetuity) interest payments on that investment will continue to burden the firm's current account.

Necessary conditions for a minimum of (3.3.16) subject to (3.3.15) are as follows:

$$\left.\begin{array}{l} w_1 - \lambda f_1(x_1^1, X_2^0) \geq 0, \quad \text{if } > \text{ holds } x_1^1 = 0 \\ \left.\begin{array}{l} w_1 - \lambda f_1(x_1^2, X_2') \geq 0 \\ rW_2 - \lambda f_2(x_1^2, X_2') \geq 0 \end{array}\right\} \quad \text{if } > \text{ holds, } x_1^2 = X_2' = 0 \end{array}\right\} \quad (3.3.17)$$

where $f_1(x_1^1, X_2^0)$ is the marginal product of the current input in the old facility, $f_1(x_1^2, X_2')$ is the marginal product of the current input in the new facility and $f_2(x_1^2, X_2')$ is the marginal product of the capital input in the new facility. Of course, the production function for the new facility need not be the same as that for the old facility. Hence, if

$$\frac{w_1}{f_1(x_1^1, X_2^0)} = \lambda < \frac{w_1}{f_1(x_1^2, X_2')} \quad \text{and} \quad \frac{rW_2}{f_2(x_1^2, X_2')},$$

then the marginal cost of current and capital inputs to a new facility exceed the marginal cost of current input to the old facility, and a second facility is not installed.[19] If

$$\frac{w_1}{f_1(x_1^1, X_2^0)} = \lambda = \frac{w_1}{f_1(x_1^2, X_2')} = \frac{rW_2}{f_2(x_1^2, X_2')},$$

then a second parallel facility is installed at a capacity determined by the simultaneous solution of the equality conditions in (3.3.17) and the constraint (3.3.15). If

$$\frac{w_1}{f_1(x_1^1, X_2^0)} > \lambda = \frac{w_1}{f_1(x_1^2, X_2')} = \frac{rW_2}{f_2(x_1^2, X_2')},$$

then $x_1^1 = 0$ and the old facility is replaced by a new one. These conditions state that all output requirements will be

---

[19] See Samuelson's *Foundations*, pp. 69–70, for a discussion of boundary or corner minima. We are assuming here that production in a given facility always requires some positive amounts of both inputs so that if the second facility is installed at all, it will be operated with some positive consumption of the current input.

met by the existing facility as long as the marginal cost of the current input to that fixed facility is smaller than the "long-run" marginal cost of the second facility. Once output reaches a level that warrants the construction of a new facility, the two facilities are operated so as to equate the marginal cost of the current inputs to each facility with the marginal cost of the capital input to the new facility. Finally, if output rises sufficiently, the marginal cost of operating the first facility may become greater than the marginal cost of inputs to a new facility. Hence, the fixed capacity of the first facility is rendered entirely obsolete.

Profit will also be maximized if we add to (3.3.17) the condition that

$$\lambda = MR'. \tag{3.3.18}$$

Where it pays to install a second parallel facility the conditions (3.3.17) and (3.3.18) require $SMC_1 = SMC_2 = LMC_2 = MR'$, which implies that the firm is in a new state of long-run equilibrium (we ignore the important industry effects that apply in pure and monopolistic competition).

These conditions are applied in the diagram of Fig. 3–3 along with the closure condition on output, $y = y_1 + y_2$, to determine the equilibrium output of each facility, viz., $y_1 = y_1'$, $y_2 = y_2'$. The geometry of this feat is accomplished by sliding to the right a line parallel to LMC_1, with origin always at P' on the dotted horizontal line $PP'S$, until a perpendicular from P' intersects the SMC_1 curve at a horizontal level (see point A_1) equal to the level at which the constructed line intersects MR' (see point B). At the point B where the new long-run cost curve LMC_2 intersects MR', we can construct the short-run cost curve SMC_2 for the new facility. At points A_1 and B we have the solution $y_1 = y_1'$ and $y_2 = y_2'$ such that $y_0' = y_1' + y_2'$ and $SMC_1 = SMC_2 = LMC_2 = MR'$. This solution can be compared with the situation in which the firm does not enter the industry until after MR has risen to MR'. In this case the firm has no incumbent facility and proceeds to build one large facility which produces the output $\hat{y} > y_0'$.

If at some later date a further increase in demand causes marginal revenue to rise to MR″ the optimal short-run response is to adjust the output of each facility until SMC_1 = SMC_2 = MR′ > LMC_2. At this point the installation of a third facility may be in order, the analysis proceeding exactly as before. The sequence of scalloped curves AA', BB', and so forth, constitutes the sequence of short-run production responses of the firm employing infinitely durable goods. The points A, B, etc., represent the sequence of long-run responses and serve as pivotal points to stake out the successive short-run response possibilities.

The response of our profit maximizing firm to decreases in demand is shown in Fig. 3–4. The firm having initially in-

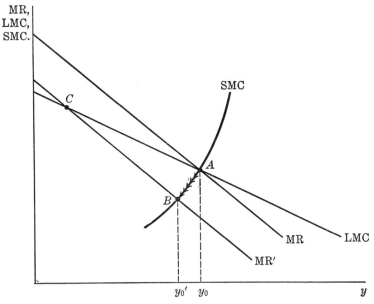

Fig. 3–4. The output response to a decrease in demand.

vested in $X_2{}^0$ units of capital, produces y_0 units at the point A where SMC = LMC = MR. If demand falls so that marginal revenue declines to MR′, then the firm will find it profitable to contract output along SMC to B where SMC

= MR$'$ < LMC. The point B is not only the best short-run adjustment in the new demand environment; it is also the best long-run response except in the event that it pays to discard the existing facility and install a new smaller facility. This is technically possible since the replacement alternative contained in the conditions (3.3.17) also applies for a decline in output, that is, for $y' < y$. For the industry as a whole, however, the entire stock of existing facilities must be held by someone as long as units of this size have any positive marginal revenue productivity. A decrease in demand will cause a commensurate decrease in the market value of existing facilities. We will adhere to the assumption that the optimal long-run response to a decrease in output is to retain the existing facility.

Turning next to an analysis of the firm's demand for current and capital inputs, our major task will be to construct the firm's *ceteris paribus* demand reaction to changes in each of the prices of these inputs as determined in their corresponding markets external to the firm. Just as in deriving the firm's output response we found the "virtual" marginal cost function in (3.3.8) to be of pivotal interest, so, likewise, we shall find the "virtual" demand functions (3.3.6) and (3.3.7) to be at the center of our analysis of the firm's demand response to changes in input prices.

THE DEMAND FOR A CURRENT INPUT

Consider first the firm's demand for the current input. In illustrating the possible response of the firm to an increase in the price of the current input we shall work with two diagrams, Fig. 3–5, representing the related output responses, and Fig. 3–6, portraying the current input responses of the firm. In Fig. 3–5, the firm's initial output equilibrium is represented by P where MR = LMC$_1$ = SMC$_1$.[20] The dotted

---

[20] We assume imperfect competition in the product market, and hence a declining MR curve. The analysis to follow applies, however, in pure competition provided our theory of the firm contains some device for limiting output, such as a rising supply function of funds, capital rationing, uncertainty, and so forth.

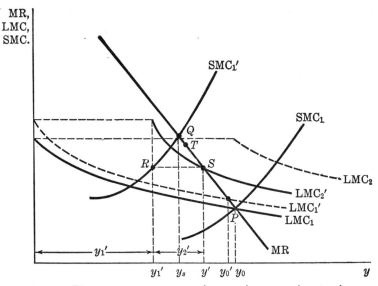

Fig. 3–5. The output response to an increase in current input price.

curve LMC_2 is the long-run marginal cost curve for a potential initial second facility whose output could be added to that of the first facility. It is evident that initially only the one facility is optimal. In Fig. 3–6, the firm's initial equilibrium with respect to the current input is represented by P' or the point (w_1, x_1^0) on $d_1 d_1$. The curve $d_1 d_1$ is the *ceteris paribus* demand function (3.3.13) or the marginal revenue productivity of the current input. This schedule represents all the different hypothetical consumption rates of input Number 1 that would occur at corresponding prices for input Number 1 for a given interest rate and a given price, W_2, for the capital input. Each point on $d_1 d_1$ assumes an optimal investment in the capital input based upon the price constellation, w_1, r, and W_2. Once the investment occurs, the demand function $d_1 d_1$ completely loses its significance for the description of the firm's response pattern.

Starting from this initial state of equilibrium, with an investment X_2^0 and the firm consuming x_1^0 of the current input, assume that we have an unanticipated *ceteris paribus* in-

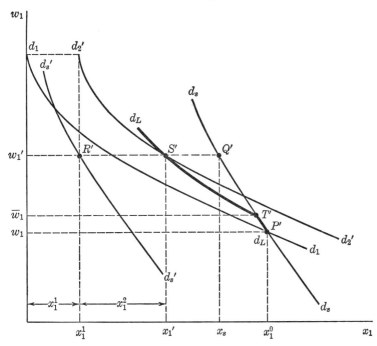

Fig. 3–6. Deviation of long-run demand for a current input.

crease in the price of the current input from w_1 to w_1'. The new price is expected to prevail permanently. The firm's profit maximizing response to this change in data will be to adjust its demand for the current input up along the short-run demand curve $d_s d_s$ to the level x_s corresponding to w_1', at point Q' in Fig. 3–6. This increase in the price of the current input will cause a rise in the short-run marginal cost curve, say from SMC_1 to SMC_1' as shown in Fig. 3–5. The firm's output response will be to move up along MR to Q where $SMC_1' = MR$, and output is $y_s = f(x_s, X_2^0)$. These shifts constitute the firm's Marshallian short-run response, and can be made as soon in calendar time as the flow of the current input can be reduced to x_s. At the temporary equilibrium represented by Q and Q', the firm is using its existing (previously "long-run" optimal) facility less intensively.

We now have

$$\mathrm{MR}(y_s) = \frac{w_1'}{f_1(x_s,X_2^0)} \lesseqgtr \frac{w_1'}{f_1(x_1^2,X_2')}, \frac{rW_2}{f_2(x_1^2,X_2')} \quad (3.3.19)$$

with $x_1^2 = X_2' = 0$, that is, marginal revenue equals the short-run marginal cost of operating the present facility which in turn may now be less than, equal to, or greater than, the marginal cost of each of the current and capital inputs to a potential new parallel facility. If the less than or equal sign holds, for all x_1^2, X_2', the firm cannot improve on its temporary equilibrium position, and Q and Q' represent the firm's long-run as well as short-run equilibrium response. If the greater than sign holds for some x_1^2, X_2', then it may pay the firm to install an additional parallel facility of size $X_2' > 0$, and consuming $x_1^2 > 0$ units of the current input, such that

$$\mathrm{MR}(y') = \frac{w_1'}{f_1(x_1^1,X_2^0)} = \frac{w_1'}{f_1(x_1^2,X_2')} = \frac{rW_2}{f_2(x_1^2,X_2')}, \quad (3.3.20)$$

where $y' = f(x_1^1,X_2^0) + f(x_1^2,X_2')$.

This long-run response of the firm is illustrated graphically in Figs. 3–5 and 3–6. In Fig. 3–5, when the price of the current input rises to w_1', the virtual long-run marginal cost curve for a single facility rises from LMC_1 to LMC_1'. Since, if it pays to build a new facility, equilibrium requires that $\mathrm{MR} = \mathrm{SMC}_1' = \mathrm{LMC}_2'$, as indicated in (3.3.20), the graphical output solution requires LMC_1' to be shifted to the right to form LMC_2' whose origin lies vertically above a point R on SMC_1' such that this equality holds. Total output then becomes $y' = y_1' + y_2'$, the sum of the outputs from each facility. The new long-run output equilibrium is at S with the first facility's output contracted to R. The net result is a smaller decrease in output in the "long-run" $(y_0 - y')$ than in the short-run $(y_0 - y_s)$. A still smaller decrease in output $(y_0 - y_0')$ would be possible were it not for the "irreversibility" characteristic of capital. That is, if w_1' had prevailed initially, output would be y_0'. In Fig. 3–6, representing the firm's input response, when the new facility is installed and output in the old facility is contracted, this causes a decrease in the short-run marginal revenue productivity of the current input from $d_s d_s$ to $d_s' d_s'$. The contraction of output in the old facility is achieved by reducing the consumption of the current input from x_s to x_1^1, while the output of the new facility is obtained by installing X_2' units of capital and using x_1^2 units of the current input. The equilibrium allocation of the current input to the two facilities occurs at R' and S' where the new price of the input is equal to the marginal revenue productivity of the input in each facility, and the total consumption of the current input is $x_1' = x_1^1 + x_1^2$. This is achieved graphically by sliding $d_1 d_1$ to the right to form $d_2' d_2'$ for the new facility whose origin is directly above R' such that R' and S' are at the new price level. S' is now a new point on the firm's *long-run demand curve for the current input*. The firm's short-run input response is from P' to Q', while its long-run response is from P' to S'.

The above analysis has assumed that the increase in input price was sufficient to warrant the installation of a new facility. Some minimum increase in price, say from w_1 to $\overline{w}_1$, can be expected to be required to induce the installation of a new facility. Thus, a point such as T in Fig. 3–5 and T' in Fig. 3–6 will limit the extent to which the firm's short-run adjustment will also represent its optimal long-run response. T and T' will be defined by the equality condition in (3.3.19). It follows that the firm's long-run demand curve $d_L d_L$ will follow $d_s d_s$ to T', at which point it will have a concave kink, and then pass through S' as shown.

In summary, small increases in the price of the current input will tend to raise marginal cost and induce the firm to employ less of the current input in the presence of an unchanged quantity of the durable capital good. If the price increase is large enough it may create a diminishing-returns imbalance between current and capital account costs of such magnitude that it pays to install an additional facility.

On the assumption that a decrease in the price of the current input from w_1 to w_1' causes a greater decrease in short-run than in long-run marginal costs, it is readily shown that the firm's long-run demand for the current input follows its short-run demand. This is seen by observing that

$$\text{MR}(y_s) = \frac{w_1{}'}{f_1(x_s, X_2{}^0)} < \left\{ \frac{w_1}{f_1(x_1{}^2, X_2{}')}, \frac{rW_2}{f_2(x_1{}^2, X_2{}')} \right\}$$

that is, the short-run marginal cost of the current input to the old facility is less than the marginal cost of current and capital inputs to a potential new facility, and it does not pay to add a parallel facility.

A long-run demand response to either increases or decreases in w_1 from an initial full equilibrium is illustrated in Fig. 3–7. The long-run response is identical with that of the

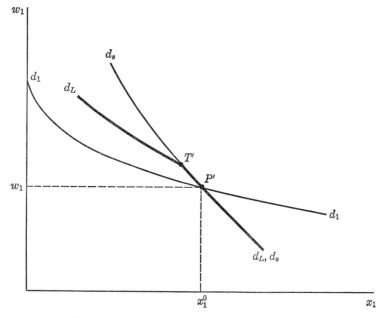

Fig. 3–7. The long-run demand for current input.

short-run for price increases that do not exceed $P'T'$ and for all price decreases. At T' and above, the resulting increase in short-run marginal cost is assumed sufficient to justify a new facility of appropriate size. The long-run demand is then $d_L d_L$ as shown.

THE DEMAND FOR AN INDESTRUCTIBLE CAPITAL INPUT

The firm's demand for the capital input is a stock demand for the good to hold. The firm's initial or virtual marginal revenue productivity demand for the capital input is shown as $D_2 D_2$ in Fig. 3–8. This schedule represents all the alterna-

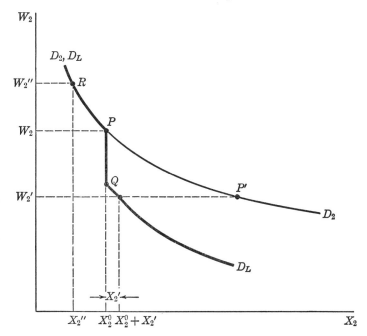

Fig. 3–8. Derivation of asset demand for a durable input.

tive hypothetical stocks of the capital input that would be optimal to install at corresponding prices for the capital input, given the rate of interest and the price of the current input. The initial equilibrium is represented by P.

Suppose that at some time after the installation of X_2^0 units of the capital input, its market price falls from W_2 to

W_2'; then

$$\text{MR}(y') = \frac{w_1}{f_1(x_s, X_2^0)} \lesseqgtr \frac{w_1}{f_1(x_1^2, X_2')}, \frac{rW_2'}{f_2(x_1^2, X_2')} \quad (3.3.21)$$

where $y_s = f(x_s, X_2^0)$ with $x_1^2 = X_2' = 0$. Furthermore, since the first equality held initially, it follows that the best *short-run* policy for the firm is to continue its previous input-output policy, that is $x_s = x_1^0$ and $y_s = y_0$. The expression (3.3.21) states that the marginal cost of current and capital inputs to a new facility priced at $W_2' < W_2$ may be greater than, equal to, or less than the marginal cost of operating the old facility. Of course, at the old price, W_2, the marginal cost of inputs to a second facility must have exceeded the marginal cost of the first facility, else the second facility would have been installed initially. If, after the fall in the price of the capital good, the marginal costs of inputs to a second facility are still greater than the marginal cost of the first facility, then the best long-run policy is to make no change in the production plan (x_1^0, X_2^0). That is, the firm maximizes profit

$$\pi = R[f(x_1^1, X_2^0) + f(x_1^2, X_2')] - w_1(x_1^1 + x_1^2) - rW_2'(X_2^0 + X_2')$$

with the previous program, namely, $x_1^1 = x_1^0$, $X_2 = X_2^0$ (which cannot be varied anyway), and $x_1^2 = X_2' = 0$. Over such a range for the decline in the price of the capital good the firm's demand for the capital good to hold is perfectly inelastic as shown by the segment PQ in Fig. 3–8. However, below some point Q it may be expected that the capital good will have become cheap enough to warrant the installation of a new facility of size $X_2' > 0$ and operated with $x_1^2 > 0$ units of the current input, such that

$$\text{MR}(y') = \frac{w_1}{f_1(x_1^1, X_2^0)} = \frac{w_1}{f_1(x_1^2, X_2')} = \frac{rW_2'}{f_2(x_1^2, X_2')}. \quad (3.3.22)$$

The demand for the additional facility will be that additional facility's marginal revenue productivity curve. Hence, below Q the firm's demand for the durable input will be less than perfectly inelastic as shown in Fig. 3–8.

Suppose that after the firm installs X_2^0 units of the capital input there is an unanticipated increase in its price from W_2 to W_2''. Now, if this price had prevailed from the beginning, the firm's equilibrium would have been at R, where it is profitable to install $X_2'' < X_2^0$ units of the capital good. Once having purchased X_2^0, is it possible for the firm to reach the point R? For the *individual firm* this is possible. The firm simply offers its capital stock of size X_2^0 to the market at the price W_2'', and proceeds to install a smaller facility of size X_2'', providing a capital gain of $(W_2'' - W_2)X_2^0$ dollars.[21] The argument here is tricky. We do not wish to suggest that the firm in question will actually achieve the move from P to R by the indicated reinvestment route. The argument is that *if* the price W_2'' were to persist, the individual firm would find it profitable to take a capital gain on its present oversized facility, and reinvest in a smaller facility. As will be shown in section 4, the price W_2'' could not in fact be maintained in the existing asset market, since all firms would offer to sell out at that price and buy smaller facilities. This flood of sell offers would depress the price until it reached W_2, causing firms to retain their existing facilities. But in order to explain such market phenomena, we must first construct the individual firm's response to all possible price changes.

It follows that above P, the firm's demand schedule follows D_2D_2, while below P the schedule is perfectly inelastic until Q is reached. Below Q it pays the firm to install a parallel facility and the schedule is less than perfectly inelastic. Hence, the firm's long-run demand for the capital good, for deviations in price from W_2, is D_LD_L as shown.

4. Indestructible Inputs and the Theory of Competitive Markets

We are now in a position to extend our theory of the capital-using firm forward into the product market and

[21] Note that the new "price" of capital, W_2'', as well as the old price, W_2, are measured per square foot or per pound or some other appropriate measure of equipment size (capacity). Such prices are unit construction costs. The selling price of the old unit of size X_2^0 is then $W_2''X_2^0$, and the selling price of the new equipment unit is $W_2''X_2''$.

backward into the input markets, and ascertain the effect on such markets of our explicit analysis of the role of indestructible durable goods in the conventional theory of the firm. In analyzing the product market we shall assume pure competition, thereby allowing a short-run industry supply curve to be defined, in the conventional manner, as the sum of the individual firm marginal cost curves.

THE PRODUCT MARKET

Imagine a competitive Marshallian industry in an initial state of long-run equilibrium in which there are no forces tending to generate a net change in the composition or size of the industry. All firms in the industry have invested in facilities of a certain size which have been determined by profit maximization principles together with whatever conditions (such as capital rationing) may serve to limit firm output. Such a state of price-quantity industry equilibrium is represented by the point P in Fig. 3–9. Think of this equilibrium occurring at the intersection of the product demand DD with the "virtual" long-run supply curve S_vS_v. The virtual long-run supply curve is a schedule of the long-run equilibrium industry outputs at corresponding alternative prices under the assumption that each firm installs initial capital facilities of an optimal size at that price. If demand is DD, the equilibrium price is p^0, and at that price if each firm installs the optimal size facility, industry output will be $\bar{y}^0$, the sum over all firm outputs.

Starting from this initial state of full input equilibrium if product demand increases from DD to $D'D'$, price and marginal revenue will rise, and, in accordance with the argument on pp. 77–82, each firm will find it profitable to adjust output upward along its short-run marginal cost curve until $P = \text{SMC}$, at which point the industry is producing $\bar{y}_s{}'$ units of output. At Q the industry is in a state of short-run equilibrium, at which point it will pay individual firms already in the industry to construct parallel facilities and/or new firms to enter and invest in durable facilities. Since, by hy-

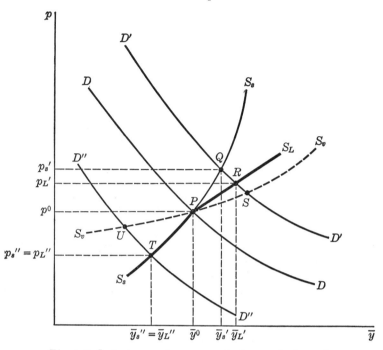

Fig. 3–9. Industry supply response to changes in demand.

pothesis, the old facilities cannot be continuously expanded
it is impossible for the industry to expand to the virtual
long-run equilibrium point S. If $D'D'$ had been the industry
demand at the beginning, then each firm would have installed capital facilities that were optimal for the price prevailing at S.[22] But once a previous equilibrium point P has
been established *any and all possible later long-run equilibria
are inescapably influenced by the position and character of that
previous equilibrium.* In the present case, the new equilibrium
will be at some point such as R where the output of the old

[22] Note that an underdeveloped region or country which lags behind in
the development of an industry of this type until the potential demand has
reached $D'D'$, will generate an equilibrium at S, and hence will have an advantage over an existing industry of the same type in another region or
country. This advantage is the natural result of growth hysteresis, and is
not dependent upon technological improvements of any kind.

facilities are augmented by that of parallel new facilities, and industry output is $\bar{y}_L{}'$. The curve PRS_L through P and R represents the long-run supply curve (not the expansion path) for alternative possible increases in demand above DD.

Starting again from the initial equilibrium P, if there is a decrease in demand from DD to $D''D''$, the industry will respond by adjusting output down along its (completely reversible) short-run supply schedule to the short-run equilibrium point T as shown in Fig. 3–9. If the industry was just normally profitable at P, then at T it is subnormally profitable. Now, since the capital input is infinitely durable the industry cannot escape the consequent decline in the market valuation of its facilities derived from the decline in product demand. The price set upon the existing stock of capital facilities will continue to fall until the industry is satisfied to hold all of this existing stock. If we imagine all capital facilities to have been financed through perpetuity bond issues, firms will be forced to reduce their interest payments to bondholders. If the bonds are debentures, their current market valuation will fall until the new interest payments provide the going yield on the new price of the bonds. If the securities are equipment bonds with the facilities themselves pledged as collateral, then bondholders may foreclose on these assets when firms default on their interest payments. But foreclosure cannot recover the original investment, with the result that bondholders bear the final capital loss.

Regardless of how one conceives of the process and incidence of financial loss taking place, the end result is the same. The existing stock of the capital facility will be held in production by someone (unless the marginal operating cost of an old facility exceeds the marginal long-run cost of a new facility), and it will pay to consume current inputs in the presence of that facility up to the point at which marginal cost is equal to the new price $p_s{}'' = p_L{}''$. Hence, T is a point of both short-run and long-run industry equilibrium, and the firm's complete long-run supply response curve is S_sPS_L for once-for-all changes in demand above and below DD.

It will be evident to the reader that in describing the supply response of an industry composed of capital using firms, we have exposed a *path-dependent process*. The state of an industry and of each firm in that industry is necessarily a function not only of all the historical changes that have occurred in the economic environment of the industry and the firm, but also the exact sequence in which these changes took place. The state of an industry and its component firms is at any time a function of the entire path traversed in the past. The character of these irreversibilities and "hysteresis effects" in the output market is illustrated in Fig. 3–10.

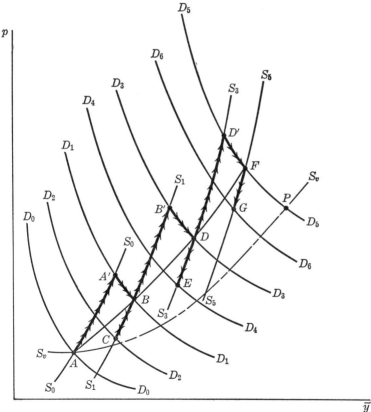

Fig. 3–10. The "hysteresis" effect in industry supply.

Suppose the industry is in initial long-run equilibrium at A with demand $D_0 D_0$ and virtual supply $S_v S_v$. Demand rises then to $D_1 D_1$. The industry responds along its short-run supply curve $S_0 S_0$ to a temporary equilibrium at A'. Some of the high cost of operating more intensively on current account at A' can be avoided by installing additional facilities. As this is done by both old and new firms, output rises until a new position of long-run equilibrium is reached at B.

Based upon the full input equilibrium at B, a new short-run supply curve $S_1 S_1$ is defined. After the new equilibrium at B has been attained, suppose there is an unanticipated decline in demand from $D_1 D_1$ to $D_2 D_2$. The industry, in accordance with the argument behind Fig. 3–9, will adjust down along $S_1 S_1$ to C, a position of both temporary and long-run equilibrium. If, after C has been attained, there is a comparative statics increase in demand to $D_3 D_3$, the industry will adjust along $S_1 S_1$ until B', a position of temporary equilibrium, is reached. At this point the industry will again expand by the construction of additional capacity until a third long-run equilibrium at D is reached. If demand continues to fluctuate about an upward trend the industry will pass from D to E, then up to D' and so forth. The expansion path of the industry is thus $A–A'–B–C–B'–D–E–D'–F–G$, and so forth. The location of each of the successive long-run equilibria A, B, D, and F depends upon all such previous points. Thus the position F depends upon where A, B, and D fall and upon the exact sequence of all previous demand increases. If the demand $D_5 D_5$ had prevailed initially in the industry, the equilibrium would have occurred at P — a point which is unattainable once the equilibrium has been established at A (or any other point) on $S_v S_v$.

THE MARKET FOR A CURRENT INPUT

In analyzing the market for a current input it might be supposed that here we can make a literal application of conventional firm and market theory. Unfortunately this is not the case, for our hypothesis that the firm employs an

irreversible and infinitely durable input substitutive for current account inputs causes hysteresis effects to reverberate
throughout every market touched by the firm.

The industry's market demand for a current input is
obtained in the conventional manner by summing over all
such individual firm demand curves as were derived in Fig.
3–7. Such an aggregate demand situation is shown in Fig.
3–11, along with the supply curve SS for the current input.

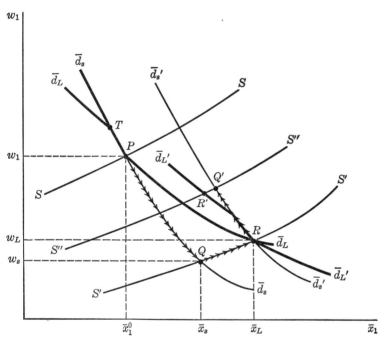

Fig. 3–11. *The market for a current input.*

With the industry initially in long-run equilibrium at P,
$\bar{d}_s \bar{d}_s$ is the aggregate short-run demand for the current input,
and $\bar{d}_L \bar{d}_L$ is the aggregate long-run demand for the input. If
we assume that all firms in the industry have identical production programs, then $\bar{d}_s \bar{d}_s$ in Fig. 3–11 is the same as $d_s d_s$
in Fig. 3–7 with a change in scale on the horizontal axis by
a factor equal to the number of firms in the industry. This

statement will not hold for $\bar{d}_L \bar{d}_L$ for prices below w_1. If the price of the current input falls, profits become abnormally high in the industry and this will tend to provide an inducement for new firms to enter. Hence, for prices below w_1, the *individual firm's* long-run demand curve will be coincident with the short-run demand curve, while for the industry this will not be the case due to the effect on aggregate demand of the entry of new firms. For price increases above w_1, the industry and firm's long-run demand curves will differ only by a scale factor. This is because an increase in costs will discourage entry, and firms in the industry will continue to employ fully their indestructible stocks of the capital input. However, if the price of the current input becomes high enough some escape will be possible through the installation of additional capacity. This is assumed to occur at T in Fig. 3–11. The price increase will not cause an exodus of firms (unless variable cost rises above receipts), because the value of the durable input will decline sufficiently to induce firms to hold the existing stock.

By appropriate use of the short- and long-run input demand curves of Fig. 3–11 we can describe the market response to changes in either demand or supply. Figure 3–11 exhibits the effect of an increase in supply from SS to $S'S'$. The first consequence is a fall in input price from w_1 to w_s as firms adjust their consumption of the current input down along their individual short-run demand curves. The corresponding industry adjustment is from P to the temporary equilibrium point represented by Q. At a price $w_s < w_1$ as shown, the industry is abnormally profitable, and new firms enter. This causes an increase in the consumption of the current input and a rise in its price until a new long-run state of input equilibrium is established at R. The industry's short-run demand response is, therefore, from P to Q, and its long-run response from P to R. At R there is now defined a new short-run demand $\bar{d}_s'\bar{d}_s'$, and a new long-run demand $\bar{d}_L'\bar{d}_L'$, for the current input based upon the new investment structure of the industry. Once the equilibrium at R is established, if supply were to decline from $S'S'$ to $S''S''$ the industry would adjust its consumption of the current input up along the new short-run demand curve $\bar{d}_s'\bar{d}_s'$ to Q'. At this price it would pay firms in the industry to construct parallel production facilities as a partial means of substituting capital for the current input, and a new long-run equilibrium would develop at R'. The entire adjustment process in the current input market is thus irreversible and dominated by path dependent phenomena. But in principle the process is orderly and predictable.

THE MARKET FOR AN INDESTRUCTIBLE DURABLE INPUT

The analysis of the market for an indestructible durable input is perhaps the most interesting task that we have to face. So much of what has to be said on this subject rests upon unfamiliar ground that considerable attention will be devoted to it.[23] The concept of the individual firm's stock

[23] It is necessary to point out that the material of this section and the parallel analysis of Chaps. IV and VI received considerable inspiration from the pioneering work in stock-flow market analysis by R. W. Clower and George Horwich. Their original contributions are contained in two papers, R. W. Clower, "Business Investment and the Theory of Price," *Proceedings of the Twenty-Eighth Annual Conference of the Western Economic Association*, 1953, pp. 22–24, and R. W. Clower, "An Investigation into the Dynamics of Investment," *American Economic Review*, XLIV (March 1954), 64–81; and a thesis recorded the same month, George Horwich, "Open Market Operations, the Rate of Interest, and the Price Level," University of Chicago Doctoral Dissertation, March 1954, Chap. I, pp. 19–25, Chap. II, and especially Chap. III. Clower is concerned with extending the conventional supply and demand analysis to the market for a durable good. The market for such goods is characterized by the fact that there is not only an existing stock supply and a stock demand to hold such goods, but simultaneously a consumption flow demand and a production flow supply of such goods into the market. Horwich is concerned with the capital market and the problem of integrating the money and securities existing asset market with the saving-investment flow equilibrium. The process involves an investigation of stock-flow relationships which is entirely analogous to that required in an analysis of the market for a durable good. In another article by Clower, "Productivity, Thrift and the Rate of Interest," *Economic Journal*, LXIV (March 1954) his stock-flow analysis of the market for a durable good is extended to the bond market. A published form of the cited thesis is contained in Horwich's "Money, Prices and the Theory of Interest Determination," *Economic Journal*, LXVII (December 1957), 625–643.

demand for a durable input was derived in Fig. 3–8. The stock demand of the industry for such an input is obtained by summing horizontally the demands of the existing firms in the industry and the demands of any new firms induced to enter the industry as a result of a decline in the prices of the input.

If, in Fig. 3–12, we assume an initial state of long-run

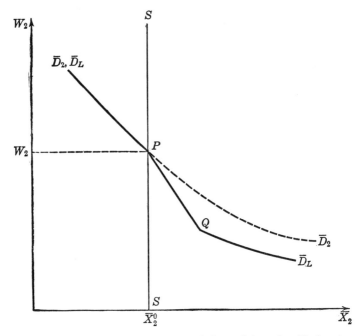

Fig. 3–12. Industry asset supply and demand for a durable input.

equilibrium in the industry, as represented by P in the durable good market, then $\bar{D}_L\bar{D}_L$ represents the industry's demand for the input to hold as a function of price movements above and below W_2. An increase in the price of the good above W_2 (if maintained) will induce firms to sell out their existing facilities, and reinvest in less capacity thereby enjoying a capital gain on the original capital. However, if the price were to rise in this manner it could not be maintained since the market value of each firm's capital facilities would then exceed the value imputed to such facilities by the output market. Firms would elect to sell out until W_2 was again restored. If price falls below W_2, new firms may be induced to enter the industry and thereby increase the stock of the durable input desired by the industry. If, in Fig. 3–12, price falls to below the point Q, which corresponds to Q in Fig. 3–8, it will pay old firms in the industry to install parallel facilities and further augment the demand for the asset. The existing supply of the good is X_2^0 as represented by the perfectly elastic supply line SS. The dotted curve $\overline{D_2D_2}$ is the industry's virtual demand for the capital good, and is simply the horizontal summation of the individual firm's virtual demands as represented by D_2D_2 in Fig. 3–8. It is a schedule of all the hypothetical alternative "amounts" of the capital good that would be installed at corresponding prices which might have prevailed at the time the firms in the industry made their investment decisions. Once all firms have invested in optimal stocks of the good, only $\overline{D_LD_L}$ is relevant for the analysis of the industry's (once-for-all) response to decreases in the price of the durable input.

The stock schedules of Fig. 3–12 are not sufficient to describe fully the forces at play in our durable input market. There is, in addition, a flow supply to the market as illustrated in Fig. 3–13.[24] This is a schedule of the various quantities of the capital facility that will be constructed per year as a function of the price of the facility. For example, if the capital good is gas pipelines, then an increase in the price of installed pipes will induce construction companies to increase their rate of pipeline production. Since our capital good is indestructible, there exists no flow demand for the resource. Without capital consumption there can be no flow (replacement) demand for a capital good. If our pipelines were subject to technological displacement and/or significant year-to-year deterioration, an industry flow demand for the good would exist. The analysis would follow that of Clower's

[24] See Clower, "An Investigation into the Dynamics of Investment," pp. 67–68.

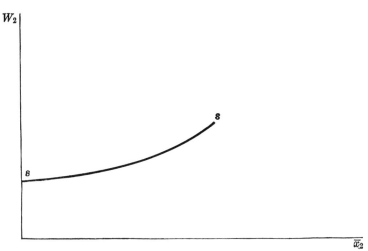

Fig. 3–13. Flow supply of new durable input.

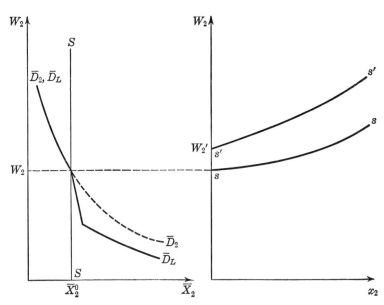

Fig. 3–14. The pricing of a durable input.

for "original and indestructible" goods except that our durable good is producible and not original.[25]

Figure 3–14 illustrates the initial state of industry equilibrium with respect to the capital good. The industry has acquired optimal holdings of the durable good at the price W_2, which in turn cannot exceed the supply price of the first produced unit of the durable good (the ss intercept), that is, in equilibrium there must be no incentive for additional units of the good to be constructed and thus add to the existing equilibrium stock, X_2^0. If there is a decrease in supply from ss to $s's'$, as shown in Fig. 3–14, then the producing industry would stand ready to produce and sell the first additional unit of the good at an offer price W_2'. But there should be no takers at this price. Any new firm entering the industry can do better by buying out one of the existing firms. Indeed, such an entering firm cannot be normally profitable at any price in excess of W_2. Each firm in the industry has, by hypothesis, adjusted its investment in the durable good until its imputed value (discounted revenue productivity) is equal to W_2. Any such firm with a desire to leave the industry because of fortuitous circumstances would, ideally, set W_2 as its minimum supply price. Hence, a decrease in the flow supply of the durable good can cause no change in its equilibrium price because there is no mechanism for decreasing the stock supply SS. Furthermore, the asset demand curve $\overline{D}_L\overline{D}_L$ would have to rise by the threshold distance $W_2' - W_2$ before potential new production of the asset can be effective.

The adjustments that follow an increase in supply from ss to $s's'$ are shown in Fig. 3–15. The industry is initially in long-run equilibrium at P with respect to the existing asset market and Q with respect to additions to that market. With the increased supply and resulting decline in the minimum supply prices for producing various quantities of the

---

[25] *Ibid.*, pp. 65–67. Also, see Clower, "Productivity, Thrift and the Rate of Interest," pp. 108–110, for a discussion of the demand and supply of new bonds. If Clower's bonds were perpetuities, there would be no flow demand and the analysis would correspond to ours.

durable good, the producing industry is willing to construct
new facilities at the rate QR per year at the going market
price W_2. The moment such construction activities get under
way and the new supplies of the good start coming into the
market the supply SS of the existing asset drifts to the right

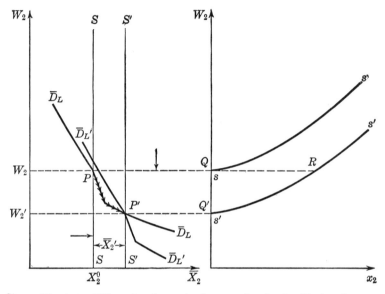

Fig. 3–15. Effect of a change in flow supply of a durable input.

and the price of the good begins to fall. The market con-
tinues to move down along $\overline{D}_L\overline{D}_L$ as SS moves to the right
until the price level reaches W_2', at which point the pro-
ducing industry no longer has an incentive to add to the
existing stock of facilities.

The new long-run equilibrium is at P' and Q' where $S'S'$
intersects $\overline{D}_L\overline{D}_L$. The adjustment process has involved the
construction of new facilities and the entry of new firms.
Therefore, based upon the new industrial structure, at P'
there will be defined a new irreversible long-run input de-
mand function $\overline{D}_{L}'\overline{D}_{L}'$. Any later increase in supply beyond
$s's'$ will induce expansion down along $D_L'D_L'$. The line seg-

ment PP' is a portion of the expansion path in the durable input market.

An increase in product demand, an increase in the prices of current inputs or a decline in interest rates may cause an increase in both the firm's and the industry's demand for a capital good. In Fig. 3–16 is shown the chain of events set

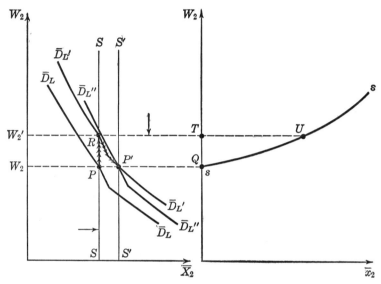

Fig. 3–16. Effect of an increase in asset demand for a durable input.

off in the capital input market by an increase in demand from $\overline{D}_L\overline{D}_L$ to $\overline{D}_L'\overline{D}_L'$. The immediate effect is an increase in the price of existing capital facilities from its previous equilibrium level W_2. If, for example, the increase in demand has been caused by a general decline in the market rate of interest, then new firms, at the price W_2, will now find it profitable to enter the industry. Potential new firms will place bids for the facilities of old firms, and this competition will drive the price of the existing facilities up to W_2' as shown. At a price W_2' the producers of this capital facility will find it profitable to construct new facilities at the rate of TU units per year. However, as such new facilities start to come into the market SS will shift to the right, and price will fall. Price will continue to fall and the existing supply to rise, as the market moves down from R along $\overline{D}_L'\overline{D}_L'$, until the new equilibrium at P' is established. At P', price has returned to its old level, W_2, and it is no longer profitable for additions to be made to the stock of facilities. Hence, an increase in demand always sets up forces which eventually cause the market for existing facilities to accommodate itself

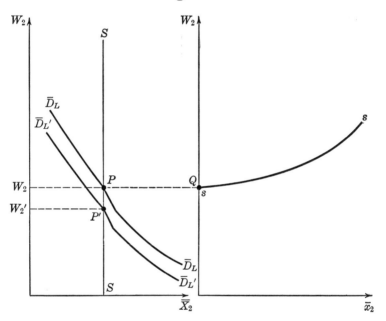

Fig. 3–17. Effect of a decrease in asset demand for a durable input.

to the flow market by lowering price until it is equal to the lowest cost at which a new facility can be produced. The rise in price from W_2 to W_2' is an ephemeral adjustment in the market allocation process.[26] Once the market finally arrives at the new long-range equilibrium level P', a new durable input demand curve $\overline{D}_L'\overline{D}_L'$ will be defined based

[26] See Horwich, "Money, Prices and the Theory of Interest Determination," pp. 631–633.

upon the new structure of the industry. The process is completely irreversible.

The effect of a decrease in demand from $\overline{D}_L\overline{D}_L$ to $\overline{D}_L'\overline{D}_L'$ is shown in Fig. 3–17. Price will fall from W_2, the previous equilibrium level, to W_2' which is below the minimum supply price of a new unit of the capital facility. This equilibrium is stable since there is no incentive for new facilities to be constructed.

Chapter IV

The Theory of Production and Investment: Capital Goods with Fixed Life

1. The Theory of the Firm under Fixed Replacement Policies

In the previous chapter we have laid the groundwork and explored the market implications of a theory of the capital-using enterprise under the assumption that capital goods were of infinite durability, continuously variable in amount prior to installation, and nonoriginal. With the tools that we now have at our command, it will be relatively easy to extend the analysis to capital goods subject to deterioration and obsolescence, and thereby requiring regular replacement. In this chapter we shall assume that capital goods require replacement at fixed intervals; in other words, that replacement policy is not to be regarded as a decision variable. This case might apply to capital goods whose life was determined primarily by technical considerations or obsolescence factors of known timing.

CHOICE OF TECHNIQUE

Again it will be assumed that there is one current input and one capital equipment input to production, except that the equipment has a fixed life of L years at the end of which time it must be replaced. If the horizon is infinite then the annual outlay for the current input is w_1x_1 as before. Also, as in the case of infinitely durable capital, total investment is W_2X_2. However, since the life of the capital input is L years, the process requires an initial outlay of W_2X_2 dollars, and "replacement" or reinvestment outlays of W_2X_2 dollars every L years thereafter. Using continuous discounting at an instantaneous rate r, the present value of an outlay of W_2X_2 dollars every L years is

$$W_2X_2(1 + e^{-rL} + e^{-2rL} + e^{-3rL} + \cdots) = W_2X_2/(1 - e^{-rL}).$$

Expressed as a cost on current account, capital cost becomes $rW_2X_2/(1 - e^{-rL})$, which might be the annual service charge paid by the firm to the bank or to bondholders depending upon the source of funds. Therefore, the expression for total current cost is

$$C = w_1x_1 + rW_2X_2/(1 - e^{-rL}). \tag{4.1.1}$$

In this expression it is assumed that the capital good requires no maintenance and has no salvage or resale value at the end of its life. The second term in (4.1.1) is the "depreciation" on the investment W_2X_2. The quantity $rW_2/(1 - e^{-rL})$ is the flow "price" of physical capital. It is interesting to note that if rL is small, so that r^2L^2 becomes negligible, then we can approximate e^{-rL} by the first two terms of its series expansion, $1 - rL$, and the depreciation charge $rW_2X_2/(1 - e^{-rL})$ becomes simply W_2X_2/L. Hence, for very small rates of discount and/or short-lived capital goods, we obtain the ordinary straight-line depreciation charge which is virtually universal in business practice.

If we minimize (4.1.1) subject to a production function constraint of the form (3.3.1) we obtain necessary conditions of the form

$$\frac{w_1}{f_1} = \frac{rW_2}{(1 - e^{-rL})f_2} = \lambda. \tag{4.1.2}$$

These conditions together with the production function determine equilibrium values for x_1, X_2, and λ, namely,

$$x_1{}^0 = d_1\left(w_1, \frac{rW_2}{1 - e^{-rL}}, y\right), \tag{4.1.3}$$

$$X_2{}^0 = D_2\left(w_1, \frac{rW_2}{1 - e^{-rL}}, y\right), \tag{4.1.4}$$

$$\lambda^0 = \lambda\left(w_1, \frac{rW_2}{1 - e^{-rL}}, y\right), \tag{4.1.5}$$

assuming a neoclassical interior solution. Again, from the convexity properties of the production function, certain qualitative properties of the input demand functions can be deduced. Thus, *ceteris paribus*, the greater is the price of input Number 1, the smaller is $x_1{}^0$, the larger is $X_2{}^0$, and the greater is the firm's optimal investment $W_2X_2{}^0$. Similarly, the lower is the unit investment cost, W_2, the lower is the rate of interest, r, or the greater the durability of equipment, L, the smaller is $x_1{}^0$ and the larger is $X_2{}^0$.[1]

---

[1] The above analysis assumes an infinite horizon. It is worth noting that the solution is independent of the horizon if the horizon is an integral multiple of equipment life. If we assume a finite planning horizon of $T = nL$ years, that is, the horizon extends over n replacement cycles, then we minimize

$$C = w_1x_1 + \frac{r}{1 - e^{-rnL}} [W_2X_2 + W_2X_2e^{-rL} + \cdots$$

$$+ W_2X_2e^{-(n-1)rL}] = w_1x_1 + \frac{rW_2X_2}{(1 - e^{-rL})},$$

subject to the production function constraint, and get the condition (4.1.2). Upon reflection the reason for this will be quite evident. If the life of equipment is fixed, the amount of investment per L year period is fixed, and the annual cost of capital is the same whether the planning horizon is 1, 2, or n replacements long. The annual cost of a dollar's worth of investment, $r/(1 - e^{rL})$, is the same independently of how many reinvestments are anticipated as long as the same discount rate is applied. From another point of view, the payment required to service an L year renewable loan is independent of the number of times it is renewed.

If we allow output to be a decision variable and assume that output is determined by the condition that marginal current revenue equals marginal current cost, we get the marginal revenue productivity demand functions

$$x_1^0 = d_1\left(w_1, \frac{rW_2}{1 - e^{-rL}}\right), \qquad (4.1.6)$$

$$X_2^0 = D_2\left(w_1, \frac{rW_2}{1 - e^{-rL}}\right). \qquad (4.1.7)$$

THE FIRM'S OUTPUT EQUILIBRIUM

Our previous analysis of the response of the capital-using enterprise to changes in demand can now be extended to the case in which the capital good must be replaced at fixed intervals. We begin with a firm in long-run equilibrium producing y units of output with x_1^0 units of a current input and X_2^0 units of machine capacity requiring replacement every L years, with MR = SMC$_1$ = LMC$_1$, as shown in Fig. 3–3. Suppose $U < L$ years have elapsed since the present equipment was installed. Then the firm's equipment has been in use for U years and has left $L - U$ years of useful life. If in this situation there is a permanent increase in product demand which raises MR to MR′, the firm's immediate response will be to adjust the current input upward to a level x_s such that MR′ = $w_1/f_1(x_s, X_2^0)$, as indicated by point A' in Fig. 3–3. So far, the response is the same as the case in which the capital good is indivisible and indestructible.

The firm's longer-run response on capital account depends upon what is assumed about the divisibility of the capital equipment. If the capital good were more or less continuously expansible, then the firm would elect to expand its investment from X_2^0 to $\hat{X}_2$ and operate at C in Fig. 3–3 where

$$\mathrm{MR}'(\hat{y}) = \frac{w_1}{f_1(\hat{x}_1, \hat{X}_2)} = \frac{rW_2}{f_2(\hat{x}_1, \hat{X}_2)[1 - e^{-rL}]}. \qquad (4.1.8)$$

Where the capital good is divisible this action can be taken at any time T after the increase in demand, where $U \leq T \leq L$. There is no incentive to delay expansion until the incumbent equipment is discarded. In taking this action the firm now operates two machine groups. The first, composed of X_2^0 units, is replaced every L years. The second, composed of $\hat{X}_2 - X_2^0$ units, is also replaced every L years, but the replacement dates lag those of the first chain by T years. To take a concrete illustration, suppose our firm is a trucking company and that the appropriate production function arises out of the queuing process discussed in Chapter III. In that process, the *number* of trucks, X_2, was a substitute for man-hours of repair labor, x_1. When the increase in demand occurs, the firm has a stock of X_2^0 trucks of age U years. The long-run response to the increase in demand is to purchase $\hat{X}_2 - X_2^0$ new trucks. The firm now operates two parallel truck replacement chains. The assumption here is that investment expansion occurs by purchasing several standard units of the capital good.

If investment in the capital good is a matter of choosing a facility of appropriate size, our situation is that of section 3, Chapter III, with the very important difference that the good requires replacement every L years, making it *possible* for the firm to escape the effects of irreversibility. In this case our analysis will be based upon the assumption that the firm operates at the temporary equilibrium A' in Fig. 3–3 for the remaining life of the incumbent facility ($L - U$ years), at the end of which time it may reinvest at a higher level employing $\hat{X}_2$ units of capital and consuming $\hat{x}_1$ units of the current input, as given by (4.1.8).[2]

The firm is seen to reach the long-run equilibrium at C in Fig. 3–3 by either of two routes. If the capital good is continuously expansible, the firm reaches C using parallel

---

[2] Note that the firm's response could take the form of installing a second parallel facility of optimal size which is then replaced every L years. The greater the remaining economic life of equipment, $L - U$, the more likely is the parallel facility response to be the firm's best course of action. Such a response introduces irreversibilities of the same kind as those discussed in Chapter IV even though equipment has a finite life.

machine chains with staggered replacement dates without waiting until the incumbent capital requires replacement. If the capital good cannot be expanded continuously once installed, the firm may reach C by reinvestment at the required level at the time the incumbent facilities are discarded.

The response of the firm to a decrease in demand which causes marginal revenue to fall from MR to MR′ is shown in Fig. 3–4. The short-run response is to utilize existing facilities less intensively by consuming less of the current input, thereby moving from the initial long-run equilibrium at A to the temporary equilibrium at B. This temporary equilibrium is then maintained until such time as the replacement of the existing facilities is in order. Then the firm reinvests at a lower level, such that

$$\text{MR}' = \frac{w_1}{f_1(\hat{x}_1, \hat{X}_2)} = \frac{rW_2}{f_2(\hat{x}_1, \hat{X}_2)(1 - e^{-rL})},$$

and reaches the new long-run equilibrium at C in Fig. 3–4. Hence "replacement" may provide the mechanism whereby the firm can escape over-investment in facilities, and, depending upon the durability of the equipment, the adjustment process eventually can be reversed even in the case of indivisible capital goods.

2. The Output and Input Markets

It should be relatively easy now for the reader to reconstruct the arguments of section 3, Chapter III, concerning the firm's demand for current and capital inputs under the assumption that the capital input requires replacement at fixed intervals. We shall put aside any such detailed analysis and proceed to a brief examination of the output market and the capital input market for an industry composed of competitive firms employing capital goods requiring replacement at equidistant intervals.

The output response of such an industry to an increase in demand will follow the traditional Marshallian analysis. Referring to Fig. 3–9, an increase in demand will induce firms to operate at high short-run cost, with the market rising from an initial long-run equilibrium at P to the new short-run equilibrium at Q. As the fixed life of the existing stock of capital in the industry is expired, each firm will reinvest at the levels indicated by the new marginal productivity conditions. As a consequence, the industry will move toward a new long-run equilibrium at S, where $D'D'$ intersects S_vS_v in Fig. 3–9. Where the capital asset is subject to deterioration and must be replaced, the supply function S_vS_v is not a virtual relationship as in the case of indestructible capital goods. Any point on S_vS_v is attainable after an appropriate change in demand. In this case the "long-run" is a period not exceeding L years — the maximum life of capital existing in the industry at any time.

THE MARKET FOR DURABLE INPUT

Turning now to the market for the replaceable durable good employed by firms in the industry, we note that any point on the individual firm's marginal revenue productivity demand curve for the durable input is attainable through replacement policy. Thus D_2D_2 in Fig. 3–8 represents the firm's long-run demand for the durable input to hold. The irreversible demand function D_LD_L in Fig. 3–8 does not apply when we consider capital assets which must be replaced every L years. A change in the price of the durable input will induce corresponding changes along D_2D_2 in the quantity of the asset that the firm will desire to hold in stock. The adjustment period will be $L - U$ years in the case of a factor price change occurring when the existing capital facilities are of age U. In Fig. 3–8 a decline in price from W_2 to W_2' will, after a lag of $L - U$ years, induce the firm to reinvest at a level indicated by the point P'.

The long-run demand for the durable input by the industry as a whole is the sum of these individual stock demand functions. Notice that such an industry demand function represents a demand for *new* units of the durable asset, since we have formulated the individual demand functions in terms of new equipment units. The problem of used assets did not arise in the case of indestructible capital goods because used equipment and new equipment of the same size were equally desirable. In the case of capital goods with finite lives we cannot avoid explicit consideration of the used equipment market. In particular, it is necessary to develop a net stock demand function for new capital units as well as a flow replacement demand for new units of capital. Since the existing stock of equipment in each age class forms a set of predetermined variables, we can always find the net stock demand for new equipment by subtracting the total stock of used equipment (which must be held by someone) from the total stock demand function obtained by summing over individual firm stock demand functions. Such a procedure assumes a perfect market for used as well as new assets whereby the value of used equipment per year of remaining life is always equal to the value of new equipment per year of useful life. In effect the asset market is simply a mechanism for placing a value on equipment-years of "service." More explicitly, if $W_2{}^U$ is the price of a unit of the capital good of age $U(U = 1,2, \cdots, L - 1)$, then given the price of new durable goods, W_2, the used market generates a set of $L - 1$ prices such that $W_2{}^U/(L - U) = W_2/L$, where $U = 1, 2, \cdots, L - 1$. Hence, under the assumption that the market always places a value on used equipment such that every firm is indifferent between satisfying its stock requirements with new or with old equipment, it is possible to analyze the market for a durable good in terms of the market for new units of the good.

For expository purposes we shall take two approaches to the analysis of the durable asset market. In the first instance, we shall ignore any detailed consideration of the used market, and simply take as given a net stock demand function for new equipment. In particular we shall ignore any influence that the age distribution of equipment might exert on the pricing of new and old equipment. In the second approach we shall give explicit attention to the used equipment market, showing how the net stock demand for new equipment can be derived, and the manner in which the age distribution of equipment influences the pricing of both old and new equipment.

For the moment we assume the existence of a net stock demand for new equipment $\overline{X}_2 = \overline{D}_0(W_2)$, represented by $\overline{D}_0\overline{D}_0$ in Fig. 4–1, and a replacement flow demand function, $\overline{x}_2 = \overline{d}(W_2, L)$, represented by $\overline{d}\overline{d}$ in Fig. 4–1. If the total

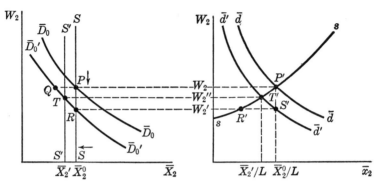

Fig. 4–1. The pricing of a replaceable durable input.

stock demand for equipment, obtained by summing over all individual firm stock demand functions, is $\overline{D}(W_2)$, and if we assume a uniform age distribution of equipment, then $\overline{x}_2 = \overline{d}(W_2, L) = \overline{D}(W_2)/L$, since the life of equipment is fixed technically at L. Under such assumptions, the aggregate stock demand function differs from the flow demand function only by the fixed scale factor, $1/L$. SS is the fixed stock supply of new equipment in the initial equilibrium state of the market while ss is the producing industry's flow supply of the durable input giving the various amounts of new units of the good that will be produced per unit time as a function of its price.

Initially it will be supposed that the market is in a state of long-run equilibrium at P in the existing asset market and, simultaneously, at P' in the "flow" market, where the annual quantity of new durable goods that the producing industry finds profitable to produce is just equal to the average rate at which the existing stock requires replacement. Of course the two markets are indistinguishable and inseparable. In this equilibrium state, the price of new equipment is W_2, and firms desire to hold a stock of the good just equal to its existing supply, $\overline{X}_2{}^0$, and the supply of newly produced units coming into the market is just equal to the equilibrium replacement demand $\overline{X}_2{}^0/L$. Now, suppose there is a general fall in the asset demand for the durable good from $\overline{D}_0\overline{D}_0$ to $\overline{D}_0'\overline{D}_0'$. This might be the result of a general rise in interest rates. Since $\overline{d}$ and $\overline{D}_0$ cannot shift independently, there must occur a corresponding decline in the long-run replacement demand from $\overline{d}\overline{d}$ to $\overline{d}'\overline{d}'$. Under the new conditions of demand, firms will desire to hold a smaller stock of the capital good. Therefore, since the actual stock is temporarily constant at $\overline{X}_2{}^0$, an excess stock supply of the good given by PQ will develop at the existing equilibrium price W_2. Firms will try to get rid of their unwanted supplies of the good by offering them to the market for sale, causing market price to fall until it reaches W_2'. At this level the existing asset market is in temporary equilibrium at R. However, at the price $W_2' < W_2$ the producing industry will desire to supply a smaller quantity of new units of the good per period with the result that there will be an excess demand for the good on flow account, and a smaller quantity of newly produced goods will be flowing into the market than are currently being discarded. The excess long-run flow demand at W_2' is $R'S'$. Since more units of the durable good are being discarded than produced, the existing stock of the good will decline. But as the stock declines an excess demand will tend to form in the existing asset market causing price to rise. Price will continue to rise, the instantaneous stock to fall, and the excess replacement demand to fall, until price reaches W_2''. At this price the market is in a new state of long-run equilibrium at T and T', with firms desiring to hold the existing stock of $\overline{X}_2'$ units of the capital good, producers desiring to supply $\overline{X}_2'/L$ units of the good per period, and firms discarding $\overline{X}_2'/L$ units per period.

The reverse of the above process occurs when there is an increase in demand. Similarly, it is relatively simple to trace through the repercussions of changes in the flow supply function, ss. The reader will find it relatively easy to trace through the adjustment process that follows a change in any of the schedules or parameters of Fig. 4–1. Observe, however, that the existing asset market has only a transient influence on the pricing of a durable input. In the long pull the existing asset market always accommodates itself, through changes in SS, to the flow supply and replacement demand conditions prevailing in the market.

THE MARKET FOR NEW AND USED DURABLE INPUT

Having sketched the general outlines of a theory of the pricing of durable goods with finite lives, we turn now to a more detailed consideration of the role of new and used durable goods in the pricing process. As before, we have given the total stock demand for a durable input, $\overline{D}(W_2)$, obtained by summing over all individual firm stock demand functions. The net stock demand for new durable input units can be derived from $\overline{D}(W_2)$, depending upon the age distribution of the used stock of durable inputs. It will simplify things analytically and conceptually if we assume a uniform age distribution of equipment assets, and think of such assets as aging in discrete one-year intervals, that is, we let S_0 be the existing stock of new freshly produced assets, S_1 be the stock of assets one year old, and so forth, with S_{L-1} representing the stock of assets having only one remaining year of useful life. The assumption of an initial uniform age distribution of equipment means that $S_0 = S_1 = S_2 = \cdots = S_{L-1}$. This assumption presupposes that the annual rate of installation of new equipment was constant in the process of building up the existing stock.[3] Under these assumptions the net stock demand for new units of durable input is simply $\overline{D}_0(W_2) = \overline{D}(W_2) - S_1 - S_2 - \cdots - S_{L-1}$. All of the existing stock of used assets must be held by someone in the industry, since the price of such assets will always seek a level such

---

[3] See Lutz and Lutz, *Theory of Investment of the Firm*, pp. 108–109.

that it will be a matter of indifference to individual firms whether they satisfy their stock requirements with new or used assets. The condition, therefore, for equilibrium in the existing new asset market is $S_0 = \overline{D}_0(W_2)$. Given the predetermined stocks $S_1, S_2, \cdots, S_{L-1}$, this condition determines W_2, the equilibrium price of existing new assets. If $s(W_2)$ is the supply function of new durable goods to the market, then in a state of long-run competitive equilibrium in which the replacement rate is equal to the production rate for new assets, we have $s(W_2) = S_{L-1}$. Since

$$\sum_{i=0}^{L-1} S_i = LS_{L-1} = \overline{D}(W_2),$$

this condition can also be written $s(W_2) = S_{L-1} = \overline{D}(W_2)/L$. In summary, given the stock of used assets in each age class, we have long-run equilibrium if the price W_2, at which firms desire to hold the existing stock of new assets, S_0, is also the price at which the annual production of new durable goods is equal to the replacement demand rate. With the price of new durable goods thus determined, the demand for used durable goods in each age class is perfectly elastic with

$$W_2^1 = \left(\frac{L-1}{L}\right) W_2, \ W_2^2 = \left(\frac{L-2}{L}\right) W_2, \cdots, \ W_2^{L-1} = \left(\frac{1}{L}\right) W_2.$$

The equilibrium conditions and the process of adjustment to a change in demand is demonstrated for the case $L = 3$ in Fig. 4–2(a)–(d). In Fig. 4–2(a) is shown an initial state of long-run equilibrium with the uniform age distribution of new and used assets given by $S_0 = S_1 = S_2$ as shown. $\overline{D}_0\overline{D}_0$ is the stock demand for new durable goods, where $\overline{D}_0 = \overline{D}(W_2) - S_1 - S_2$; ss is the flow supply of new units of the good; and the replacement flow demand function is $\overline{d}\overline{d}$, where $\overline{d} = \overline{D}(W_2)/3$. At the equilibrium price W_2^0, the stock demand for new durable goods is equal to the existing supply, that is, $\overline{D}_0 = S_0$ (at P), and the rate of production of new durable goods is equal to the replacement demand rate, that is, $\overline{x}_2^0 = \overline{d}$ (at P'), where $\overline{d} = S_2 = S_1 = S_0$. The demand function $\overline{d}\overline{d}$ is shown dotted since, as will be evident, it plays no independent role in the equilibrating process.[4] Also at the price $W_2{}^0$ the stock demand for one-year-old assets is perfectly elastic as indicated by $\overline{D}_1\overline{D}_1$, at the equilibrium price $W_2{}^1 = \frac{2}{3}W_2{}^0$, while the stock demand for two-year-old assets is $\overline{D}_2\overline{D}_2$ with $W_2{}^2 = \frac{1}{3}W_2{}^0$ as shown in Fig. 4–2(a). Of course, $W_2{}^3$ equals zero because three-year-old assets have no value since, by hypothesis, they have exhausted their lives.

Beginning with this initial long-run equilibrium state, suppose total asset demand $\overline{D}(W_2)$ rises to $\overline{D}'(W_2)$. Since S_1 and S_2 are fixed, this causes an increase in new asset demand from $\overline{D}_0\overline{D}_0$ to $\overline{D}_0'\overline{D}_0'$, as shown in Fig. 4–2(a), where $\overline{D}_0'$ $= \overline{D}'(W_2) - S_1 - S_2$. Similarly, the long-run replacement demand curve rises from $\overline{d}\overline{d}$ to $\overline{d}'\overline{d}'$. At the previous equilibrium price, $W_2{}^0$, there is now an excess stock demand for new durable goods which causes their price to rise. However, any tendency for the price of new durable goods to rise relative to used equipment causes demand to shift to the latter. Hence, as W_2 rises, $W_2{}^1$ and $W_2{}^2$ rise *pari passu*. New asset prices continue rising until a short-run equilibrium at R is reached where price is W_2', the demand for one-year and two-year-old assets are $\overline{D}_1'\overline{D}_1'$ and $\overline{D}_2'\overline{D}_2'$ and their prices $\frac{2}{3}W_2'$ and $\frac{1}{3}W_2'$ respectively.

At the price W_2' producers desire to build more new units of the durable good than are required for replacement purposes. Specifically, let us suppose that producers correctly anticipate the new long-run replacement demand conditions $\overline{d}'\overline{d}'$, thereby scheduling an increase in annual production

---

[4] Fundamentally, the replacement demand rate is S_2, the number of units that will exhaust their lives in the current period. But with a uniform age distribution of equipment $S_0 = S_1 = S_2$, we can draw a $\overline{d}\overline{d}$ curve as shown, which is the locus of points one-third of the horizontal distance from the price axis to the given aggregate stock demand function $\overline{D}(W_2)$. Since an initial equilibrium requires $\overline{d} = S_0 = S_1 = S_2$, the various points on the dotted curve $\overline{d}\overline{d}$ correspond to different assumptions concerning the initial equilibrium state of the market. We include $\overline{d}\overline{d}$ in the diagram only because it is a useful bench mark. Note, by way of comparison, that $\overline{D}_0\overline{D}_0$ is the locus of points obtained by horizontally subtracting the constant $2d = 2S_0 = 2S_1 = 2S_2$, from $\overline{D}(W_2)$. $\overline{d}\overline{d}$ is therefore steeper than $\overline{D}_0\overline{D}_0$.

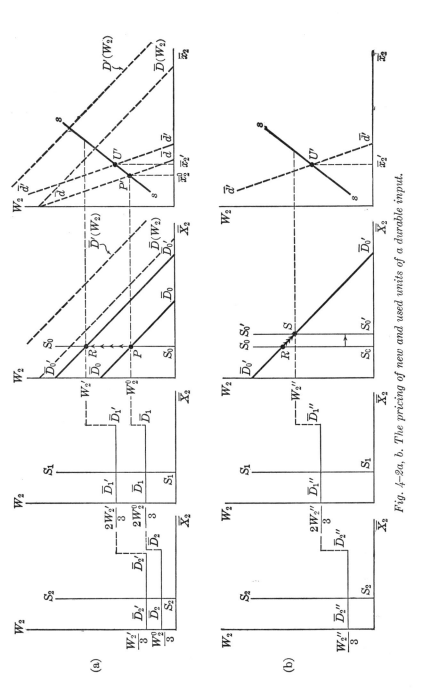

Fig. 4-2a, b. The pricing of new and used units of a durable input.

from $\bar{x}_2{}^0$ to $\bar{x}_2'$. Hence, the stock of new durable goods coming into market in the first year following the increase in demand is $S_0' = \bar{x}_2'$. Since the quantity of units discarded at the end of this first year is $S_2 = \bar{x}_2{}^0$ (the unchanged replacement demand rate), the result is an increase in aggregate supply from $S_0 + S_1 + S_2$ to $S_0' + S_1 + S_2$, where $S_1 = S_2 = \bar{x}_2{}^0$. The effect of the increase in new asset supply from $S_0 S_0$ to $S_0' S_0'$ is shown in Fig. 4–2(b). New asset prices fall from W_2' to W_2''. The demands for one- and two-year-old assets fall correspondingly as shown, with the price of the former becoming $\frac{2}{3} W_2''$ and of the latter becoming $\frac{1}{3} W_2''$. The result is a new temporary equilibrium at S.

During the second year following the initial increase in demand, producers again build $\bar{x}_2'$ units of new durable goods. The existing stock of new assets in this second year is again $\bar{x}_2' = S_0'$. Last year's stock of new assets now becomes the stock of one-year-old assets. Hence, $S_0' = S_1' > S_1 = S_2$, and $S_1 S_1$ rises to $S_1' S_1'$ as shown in Fig. 4–2(c). This increase in the stock of one-year-old assets lowers the stock demand for new assets from $\overline{D}_0' \overline{D}_0'$ to $\overline{D}_0'' \overline{D}_0''$, where $\overline{D}_0'' = \overline{D}'(W_2) - S_1' - S_2 < \overline{D}_0' = \overline{D}'(W_2) - S_1 - S_2$, giving a new temporary equilibrium at T. New assets now sell for W_2''', one-year-old assets sell at $\frac{2}{3} W_2'''$, and two-year-old assets go for $\frac{1}{3} W_2'''$.

The final adjustment occurs in the third year following the initiating increase in demand when the stock of two-year-old assets becomes $S_2' = S_1' = S_0' = \bar{x}_2'$, and $S_2 S_2$ rises to $S_2' S_2'$ as shown in Fig. 4–2(d). The demand for new assets is thereby lowered to $\overline{D}_0''' \overline{D}_0'''$, where $\overline{D}_0''' = \overline{D}'(W_2) - S_1' - S_2'$, giving a new long-run equilibrium at U in the existing asset market and U' in the flow market with the price of new assets W_2''''. Note that the new long-run equilibrium is specified by the intersection of ss with the new replacement demand curve $\bar{d}'\bar{d}'$. The new equilibrium is characterized by a uniform age distribution of used and new assets such that $\bar{x}_2' = S_0' = S_1' = S_2'$. In the general case where the life of equipment is L, a sequence of $L - 1$ adjustments in the stock demand schedule is required as the initial bulge in output

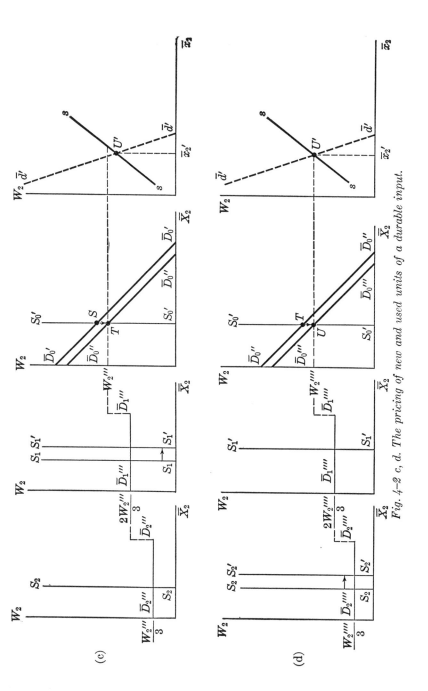

Fig. 4-2 c, d. The pricing of new and used units of a durable input.

is worked through the existing stock of assets, and a new uniform age distribution established.[5]

The analysis of investment so far has been confined to that of physical investment in durable inputs. What does our model have to say concerning the "Keynesian" investment demand schedule for a single durable good, namely, the relationship between the market rate of interest and the level of expenditure on a durable good? It is evident immediately that there are two such concepts of investment demand — the one a stock demand, the other a flow demand. In each case the rate of interest influences the demand quantity. For example, in the analysis of Fig. 4–2(a)–(d) it was found that a rise in the demand for a durable input led eventually to an increase in its price, an increase in the quantity of the input in each age class which the industry found it profitable to maintain in stock, and an increase in the equilibrium annual replacement demand for the input. Hence, it can be asserted that a *ceteris paribus* decrease in the market rate of interest (which in turn causes an increase in the demand

---

[5] The general dynamic process requires the solution of an Lth order difference equation which can be derived as follows: Let $S_U(t)$ be the stock of durable goods of age U at time t, $W_2(t)$ be the price of new durable goods at t, $s[W_2(t)]$ be the flow supply of new units to the market at t, and $\overline{D}^0[W_2(t)]$ be the aggregate stock demand for durable goods at t. Then by definition of the production and aging process we must have

$$s[W_2(t)] = S_0(t + 1) = S_1(t + 2) = \cdots = S_{L-1}(t + L).$$

Also, for any t, we must have zero total excess stock demand, that is,

$$\overline{D}^0[W_2(t)] - S_0(t) - S_1(t) - \cdots - S_{L-1}(t) = 0.$$

This difference equation system can be reduced to the Lth order equation

$$\overline{D}^0[W_2(t)] - s[W_2(t - 1)] - s[W_2(t - 2)] - \cdots - s[W_2(t - L)] = 0.$$

Also, of course, we have $W_2{}^U(t) = (L - U/L)W_2(t)$, $U = 1, 2, \ldots, L - 1$. Hans Brems works with a similar difference equation system in an input-output context. See his *Output, Employment, Capital, and Growth* (New York: Harper, 1959), chaps. xxii–xxiv.

for the capital input) will eventually increase the price of the input, increase the physical stock of the input, increase the total value of capital invested in the new and used stock of the input, and increase the flow of replacement expenditures on the asset. These results will now be derived more systematically.

Both the stock and flow investment demand (value) functions can be derived from the long-run conditions for static market equilibrium. We consider a single durable input, and assume a uniform age distribution of the input among its users. We let X be the stock supply of the durable input in each of L age classes, $D(W,r,L)$ be the total stock demand for the good (see equation [4.1.7]), and $s(W)$ be the flow supply function. The conditions for long-run static equilibrium are that total supply (XL) equal demand in the existing new and used asset market, and that the flow supply of the asset be equal to the replacement demand rate; thus,

$$XL = D(W,r,L)$$
$$D(W,r,L)/L = s(W). \qquad (4.2.1)$$

Given the rate of interest and the durability of equipment, the conditions (4.2.1) determine $X = X(r,L)$ and $W = W(r,L)$. The "Keynesian" investment flow (replacement) demand rate is $I \equiv WX$. Since the price of a unit of capital of age U must be $[(L - U)/L]W$, the total value of investment in capital goods of all ages can be written

$$K \equiv WX + \left(\frac{L-1}{L}\right)WX + \left(\frac{L-2}{L}\right)WX + \cdots + \left(\frac{1}{L}\right)WX$$
$$= \frac{WX(L+1)}{2}.$$

Hence from (4.2.1) we can write

$$\begin{cases} I = \dfrac{WD(W,r,L)}{L} = Ws(W) \\ K = \dfrac{I(L+1)}{2} \end{cases} \qquad (4.2.2)$$

These equations allow the total stock and flow investment demand schedules $K = K(r,L)$ and $I = I(r,L)$ to be determined.

The slope functions $\partial I/\partial r$ and $\partial K/\partial r$ can be obtained by appropriately differentiating the equations in (4.2.2), giving

$$\frac{\partial I}{\partial r} = \frac{W}{L}\frac{\partial D}{\partial r}\left(\frac{e+1}{e-E_W}\right) \tag{4.2.3}$$

and

$$\frac{\partial K}{\partial r} = \frac{W(L+1)}{2L}\frac{\partial D}{\partial r}\left(\frac{e+1}{e-E_W}\right) \tag{4.2.4}$$

where $e = (W/s)(\partial s/\partial W) > 0$ is the price elasticity of the flow supply function, and $E_W = (W/D)(\partial D/\partial W) < 0$ is the price elasticity of the physical stock demand function. Since $\partial D/\partial r < 0$, it follows that $\partial I/\partial r < 0$, and $\partial K/\partial r < 0$, that is, an increase in the rate of interest generates a new long-run equilibrium characterized by a lower rate of replacement investment and a lower total investment in the stock of durable inputs.[6]

By differentiating (4.2.2) with respect to L we can determine the effect of *ceteris paribus* changes in the durability of capital goods on the stock and flow investment demand functions. Hence,

$$\frac{\partial I}{\partial L} = \frac{I(E_L - 1)e}{L(e - E_W)} \tag{4.2.5}$$

$$\frac{\partial K}{\partial L} = \frac{I}{2} + \left(\frac{L+1}{2}\right)\frac{\partial I}{\partial L} \tag{4.2.6}$$

---

[6] If we let $i = (r/I)(\partial I/\partial r)$ be the interest elasticity of the Keynesian flow investment demand schedule, $k = (r/K)(\partial K/\partial r)$ be the interest elasticity of the Keynesian stock investment demand schedule, and $E_r = (r/D)(\partial D/\partial r)$ be the interest elasticity of the physical stock demand function, then from (4.2.3) and (4.2.4) we can deduce

$$i = k = E_r\left(\frac{e+1}{e-E_W}\right).$$

Since $E_r < 0$, $e > 0$, $E_W < 0$, we have $i = k < 0$.

where $E_L = (L/D)(\partial D/\partial L) > 0$ is the equipment-life elasticity of the physical stock demand function. Hence, $\partial I/\partial L \gtreqless 0$ according as $E_L \gtreqless 1$. An increase in the durability of capital goods will increase or decrease the replacement demand rate depending upon whether the physical stock demand function is relatively elastic or relatively inelastic. From (4.2.6) it is seen that if $\partial I/\partial L > 0$, then $\partial K/\partial L > 0$. If increasing the durability of capital increases the replacement demand rate, it also increases the total value of invested capital. On the other hand if $\partial I/\partial L < 0$, we could have $\partial K/\partial L \gtreqless 0$. An increase in the durability of capital that lowers the long-run replacement demand rate could be accompanied by an increase or a decrease in the total value of the stock of capital.

Chapter V

Capital Replacement Theory

1. Introduction

Before extending our theory of production and investment to capital goods whose life is a decision variable, it is necessary to explore critically the theory of economic replacement policy. This is done partly for the purpose of familiarizing the reader with replacement theory, but more specifically for the purpose of making certain amendments in the theory in order to prepare the way for a more explicit theory of production, investment, and replacement to be discussed in Chapter VI.

Modern equipment analysis has its origin in two early papers by J. S. Taylor [1] and Harold Hotelling.[2] Taylor developed, by means of a discrete period analysis, a formula [3] relating the average unit cost of the output of a machine over L years to the cost of the machine new, the scrap value of the machine after L periods of service, the machine's operating costs in each period of service up to the Lth, the

---

[1] J. S. Taylor, "A Statistical Theory of Depreciation," *Journal of the American Statistical Association*, XIX (December 1923), 1010.

[2] Harold Hotelling, "A General Mathematical Theory of Depreciation," *Journal of the American Statistical Association*, XX (September 1925), 340.

[3] Taylor, p. 1017.

output of the machine in each period, and the rate of interest. Taylor then proceeded to show how one determines L (the years of machine life) such that the unit cost of production will be minimum.

Under the stimulus of Taylor's paper, Hotelling two years later asks, "Does the manufacturer desire to make his unit cost . . . a minimum? Or may not considerations of profit lead him to scrap the machine at some different time from that which makes unit cost . . . a minimum." [4] The viewpoint is then advanced that the owner of the machine wishes to maximize the present value of the machine's output minus its operating costs. Hotelling's "fundamental formula" with continuous discounting at a constant rate of interest can be stated in the following form:

$$V(\tau) = \int_{\tau}^{L} [R(t) - E(t)]e^{-r(t-\tau)}\,dt + S(L)e^{-r(L-\tau)}$$

where $V(\tau)$ is the value of the equipment at time, τ; $S(L)$ is a function giving the scrap value at time, L; $R(t)$ is the machine's revenue at time, t; $E(t)$ is the machine's operating costs at time, t; and r is the continuous rate of interest.

Writing some years later, G. A. D. Preinreich [5] was able to show that the economic life of a single machine could not be determined in isolation from the economic life of each machine in the chain of future replacements extending as far into the future as the firm's profit horizon. Hence, Preinreich argues that the firm should maximize the present value of the "aggregate goodwill" of *all* replacements, where the "aggregate goodwill" is the present value of the earnings of the future machine replacements minus the present value of the costs of all such machines. That is, Preinreich says we must maximize the expression

$$V = \sum_{k=0}^{\infty} e^{-rkL}\left\{\int_{0}^{L} [R(t) - E(t)]e^{-rt}\,dt + S(L)e^{-rL} - p\right\},$$

[4] Hotelling, p. 341.

[5] G. A. D. Preinreich, "The Economic Life of Industrial Equipment," *Econometrica*, VIII (January 1940), 12.

where p is the cost of each new machine in the replacement chain.

These contributions brought the theory to a fairly complete form, but an important ingredient was missing, and this was recognized by all three of the writers cited. The missing spice was an adequate means of taking into account technological change or obsolescence. All the writers mentioned assumed a stationary technology in which the machines considered were to be replaced by machines of identical type. Therefore the factor which eventually made replacement economically attractive was the effect of age in causing the net earnings of a machine to decline.

The important contribution of extending the theory to account for equipment obsolescence was provided by George Terborgh.[6] No one who has surveyed the body of equipment replacement theory can fail to appreciate Terborgh's simple, yet fundamental, theoretical contribution. Terborgh contends that the replacement of an existing facility (the defender) should be conditioned by a comparison of its performance with that of the latest new comparable facility which is available (the challenger). It is the growth in the inferiority of an old asset relative to the initial performance of the latest equipment continually being made available, taking into account the appropriate capital costs and disposal values, which eventually makes it unprofitable to continue the incumbent facility in service. This growth in inferiority is called the "inferiority gradient" and is assumed to develop at a constant rate. This inferiority is composed partly of obsolescence, or the amount by which the earning rate of the latest new equipment exceeds that of the present equipment when the latter was new, and partly of economic deterioration, or the amount by which the earning rate of the incumbent facility has fallen below its original earning rate when it was new. He argues, following Preinreich, that replacement analysis cannot in general be confined to a single machine horizon.

[6] Terborgh, *Dynamic Equipment Policy.*

2. An Appraisal of Received Replacement Theory

Except for the two cited initial papers by Taylor and Hotelling the replacement literature contains no new discussion of the criteria appropriate for replacement decisions. Ever since the Hotelling paper it has been taken for granted that the appropriate replacement criterion should be the maximization of the present value of the machine's net revenue or "goodwill." It was perhaps natural for economists to develop the theory in terms of profit maximization since "machines" obviously contribute to output, which in turn has a market value. The crucial question, however, is whether or not output and/or the value of output is altered in any way by the "replacement" decision. If neither output nor selling price is influenced by the replacement decision then the decision can only be influenced by the relevant cost considerations.

Prior to the work of Terborgh there had appeared no significant treatment of the replacement problem which took account of technological change.[7] This earlier theoretical literature of replacement theory is almost wholly concerned with the replacement of machines with units of identical type. It is therefore somewhat puzzling to find such tenacious adherence to a profit maximization formulation of the model, since, in the absence of technological changes in equipment, the replacement decision cannot possibly affect either price or output. In the post-Terborghian literature,[8] where problems of obsolescence are treated explicitly, the revenue per machine is frequently assumed to decline with age and rise with technological improvements. The rational would seem to be that one expects machine output "efficiency" to fall

---

[7] There are several references in the literature which recognize the importance of obsolescence and give the subject limited analysis, as, for example, in Lutz and Lutz, *Theory of Investment of the Firm*, pp. 109–112, but these references provide only fragmentary and incomplete contributions to the analysis of obsolescence.

[8] See, for example, Armen A. Alchian, *Economic Replacement Policy* (Santa Monica: RAND Corporation, April 12, 1952), and Richard Bellman, "Equipment Replacement Policy," *Journal of the Society for Industrial and Applied Mathematics*, III (September 1955), 133–136.

with age. Then when "replacement" occurs the stock is replaced by units of greater productivity. One construction that can be put on this approach is that it views the typical equipment problem as one of piecemeal replacement of single machines so that the effect of expansions in output capacity is so small that one can ignore demand considerations. Another interpretation is that expansions can be made without lowering price (perfect market for the product) and added capacity can only be obtained through replacement; in other words, one cannot purchase another machine of the same type or new machines of smaller capacity to augment the capacity of the present machine. Unless some such assumptions are made the analysis is sure to be in error since there is no justification in arriving at a decision to burden the old machine — by comparison — with the earnings of the new capacity.

This tendency to confound replacement and expansion decisions is no doubt due to the fact that it is the machine unit (a truck, press, lathe, etc.) which is physically replaced. In the present work a clear distinction between replacement and expansion decisions will be maintained, and where the "replacement" of particular machines involves both reinvestment and expansion the appropriate adjustments will be made. We shall understand that if any qualitative or quantitative dimension of output is changed when an old machine is displaced by a new one, then, by definition, that replacement is not literal. Fundamentally our view shall be that replacement is concerned with minimizing the cost of producing a given output. The problem of expansion, whether it be bound up with the "replacement" of particular machines or not, is a problem of scale which cannot be solved without introducing demand considerations. In its pure form, replacement will be formulated as part of the problem of least cost production.[9] In this regard it is preferable to think

[9] Observe that this is roughly the position taken in the first paper on equipment theory (Taylor, note 1, above). Until the proper point of view is taken on this matter, it is very difficult to be led to a clear understanding of the relationship between equipment replacement theory and neoclassical production theory.

of machine load capacity rather than machines as the entity which is replaced. Milling machines are not replaced by milling machines — milling capacity is replaced by milling capacity. In the typical case, four new machines may replace five old machines with no change in normal output since technical changes in equipment frequently impinge upon the capacity of equipment to do work.

There is at least one important sense in which replacement policy is not strictly identified with cost minimization, and cannot be formulated independently of output and therefore revenue policy. Where equipment is subject to cost reducing technological improvements, then, as "replacements" are made in the future, the short-run cost function falls. With a declining cost curve from one replacement point to the next, profit maximization may require readjustments in output and price policy in accordance with marginal revenue and marginal cost considerations. Hence, replacement policy will affect revenue through its effect on cost and output.[10] However, unless otherwise stated, our fundamental working hypothesis will be that replacement policy is concerned with minimizing the flow cost of capital goods to the enterprise.

In the sections to follow we shall develop the relationship between the total cost function and the flow or current account cost of capital goods, assuming fixed production coefficients. Replacement policy as a means of minimizing this flow cost of capital will be derived assuming that equipment obsolescence and deterioration affect *only* operating cost per unit of equipment. After a digression on dynamic programming we shall then analyze briefly the more general cost minimization case in which technological improvements in equipment lower the input coefficients. Finally, a general profit maximization model will be developed showing a sense in which replacement policy cannot be formulated independently of output and price policy. Our objective, be-

[10] Replacement could also directly influence revenue if the age of equipment was a demand parameter. This might be the case in certain monopolistically competitive industries in which consumers favored those firms with the newest equipment. For example a milk distributor might sell more milk with shiny new trucks of the latest design, than with old trucks.

sides laying the foundation for a more general theory of the capital-using enterprise is to clarify the distinct roles that unit revenue, unit cost, and output policy can play in the equipment replacement decision.

3. Economic Replacement Policy; A Modern Synthesis

Consider a simple productive process requiring two inputs — one current input and one equipment input. Let x_1 be the consumption per unit time of the current input and X_2 be the physical stock of equipment required. If w_1 is the price of input Number 1, and w_2 is the annual cost, including investment, interest, and operating outlays, of maintaining a unit of equipment in production, then an expression for the total current account cost of the process is

$$C = w_1 x_1 + w_2 X_2. \qquad (5.3.1)$$

If we further assume that production is characterized by Walras-Leontief fixed input-output coefficients with $x_1 = ay$ and $X_2 = by$, where y is output, a is the flow coefficient, and b is a Leontief investment coefficient, then (5.3.1) becomes

$$C = (aw_1 + bw_2)y. \qquad (5.3.2)$$

Our hypothesis will be that $w_2 = w_2(L)$, that is, the annual cost of maintaining a unit of equipment in production is a (U-shaped) function of equipment age, and that a, b, and y are independent of L. For the present, replacement theory will be presented assuming that limitational inputs prevail, and that equipment obsolescence and deterioration affect only the annual cost of maintaining a physical unit of equipment in production. Our main immediate task will be to develop the age-variable components of $w_2(L)$ in detail.

In formulating a generalized statement of the equipment replacement problem within the foregoing assumptions, consider a firm with a stock of incumbent equipment that has already been purchased, and has been in service for some period of time. This equipment will have declined in "efficiency" with a concomitant rise in repair, servicing, and other operating expenses. These operating outlays can be expected to continue rising with equipment age. They will also depend upon the rate of equipment utilization. The more intensely the equipment is employed (for example, the greater the annual mileage put on a truck fleet) the greater will be these annual operating costs. We define, therefore, an operating expense function of the form $\phi_0(u_0,t)$, where u_0 is the average annual utilization rate and t is the number of additional years the incumbent equipment is continued in service.[11] If the equipment is kept for $t = L_0$ additional years,

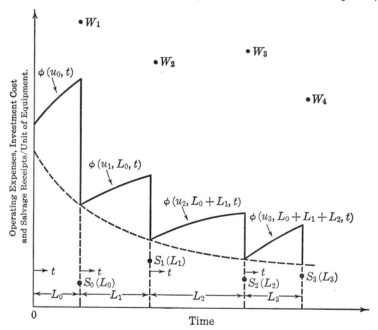

Fig. 5–1. The cost stream for a unit of equipment.

[11] Equipment operating cost depends most directly upon *cumulative use*, and perhaps also upon the current utilization rate. Equipment age is an indirect determinant of equipment operating cost due to the relation between cumulative use and age (for example, cumulative machine hours equal average rate of utilization in machine hours per month times months of equipment service). Therefore, operating costs ought to be expressed as a function of both the utilization rate and equipment age. See Vernon L. Smith, "Economic Equipment Policies; An Evaluation," *Management Science*, IV (October 1957), 26–29.

then by that time the operating expense rate will have risen
to $\phi_0(u_0, L_0)$, as shown in Fig. 5–1. The optimal replacement
date for this incumbent machinery is obtained by determining $L_0 = L_0{}^0$ such that the annual unit equipment cost, w
(hereafter in this section the subscript will be dropped), is
a minimum. Replacement policy is thus expressed in terms
of equipment life. If $L_0 = 0$, an optimal policy signals immediate replacement. If $L_0 > 0$, this represents an estimate
of how many more years the equipment should remain in
service.

The problem is still incompletely defined, since the economic life of the present equipment cannot be determined
independently of the operating performance and economic
life, L_1, of the equipment that will replace it. If the firm's
planning horizon extends beyond the life of a single replacement, then L_0 cannot be evaluated independently of the
economic life of each machine unit in the *chain* of future
replacements — L_1, L_2, L_3 and so forth — for as far into
the future as the horizon extends. Just as we associate an
operating cost function $\phi_0(u_0, t)$ with the incumbent (initial)
equipment, there will exist a similar function for each unit
of equipment in the chain of future replacements. Since
technological improvements in equipment will be assumed
to take place continually, the operating expenses of the first
replacement units will be lower the longer their purchase is
postponed. Delaying replacement permits the installation
of more advanced equipment models, but raises the operating expense of the incumbent equipment. This is true for
each member in the chain of replacements. The operating
expense function for the first replacement in the chain will
be a function of three variables — the utilization rate of the
equipment, the time at which the replacement is made (since
this determines the technological state of advancement of
the equipment to be installed), and the age of the equipment. This function can be written $\phi(u_1, L_0, t)$, and will be
an increasing function of u_1 and a decreasing function of L_0,
since the longer the incumbent equipment is held in service

the more advanced will be the replacement equipment. It will be an increasing function of t, since, once the replacement is made, operating outlays are assumed to rise with age.

Similarly, the operating cost function for the second link in the replacement chain is $\phi(u_2, L_0 + L_1, t)$, where u_2 is the utilization rate for the second machine replacement which is purchased at $L_0 + L_1$, the end of the life of the first replacement. The operating cost function for the third machine replacement is $\phi(u_3, L_0 + L_1 + L_2, t)$ and for the $n + 1$th is $\phi(u_{n+1}, \sum_{k=0}^{n} L_k, t)$. The result is a sequence of functions which generate a ragged saw-toothed operating expense profile per unit of equipment such as that shown in Fig. 5–1.

In addition to operating expenses there is one other major category of expense associated with equipment, viz., the first cost or investment cost per unit of equipment, W_k, for the kth machine replacement. Since machinery will normally have some resale, "trade-in" or salvage value at the time of replacement, W_k is not the net investment in equipment. To get net investment we must subtract $S_k(L_k)$, the salvage value of the kth machine chain which is assumed to be a decreasing function of its life.

We define an economic replacement policy to be one that minimizes w, the constant outlay stream that has the same present value as all the operating cost and net investment cost outlays associated with a unit of equipment in an infinite chain of equipment replacements. Stated in another way, we minimize the uniform continuous equivalent or "current account" cost of all future operating and capital expenditures per unit of equipment over an infinite horizon. By stating our replacement criterion with reference to a physical unit of equipment, we pave the way for an integration of replacement policy with production and investment theory in Chapter VI.

The general problem of replacement can therefore be stated in terms of minimizing an expression of the form

$$w = r \left\{ \int_0^{L_0} \phi(u_0, t) e^{-rt} \, dt - S_0(L_0) e^{-rL_0} \right\}$$

$$+ r e^{-rL_0} \left\{ \int_0^{L_1} \phi(u_1, L_0, t) e^{-rt} \, dt + W_1 - S_1(L_1) e^{-rL_1} \right\}$$

$$+ r e^{-r(L_0 + L_1)} \left\{ \int_0^{L_2} \phi(u_2, L_0 + L_1, t) e^{-rt} \, dt \right.$$

$$\left. + W_2 - S_2(L_2) e^{-rL_2} \right\}$$

.
.
.

$$+ r e^{-r(L_0 + L_1 + \cdots + L_k)}$$

$$\left\{ \int_0^{L_{k+1}} \phi(u_{k+1}, L_0 + L_1 + \cdots + L_k, t) e^{-rt} \, dt \right.$$

$$\left. + W_{k+1} - S_{k+1}(L_{k+1}) e^{-rL_{k+1}} \right\},$$

.
.
.

$$(5.3.3)$$

where r is the continuous rate of discount. This expression provides the uniform continuous cost stream whose present value is equal to the present value of the operating cost profile and the lump sum investment outlays and salvage receipts shown in Fig. 5–1. The investment cost of the incumbent equipment, W_0, does not appear in the first bracket since, by hypothesis, the incumbent equipment is a sunk investment whose capital cost should not be allowed to influence decisions. The integrals in this expression serve the purpose of discounting the operating cost stream of each replacement back to the point in time when the replacement equipment was purchased new. The exponential term outside each set of brackets then discounts all these operating cost streams back to the present on "now" in calendar time. Similarly, the second and third term inside each bracket, when discounted, determines the present value of all future investment outlays net of salvage values. The discount rate multiplying the entire expression converts the present value of all these outlays into a uniform continuous annuity. The quantity w therefore represents the annual service charge, including interest, which is necessary to meet all operating and investment expenses associated with maintaining a unit of equipment in production. This cost may vary over a wide range depending upon the values chosen for the L_k.

The formulation (5.3.3) represents a generalization and synthesis of the Preinreich-Lutz-Terborgh approach to replacement, with the major exception that, in accordance with our previous arguments, the problem has been stated in terms of cost minimization instead of profit ("goodwill") maximization. The explicit conditions for minimization of w will be derived mathematically after certain approximations and simplifications in (5.3.3), which are to be adhered to hereafter, have been introduced. For the moment let us undertake an intuitive approach to the problem of replacing incumbent units of equipment. At any point in time along the replacement chain consider the alternatives of continuing the incumbent equipment in operation for an additional "year," versus replacing the equipment with units of the latest model available. These are mutually exclusive alternatives. If the incumbent equipment is held an additional year, the firm will incur direct costs equal to the next-year operating expenses of such equipment. The additional year of service will also lead to three opportunity costs, two of which cause an increase and one a decrease in the avoidable cost of delaying replacement for an additional year. As a consequence of holding the incumbent equipment another year, it suffers a decline in salvage value. This decline in salvage value plus one year's interest on the salvage proceeds, which are foregone as a result of the decision not to replace immediately, constitute two indirect, but avoidable, costs that are chargeable to this decision. A third opportunity cost is quite subtle and very easy to overlook entirely. The key to this cost component is to be found in the fact that changing the replacement date of any unit in the infinite equipment chain affects all future replacement dates. Where successive equipment units in the chain are characterized by technological improvements that lower operating costs, the decision to retain the incumbent equipment another year means that replacement, if it takes place the following year, can be made with equipment of lower operating cost performance. Furthermore, all future replacements are moved forward in time with resulting improvements in their performance. The interest on the present value of all these future cost savings represents a gain to be charged in favor of the additional year's service from the incumbent equipment. Hence, the net cost of holding the incumbent equipment in service for one additional year is the next-year operating cost of the equipment, plus the decline in salvage value due to another year's service, plus the interest on the salvage proceeds foregone for another year, minus the interest on the present value of all future cost savings resulting from the fact that a delay in replacement now causes all future replacements to be delayed and thereby to be effected with improved equipment. When this net cost is equal to the uniform equivalent of all future equipment expenses, assuming optimal future replacement policies, it is time to discard the incumbent equipment.[12] This marginal condition will be further elucidated shortly.

In the expression (5.3.3) it has not been assumed that the economic lives of successive units in the replacement chain were equal.[13] For the case of an infinite chain of machines, not subject to obsolescence, Preinreich has shown that the economic lives of all machine units in the chain converge to equality.[14] Two considerations are favorable to simplifying

[12] This condition in profit ("goodwill") maximization form was derived first by Preinreich (note 5 above, p. 17), and is discussed by the Lutzes, pp. 106–107, for equipment not subject to technological improvements, that is, both Preinreich and the Lutzes deal with equipment which is to be replaced by units of identical type. Terborgh, chaps. v and vi, employs this condition to define an optimal policy where equipment is subject to obsolescence. See his analysis of the "adverse minimum" of "challenger" and "defender" machines in the cited chapters.

[13] See Lutz and Lutz, pp. 106–107.

[14] See Preinreich, p. 17. The proof is cumbersome. An extension or denial of the theorem has not been provided where machines are subject to obsolescence.

the criterion function (5.3.3) by assuming replacements (beginning with the first) to be spaced at equidistant intervals. The mathematical procedure of exponentially discounting the cost stream of future replacements causes the earlier machines in the chain to exert a much greater influence on w than the later machines. The series tends to converge rapidly for medium to long-lived equipment so that differences in L_k for k beyond the first few replacements exert a very minor influence on w. Also, in the face of steady technological improvement in equipment, the economic life of equipment does not change abruptly from one replacement to another. Such an erratic phenomenon is characteristic only of equipment that experiences spectacular changes. In the analysis to follow, (5.3.3) will be simplified by introducing the approximation $L_1 = L_2 = L_3 = \cdots = L$. In effect, the influence that all future replacement decisions have upon the decision to replace the incumbent equipment, is being telescoped by this procedure into the choice of an "average" or approximate economic life for these future machines. The more spectacular and sporadic the changes in equipment, and the lower the discount rate, the more error may be introduced by this approximation.

Under an equidistant replacement policy for all future equipment beyond the incumbent machinery, assuming a constant rate of equipment utilization, and assuming no change in the investment cost of future equipment (that is, $W = W_k$), equation (5.3.3) can be written

$$w = r \left\{ \int_0^{L_0} \phi_0(t) e^{-rt} \, dt - S_0(L_0) e^{-rL_0} \right\}$$
$$+ re^{-rL_0} \sum_{k=0}^{\infty} e^{-rkL} \left\{ \int_0^{L} \phi(L_0 + kL, t) e^{-rt} \, dt + W - S(L) e^{-rL} \right\}.$$
$$(5.3.4)$$

Note that L_0 will not in general equal L, since the incumbent equipment by hypothesis has already been in service for some period. If we let w' be the uniform equivalent of all future equipment expenses beginning with the first replacement (the future "challengers"), the expression (5.3.4) can be written

$$w = r \left\{ \int_0^{L_0} \phi_0(t)e^{-rt} \, dt - S_0(L_0)e^{-rL_0} \right\} + w'e^{-rL_0}. \quad (5.3.4')$$

Equation (5.3.4), or some variant thereof, forms the substructure of all contemporary approaches to applied replacement analysis. In most applications, however, linear approximations to the ϕ-functions and salvage value functions are employed and seem to be entirely satisfactory.[15] Linear approximations to ϕ_0 and ϕ in (5.3.4) and (5.3.4') are as follows:

$$\left. \begin{array}{l} \phi_0(t) = E_0 + \beta_0 t; \, E_0, \, \beta_0 \geq 0 \\ \phi(L_0 + kL, \, t) = E - \alpha(L_0 + kL) + \beta t; \\ \qquad k = 0, 1, 2, \cdots; \, E, \, \alpha, \, \beta \geq 0, \end{array} \right\} \quad (5.3.5)$$

where

β_0 is the rate at which the operating expenses of the currently employed equipment rise with age. This parameter measures the rate at which economic deterioration occurs in a unit of equipment.

β is the rate at which the operating expenses of future machine replacements are expected to rise with their ages.

E_0 is the present or initial ($t = 0$) operating expense rate per unit of the incumbent equipment.

E is the initial or first-year operating expense rate of the best currently available model of new equipment which would be installed if the incumbent equipment were discarded at $L_0 = 0$.

α is the rate of technological change, measured by the amount that the initial operating cost rate of new equipment falls each year as a consequence of model improvements.

The equipment utilization rate, u, will affect these parameters, but for the present analysis this is assumed to be constant.

[15] Terborgh, who has directed by far the most ambitious program of applied replacement reasearch, uses linear obsolescence rates throughout most of his work. See Terborgh, chap. ix, and the *MAPI Replacement Manual* (Chicago: Machinery and Allied Products Institute, 1950), chap. vi.

The operating expense profile per unit of equipment will now appear as shown in Fig. 5–2. It should be borne in mind that E_0 and E are fixed only in relation to the origin 0, which in turn is constantly moving forward in calendar time. For example, the value of E_0 depends upon the period that

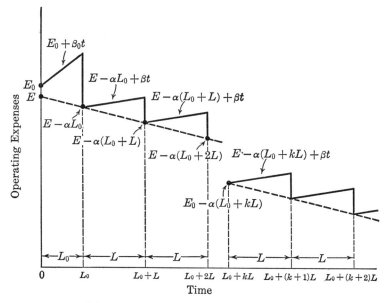

Fig. 5–2. A linear operating expense profile.

has elapsed since the incumbent equipment was installed. Remember that time, t, in Fig. 5–2 refers to time in terms of equipment age, and not calendar time. The capital-using firm on some calendar date is considered to be at the origin 0 looking forward to the indicated operating expense profile. As time passes, the firm moves forward along this profile incurring the variation in expenses indicated by the graph.

The last parameter defined above, α, deserves further discussion. Each year a number of improvements may be embodied in a particular type of equipment being produced by the manufacturers of the good. Some of these improvements will be very insignificant and some may be quite important, costwise, to the users of the equipment. We assume that the net effect of such improvements will be to decrease the operating cost per unit of equipment by cost reducing changes and attachments which cannot be embodied in earlier models produced in previous years. Each year such improvements may be expected to lower the new machine's operating expense function below that of the machines produced in the previous year. In the approximations (5.3.5) it is assumed that such technical changes do not alter the (linear) shape of the operating cost function or its slope, but instead shift the operating cost function downward at a constant average rate per year, α. Clearly we are not concerned here with sudden, major, technological changes — the kind that produce such enormous savings that it pays to scrap even new equipment of the old type and shift to the latest model. Such discontinuous innovations have been afforded abstract treatment in the literature,[16] but do not seem to be characteristic of the typical pattern of technological advance experienced by many varieties of industrial equipment. An excellent illustration is to be found in the development of the internal combustion engine. This development has been characterized by a gradual steady improvement in the various operating components of the engine with consequent improvements in automobiles, trucks, tractors, and other types of equipment which make use of this source of motive power. Thus trucking firms are faced with making vehicle purchasing decisions not unlike the kind considered here. Similar decisions are faced in the purchase of locomotives, buses, machine tools, farm implements, textile machinery, pumping equipment, and so on throughout, perhaps, most of the range of durable equipment. Of course in some cases the steady progress of technological change will be punctuated from time to time with innovational upheavals. For example, the steam locomotive enjoyed many improvements over the years before the appearance of the diesel, which in turn rapidly displaced steam power. Since

[16] See Lutz and Lutz, pp. 109–112.

the changeover, diesel improvements have proceeded at a steady, more pedestrian, pace.

Where major innovations have been initiated there is no substitute for a specific factual analysis of the new product in evaluating its effect on replacement policy. But in the absence of, or supplementary to, such remarkable changes, the irregular plodding growth of technology is easily taken into account, and the approximations suggested here are designed for precisely such circumstances. Generally, as a working hypothesis, we will identify steady year-to-year improvements in equipment with reductions in operating expenses per unit of capital equipment, while major innovations will be identified with changes in the production function that require new kinds of capital equipment to achieve the benefits of the innovation.

If we assume constant salvage values, S_0 and S, for the incumbent and future replacement machines, then substituting from (5.3.5) into (5.3.4') gives [17]

$$w = r \left\{ \int_0^{L_0} (E_0 + \beta_0 t) e^{-rt} \, dt - S_0 e^{-rL_0} \right\} + w' e^{-rL_0} \qquad (5.3.6)$$

with

$$w' = r \sum_{k=0}^{\infty} e^{-rkL} \left\{ \int_0^L [E - \alpha(L_0 + kL) + \beta t] e^{-rt} \, dt \right. $$
$$\left. + W - S e^{-rL} \right\} \qquad (5.3.7)$$

$$= E - \alpha L_0 + \frac{\beta}{r} + \frac{r(W - S e^{-rL}) - (\alpha + \beta) L e^{-rL}}{1 - e^{-rL}}$$

[17] In equations (5.3.6) and (5.3.7) we have assumed (see Fig. 5–2) an operating cost function whose obsolescence component declines linearly through time. It follows that eventually operating costs must become negative with the result that in equations (5.3.6) and (5.3.7) the discounting process is eventually applied to negative costs. It might be supposed that W and w' are thereby given a sharp downward bias. The conclusion is true only if α is large relative to the other parameters in the operating cost function. We assume that in normal applications the discounting process causes (5.3.7) to converge so rapidly that only the first few replacement machines have any appreciable influence on the results. Hence, the linear approximations do not have to hold for any considerable distance into the future. We could have assumed that obsolescence causes an exponential decay in operating costs,

Minimizing w, we set $\partial w/\partial L_0 = 0$; and

$$\partial w/\partial L = e^{-rL_0}(\partial w'/\partial L) = 0.$$

This operation gives

$$E_0 + \beta_0 L_0{}^0 + rS_0 - \frac{\alpha}{r} = w'^0 \qquad (5.3.8)$$

and

$$(\alpha + \beta)(1 - rL^0 - e^{-rL_0}) + r^2(W - S) = 0, \qquad (5.3.9)$$

where $w'^0 = w'|_{L=L^0}$.

Equation (5.3.8) expresses the marginal condition for replacement, discussed verbally above, assuming equidistant replacements of future equipment, a linear operating expense function and constant salvage values.[18] The term $E_0 + \beta_0 L_0{}^0$ is the annual rate of operating expense at the time $(t = L_0{}^0)$ when replacement is optimal. Since a constant salvage value is assumed, there can be no decline in salvage value. Hence, only the interest on the salvage value, rS_0, appears as an opportunity cost in the replacement decision rule. Finally, the term α/r measures the rate at which annual equipment cost declines with each year the replacement is delayed. Therefore, the sum $(E_0 + \beta_0 L_0{}^0) + rS_0 - (\alpha/r)$ represents the additional total cost (including both direct and opportunity costs) of holding a unit of the incumbent equipment an additional year. When this sum has risen to equality

---

i.e., $\phi(L_0 + kL, t) = Ee^{-a(L_0+kL)} + \beta t$, $k = 0, 1, 2, \ldots$ where a is now the percentage rate of decline in operating cost due to technological improvements. However, with our reservations concerning the rapid convergence of (5.3.7), linear approximations serve admirably for illustrative purposes, and the way is prepared to compare our analysis with that of Terborgh.

[18] The more general nonlinear condition corresponding to (5.3.8) is obtained by differentiating (5.3.4') with respect to L_0. This gives

$$\phi_0(L_0) - S_0'(L_0) + rS_0(L_0) + \frac{1}{r}\frac{\partial w'}{\partial L_0} = w'.$$

The expression on the left is the cost of holding the incumbent equipment in service an additional year, that is, the next-year operating cost plus the decline in its salvage value plus interest on the salvage proceeds minus the interest on the present value of all future savings resulting from another year's delay in replacement. The term on the right is the uniform equivalent of all future equipment outlays.

with w'^0, the discounted annual cost of installing and maintaining new equipment and following an optimal replacement policy forever after, the incumbent equipment should be discarded. From (5.3.8) this occurs when

$$L_0^0 = \frac{w'^0 - E_0 - rS_0 + \alpha/r}{\beta_0}. \qquad (5.3.10)$$

The diagram in Fig. 5–3 illustrates the equilibrium conditions (5.3.8), and the determination of the optimal service

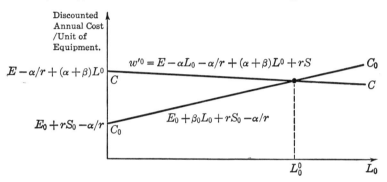

Fig. 5–3. Optimal replacement of incumbent equipment.

life of the incumbent equipment, given the optimal service life, L^0, of future replacements. The curve C_0C_0 represents the annual average cost of retaining the incumbent equipment one additional "year" as a function of the age of that equipment. CC represents the annual average cost if new equipment is installed at L_0 and optimal replacement policies followed thereafter.

The economic life of each member in the chain of future replacements, L^0, is determined by the implicit expression (5.3.9). A simple expression for w'^0 can be obtained by substituting for e^{-rL_0} from (5.3.9) into (5.3.7) giving

$$w'^0 = w|_{L=L^0} = E - \alpha L_0^0 - \frac{\alpha}{r} + (\alpha + \beta)L^0 + rS.^{19} \quad (5.3.11)$$

---

[19] Note that if incumbent and replacement equipments differ only by the effect of the linear obsolescence rate, then $E = E_0$, $\beta = \beta_0$, and $S = S_0$, and

From (5.3.9) it is seen that there exists no explicit solution for L^0. However, if rL^0 is small, we can approximate e^{-rL_0} with the first three terms of its Taylor series expansion,[20] or

$$e^{-rL^0} \cong 1 - rL^0 + (rL^0)^2/2. \qquad (5.3.12)$$

Now, substituting from (5.3.12) into (5.3.9), the optimal life of each unit of equipment in the infinite sequence of future replacements is

$$L^0 \cong \left(\frac{2(W - S)}{\alpha + \beta}\right)^{\frac{1}{2}}, \qquad (5.3.13)$$

and, using this approximation, w'^0 can be written

$$w'^0 \cong E - \alpha L_0{}^0 - \alpha/r + [2(W - S)(\alpha + \beta)]^{\frac{1}{2}} + rS. \quad (5.3.14)$$

The square root formula (5.3.13) is identical with that of Terborgh,[21] as will be demonstrated in the next section. Terborgh calls the quantity w'^0, the "adverse minimum" of the "challenger" machines. In Terborgh's analysis $(\alpha + \beta)$ is called the "inferiority gradient," or the rate at which the presently available "challenger" (the prospective replacement for any incumbent equipment) becomes inferior rela-

---

substituting (5.3.11) into (5.3.8) gives $L_0{}^0 = L^0$. The economic life of the incumbent equipment is equal to that of future replacement equipment if they exhibit the same obsolescence, deterioration, and salvage characteristics.

[20] If we write e^{-rL^0} as the first three terms of its Taylor series plus remainder, R_2, we get

$$e^{-rL^0} = 1 - rL^0 + \frac{(rL^0)^2}{2} - \frac{(rL^0)^3}{3!} e^{-\xi rL^0}, \quad 0 \le \xi \le 1.$$

The error in dropping terms beyond the third is

$$R_2 = \frac{(rL^0)^3}{3!} e^{-\xi rL^0} \le \frac{(rL^0)^3}{3!}.$$

Hence, the error in approximating e^{-rL^0} with the quadratic $1 - rL^0 + (rL^0)^2/2$ cannot exceed $(rL^0)^3/6$. For example, if $r = 0.06$ and $L^0 = 10$, then $R_2 \le 0.036$. The shorter the economic life of future replacement machines, and the lower the rate of discount, the smaller will be the error, R_2. A small value of R_2 does not, however, imply that the error in the solution L^0 will be correspondingly small.

[21] Terborgh, p. 254.

tive to the performance of future new machines during their first year of operation. In our analysis the so-called inferiority gradient is separated into two components — that due to technological change, α, and that due to deterioration, β. Remember, however, that the parameter α in our analysis reflects only those technological changes that influence operating cost per unit of equipment. This is in keeping with our strict distinction between cost effects and demand effects. Terborgh includes all improvements in new equipment in arriving at his computation for the inferiority gradient, but insofar as such improvements affect product demand as opposed to cost, one cannot ignore an explicit analysis of demand.

4. An Exposition of Terborgh's Replacement Formulas

Terborgh's prescription for replacement is essentially that developed in the last section. According to Terborgh we allow the current "challenger" to displace the incumbent "defender" the moment the discounted annual cost [22] of keeping the incumbent equipment rises above the discounted annual cost ("adverse minimum") of all future replacement machines, where the latter are assumed to be replaced optimally. As we have stated previously, this condition had already been derived by Preinreich and the Lutzes. Terborgh's special contribution to replacement theory has been (1) the extension of this marginal replacement condition to the important case in which equipment is subject to obsolescence, and (2) the derivation of simple formulas for the computation of the economic life of future "challengers," and their corresponding discounted annual cost, based upon simple intuitive time averages of the various components of equipment cost. Our exposition will employ Terborgh's analysis within the context and notation of our previous formulation of the general problem.[23] It will be shown that Terborgh's analysis

---

[22] Terborgh discounts capital cost plus "operating inferiority," where the latter includes revenue as well as cost considerations. We will continue to formulate our analysis in terms of cost.

[23] See Terborgh, chaps. vi and vii, especially pp. 92–100.

is essentially equivalent to the approximate expressions (5.3.13) and (5.3.14), which were derived using linear operating expense functions and constant salvage values.

Consider a unit of equipment with service life extending over a period of length L. Suppose it is known that the operating cost rate, in dollars per year, for this equipment rises with age, t, according to the linear function $E + \beta t$. Then the *average* annual operating expense of this equipment over a life of L years is $E + \beta L/2$ as shown in Fig. 5–4.

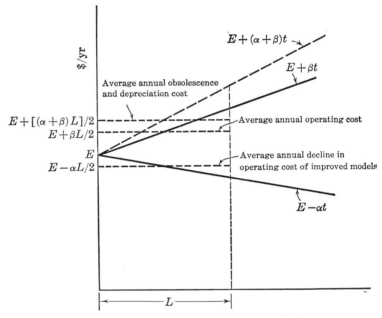

Fig. 5–4. Some average annual cost approximations.

There are three other costs associated with the maintenance of a unit of equipment in production. One is the asset's first or capital cost, and we suppose this to be allocated to current account by the favored method of straight line depreciation. Since the equipment is assumed to have some salvage value the net capital cost to be allocated is $W - S$. The net investment cost of equipment on current account is therefore

$(W - S)/L$. Another cost is the interest on this capital investment which can be approximated by $i(W - S)$. The third cost is the opportunity cost of *not* replacing each year with the best newly produced equipment, or, alternatively, it is the cost savings foregone by continuing the present equipment in service *after* better equipment has been made available. If the initial operating cost rate of new equipment available at time t is $E - \alpha t$, where α represents a measure of the rate of equipment obsolescence, then the average annual obsolescence charge on the incumbent equipment is $\alpha L/2$. This is the average annual opportunity cost of holding the incumbent equipment for L years. Hence, the total of operating and obsolescence cost is $E + [(\alpha + \beta)/2]L$ per year for a life of L years, and represents, in Terborgh's language, the annual rate at which the incumbent equipment becomes inferior to the latest "challengers." [24]

Taking account of these four elements of cost — operating, obsolence, interest, and capital cost — the average annual equipment cost is $E + [(\alpha + \beta)/2]L + [(W - S)/L] + i(W - S)$. When we consider replacements beyond the incumbent equipment this cost function is simply repeated over the life of each asset, except that it is shifted downward by the amount αL with each new replacement. Hence, in order to deduce the final form of the equipment cost function we must subtract a term to account for this decline in cost due to technological improvements beyond the life of the first equipment in the chain. The annual cost rate falls at the rate α. The present value of an infinite cost stream growing steadily at the rate α is α/i^2 where i is the annual compound rate of interest, and the constant annual cost stream with the same present value is $i(\alpha/i^2) = \alpha/i$. If, therefore, we subtract α/i from the other cost elements we obtain the final form for the average annual equipment cost rate, namely,

$$w' = E + \left(\frac{\alpha + \beta}{2}\right)L + \frac{W - S}{L} + i(W - S) - \frac{\alpha}{i}. \quad (5.4.1)$$

[24] Note that α and β have the dimensions $\dfrac{[\text{Dollars}]}{[\text{Equipment Units}][\text{Time}]^2}$. They are rates of change of rates of change, that is, accelerations.

If the economic life L is chosen so as to minimize w', the unit annual equipment cost, then it is necessary that $\partial w'/\partial L = 0$, or

$$L^0 = \left(\frac{2(W - S)}{\alpha + \beta}\right)^{\frac{1}{2}}. \tag{5.4.2}$$

This expression is identical with that of (5.3.13). Substituting from (5.4.2) into (5.4.1) to obtain the annual equipment cost rate under an optimal replacement program, gives

$$w'^0 = E + [2(W - S)(\alpha + \beta)]^{\frac{1}{2}} - \alpha/i + i(W - S), \tag{5.4.3}$$

which differs only by a constant from (5.3.14).

These results demonstrate that our mathematical formulation of a "crude intuitive approach" based on simple averages gives the same economic life and approximately the minimum annual equipment cost ("adverse minimum") formulas as were obtained in (5.3.13) and (5.3.14) by the modified Preinreich-Lutz continuous discounting approach using a linear operating cost function. Hence, the simple annual average cost approach of Terborgh is equivalent in its essentials to the continuous discounting analysis. In much of our later investigation, the expression (5.4.3) will be employed to estimate the "flow price" of a capital good whose replacement is subject to economic considerations.

5. Optimal Policy; Dynamic Programming

Richard Bellman has applied the technique of dynamic programming to the formulation of replacement policy.[25] This technique, besides illuminating the structure of replacement decision problems, provides a convenient computational routine applicable to tabular as well as analytical representations of the operating expense function.

Bellman employs a discrete discounted net revenue maximization model, which in our exposition will be converted to a cost minimization model in keeping with our previous analysis. We begin by defining the function $f(t)$ as the present

---

[25] Bellman, "Equipment Replacement Policy."

discounted value of all capital and operating costs associated with a machine of age t years employing an optimal replacement policy, where $t = 0, 1, 2, 3, \cdots$. At any time t there are two alternatives facing the equipment manager. He may keep the machine for another time period, that is, until $t + 1$, or he may purchase a new machine. If he keeps the incumbent machine, then $f(t)$ satisfies the relation

$$f_K(t) = \phi(t) + (1 + i)^{-1}f(t + 1), \qquad (5.5.1)$$

where $\phi(t)$ is the operating cost of the equipment at time t. The cost associated with this action is the operating cost of the machine for an additional period plus the discounted future cost employing an optimal policy. If a new machine is purchased at t, then

$$f_P(t) = W - S + \phi(0) + (1 + i)^{-1}f(1). \qquad (5.5.2)$$

The cost associated with this alternative is the net capital cost of purchasing a new unit of equipment, plus the first year operating expenses of the unit, plus the discounted future cost employing an optimal policy.

A functional equation for $f(t)$ can now be defined as follows:

$$f(t) = \min \begin{cases} f_K(t) = \phi(t) + (1 + i)^{-1}f(t + 1) \\ f_P(t) = W - S + \phi(0) + (1 + i)^{-1}f(1). \end{cases} \qquad (5.5.3)$$

Bellman argues (in the case of no technological change) that an optimal policy requires a new machine to be kept until it is L years old and then a new machine purchased. For a sequence of L years $f(t)$ will appear as follows:

$$\begin{aligned} f(0) &= \phi(0) + (1 + i)^{-1}f(1) \\ f(1) &= \phi(1) + (1 + i)^{-1}f(2) \\ &\;\cdot \\ &\;\cdot \\ &\;\cdot \\ f(L - 1) &= \phi(L - 1) + (1 + i)^{-1}f(L) \\ f(L) &= W - S + \phi(0) + (1 + i)^{-1}f(1). \end{aligned} \qquad (5.5.4)$$

Solving for $f(0)$ by recurrent substitution yields

$$f(0) = \frac{\sum_{t=0}^{L-1} (1 + i)^{-t}\phi(t) + (1 + i)^{-L}(W - S)}{1 - (1 + i)^{-L}}. \quad (5.5.5)$$

If an optimal replacement policy requires $f(0)$ to be a minimum, we see that optimal equipment life is obtained by finding the value of L that minimizes the right side of (5.5.5). But what is the right side of (5.5.5)? It is simply the present value of the cost stream associated with an infinite chain of future replacements. If we convert $f(0)$ to a cost on current account by multiplying both sides by i, the right side of (5.5.5) becomes

$$\frac{i\sum_{t=0}^{L-1} (1 + i)^{-t}\phi(t) + i(1 + i)^{-L}(W - S)}{1 - (1 + i)^{-L}},$$

which is the discrete annual compounding form for equation (5.3.4) assuming no technological change, constant salvage values, and $L_0 = L$ (the incumbent equipment is a new machine). Hence, a dynamic programming formulation of the replacement problem, in which an optimal policy is defined implicitly by (5.5.3), permits one to deduce the variational criteria of Preinreich, Lutz, and Alchian. In this sense the dynamic programming and variational approaches are equivalent.[26]

6. Replacement Policy and Production Coefficients

In the argument of sections 2 and 3, it was held that replacement policy should be concerned primarily with minimizing the flow cost of capital to the productive process. The phenomenon of obsolescence took place because of technological improvements that reduced operating expenses per unit of equipment. This view represents a polar case and

---

[26] For an application of the dynamic programming approach to a numerical example involving technological improvement, see Stuart E. Dreyfus, "A Generalized Equipment Replacement Study," P-1039, RAND Corporation, March 15, 1957.

is of great value in clarifying the connection between replacement policy and the classical theory of cost and production. However, the replacement of old equipment with new may be motivated by cost considerations other than those affecting operating expenses, and our analysis is capable of extension in this direction.

In classical production theory technological change takes the form of shifts in the production function. An examination of many production processes will reveal that such changes in input-output technique are made possible by the installation of new equipment. In such processes the "replacement" decision is the crucial mechanism whereby new input-output techniques are introduced. We shall now proceed to introduce these considerations into formal analysis, retaining, for the present, our assumption of fixed production coefficients.

In the case of a production process with one current input and one capital input (in addition, that is, to the age-variable maintenance and servicing inputs which constitute the "logistic" support given the capital input), it is assumed that equipment improvements take the form of progressively lowering both the current input consumption per unit of output and the capital input requirements per unit of output. Specifically, we assume that the flow and the capital coefficients are each decreasing functions of time measured in terms of the chronological chain of machine replacements. For the new equipment models becoming available each year these coefficients are steadily declining, but it is only through "replacement" that the benefits of this decline can be achieved by the firm. Suppose machine units purchased now exhibit a flow coefficient $a(0)$. If the units are retained L_1 years and replaced with new units, then the flow coefficient becomes $a(L_1) < a(0)$. If the second link in the machine chain is retained L_2 years, then the flow coefficient over the life of the third replacement unit will be $a(L_1 + L_2) < a(L_2) < a(0)$, and so forth. It is assumed that the capital coefficient declines in a similar manner. Again, if we assume an equidistant replacement policy, then the flow and capital coefficients for our simple process can be written

$$\begin{cases} a = a(kL) \\ b = b(kL) \end{cases} \quad k = 0,\ 1,\ 2,\ \cdots \tag{5.6.1}$$

Under this hypothesis we can no longer identify replacement policy with minimizing the flow cost per unit of equipment, that is, w_2 in equation (5.3.2). Replacement now affects the entire cost structure and an optimal policy clearly requires us to minimize total cost per unit of output with respect to equipment life. If the operating expense function per unit of equipment is $\phi(kL,t)$, while the purchase price of equipment (input number 2), W_2, and its salvage value S_2 are assumed constant *per unit of output*, then equation (5.3.2), representing total current account cost, must be written

$$C = r \sum_{k=0}^{\infty} e^{-rkL} \Big[\int_0^L \big[w_1 a(kL) + b(kL)\phi(kL,t) \big] e^{-rt}\, dt \\ + W_2 - S_2 e^{-rL} \Big] y. \tag{5.6.2}$$

As an illustration of the determination of an optimal replacement policy that minimizes (5.6.2), consider the case in which equipment operating expenses are not affected by technological change or deterioration, that is, where $\phi(kL,t) = E$, a constant over the life of the asset. Also, in keeping with Terborghian linearity, assume that $a(kL) = A - mkL$ and $b(kL) = B - nkL$. Current input requirements per unit of output are thus assumed to decline at the constant linear rate m, while capital stock input requirements per unit of output decline at the constant linear rate n. These declines benefit the firm only through the equipment replacement decision. Hence, (5.6.2) can be written [27]

$$C = r \sum_{k=0}^{\infty} e^{-rkL} \Big\{ \int_0^L \big[w_1(A - mkL) + E(B - nkL) \big] e^{-rt}\, dt \\ + W_2 - S_2 e^{-rL} \Big\} y \tag{5.6.3}$$

$$= \Big\{ (w_1 A + EB) - \frac{(w_1 m + En)L e^{-rL} - rW_2 + rS_2 e^{-rL}}{1 - e^{-rL}} \Big\} y.$$

[27] It is assumed that the expression converges rapidly compared with the rate at which the linear approximations to $a(kL)$ and $b(kL)$ approach zero.

In this equation the obsolescence rate, which is analogous to α in equation (5.3.7), is $w_1m + En$. If the firm purchased new equipment every year, the result would be an annual decline in the cost of input number 1 per unit of output equal to w_1m dollars. Similarly, since E is the operating cost per unit of equipment and n is the annual decline in equipment stock requirements per unit of output, it follows that En would be the annual decline in equipment-operating cost per unit of output under an annual replacement policy. Minimizing (5.6.3) by setting $\partial C/\partial L = 0$ gives

$$(w_1m + En)(1 - rL^0 - e^{-rL^0}) + r^2(W_2 - S_2) = 0. \quad (5.6.4)$$

The similarity between (5.6.4) and (5.3.9) and between (5.6.3) and (5.3.7) will be evident upon comparison. Note, however, that (5.3.7) minimizes the flow cost per unit of equipment while (5.6.4) minimizes the total cost of the productive process per unit of output. If e^{-rL^0} is approximated by the first three terms of its Taylor expansion, the result is the familiar square-root formula

$$L^0 = \left(\frac{2(W_2 - S_2)}{w_1m + En}\right)^{\frac{1}{2}}. \quad (5.6.5)$$

Having investigated the manner in which replacement policy under a cost minimization criterion can influence either the current account cost of a unit of equipment or, more generally, the cost of production per unit of product, we turn next to a discussion of the sense in which replacement policy is inseparable from output (price) policy under a profit maximization criterion.

7. Replacement Policy, Output Policy, and Profit Maximization

Suppose the firm desires to maximize the discounted current account equivalent of all future receipts minus all future outlays, that is, current account profit. It will be assumed that the firm establishes its output, and therefore price policy, at the beginning of the life of each equipment replacement, and maintains that policy over the life of that equipment. At each replacement date, the firm reviews its output policy and equipment stock requirements in the light of the improved equipment technology that will be purchased. Hence, the firm chooses replacement policy, L, and, at the beginning of each equipment operating period, the level of output y_k, $k = 0, 1, 2, \cdots$, that is to say, y_1 is chosen and maintained for the time period from $t = 0$ to $t = L$, y_2 is set for the period $t = L$ to $t = 2L$, and so forth.

If the revenue stream over the life of the kth equipment investment is $R^*(y_k)$, then the capital value of that stream at the time the kth equipment link is purchased is $R(y_k,L)$ $= [(1 - e^{-rL})/r]R^*(y_k)$. For an infinite machine chain the current account revenue for the enterprise is thus

$$r \sum_{k=0}^{\infty} e^{-rkL} R(y_k,L) = r \sum_{k=0}^{\infty} e^{-rkL} \left(\frac{1 - e^{-rL}}{r} \right) R^*(y_k).$$

The expression for total current account cost is assumed to be the same as that given in (5.6.2) except that output is now allowed to vary from one equipment life period to the next. If we let $c(kL,L)$ stand for the expression in the brackets in (5.6.2), that is, for the capital value, at the time the kth equipment stock is purchased, of all the investment and operating costs associated with that equipment, then total current account cost can be written

$$r \sum_{k=0}^{\infty} e^{-rkL} c(kL,L) y_k.$$

Current account profit is then

$$\pi = r \sum_{k=0}^{\infty} e^{-rkL} \{R(y_k,L) - c(kL,L)y_k\}. \qquad (5.7.1)$$

Maximizing π by setting $\partial \pi / \partial y_k = 0$, $k = 0, 1, 2, \cdots$, and $\partial \pi / \partial L = 0$, gives

$$\frac{\partial R(y_k^0, L^0)}{\partial y_k} = c(kL^0, L^0), \quad k = 0, 1, 2, \cdots, \qquad (5.7.2)$$

and

$$\sum_{k=0}^{\infty} e^{-rkL^0} \left\{ \frac{\partial R(y_k^0, L^0)}{\partial L} - \frac{\partial c(kL^0, L^0)}{\partial L} y_k^0 \right\}$$

$$= r \sum_{k=0}^{\infty} k e^{-rkL^0} \{ R(y_k^0, L^0) - c(kL^0, L^0) y_k^0 \}.$$

(5.7.3)

Equation (5.7.2) states that output in each period is adjusted until the marginal discounted value of the expected revenue over the life of the new equipment is equal to the marginal (in this case equal to average unit) discounted value of all costs over the period.[28] Equation (5.7.3) states that equipment service life is adjusted until the discounted value of the marginal profitability of an additional "year" of life equals the change in the discounted value of the future total profit stream resulting from lengthening all replacement intervals an additional "year." Equations (5.7.2) and (5.7.3) simultaneously determine all the y_k^0 and L^0. In this illustration an optimal replacement policy cannot be determined independently of output and therefore price policy. Hence, if pricing and replacement decisions are to be made simultaneously, the problem of cost minimization cannot logically be separated from that of profit maximization, as in the conventional static theory of the firm.

If the marginal revenue function $\mathrm{MR}(y_k, L) \equiv \partial R(y_k, L) / \partial y_k$ is a (monotonically) decreasing function of y_k, and the unit cost function is similarly a decreasing function of kL (equipment improvements lower unit cost in each replacement period), then $c_0 > c_1 > c_2 > c_3 \cdots$ as shown in Fig. 5–5. Unit cost is lowered in each successive planning period by an amount which depends upon replacement policy, L. Declining unit (and marginal) cost requires successive upward adjustments in output. Hence output and replacement policy are linked together through the mechanism of technological change. If equipment were not subject to technological improvement, then we would have $c(0, L) = c(L, L)$

---

[28] Note that we are talking about long-run marginal cost, and this condition describes a long-run planning solution.

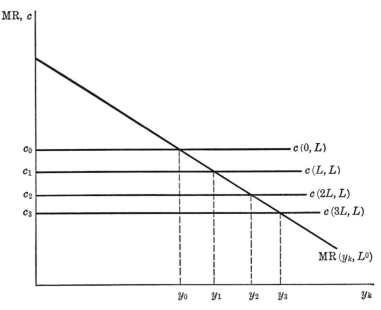

Fig. 5–5. *Output responses to technological improvements.*

$= c(2L,L) = \cdots$, and hence, with a fixed MR function, $y^0 = y_0{}^0 = y_1{}^0 = y_2{}^0 = \cdots$, that is, output would be the same in each period. Indeed, the revenue function in (5.7.1) could now be written

$$R(y_k,L) = \left(\frac{1 - e^{-rL}}{r}\right) R(y),$$

and the cost function simplified to $c(kL,L) = c(L)$, since cost is no longer influenced by technological change. Equation (5.7.1) now takes the form

$$\pi = r \sum_{k=0}^{\infty} e^{-rkL} \left\{ \left(\frac{1 - e^{-rL}}{r}\right) R(y) - c(L)y \right\}, \quad (5.7.1')$$

and (5.7.2) and (5.7.3) become

$$\frac{\partial R(y)}{\partial y} = \left(\frac{r}{1 - e^{-rL^0}}\right) c(L^0), \quad (5.7.2')$$

$$\frac{\partial c(L^0)}{\partial L} = \frac{re^{-rL^0}}{1 - e^{-rL^0}} \, c(L^0). \qquad (5.7.3')$$

From $(5.7.2')$ it is seen that output policy, y^0, is still affected by replacement policy, L^0, since the latter affects marginal cost. However, from $(5.7.3')$ we see that replacement policy becomes strictly a matter of cost minimization. In the absence of technological change it is clear that a cost minimizing replacement policy is fully equivalent to a profit maximizing replacement policy. However, an optimal output policy cannot be determined until equipment replacement policy is specified, since the latter affects cost.

In summary the situation is as follows: Cost minimization and profit maximization are separable without qualification in regard to price-output and replacement decisions if there is no technological change. If there is technological change *and* the price-output and equipment reinvestment decisions are timed concurrently, then the two criteria are not separable. The crucial assumption is concerned with the independence of price-output and replacement decisions. Thus, if price-output policies are dominated by considerations of demand and competition (as, for example, in oligopolistic industries) rather than cost, so that price-output decisions are timed independently of the replacement points, then cost minimization can be separated from profit maximization as in conventional theory.

Chapter VI

The Theory of Production and Investment: Capital Goods with Variable Life

1. The Theory of the Firm Under Economic Replacement Policies

In rounding out the fundamentals of our stock-flow theory of the capital-using enterprise, one of the remaining tasks is to extend some of the analysis of Chapters III–V to include economic replacement (or discard) policy. Our task, in effect, is to integrate the stock-flow theory of production with the theory of economic replacement, and to apply the resulting analytical framework to the theory of markets.

CHOICE OF TECHNIQUE

We shall continue to assume that there is one current input and one capital equipment input to the productive process, and that a production function constraint of the form

$y = f(x_1, X_2)$ applies. However, it is now assumed that the equipment input requires operating (including maintenance and servicing) outlays, and is subject to deterioration and obsolescence. Operating costs rise with age because of deterioration through use, while obsolescence occurs because the incumbent equipment must compete with new equipment exhibiting progressively lower and lower operating cost performance per unit of equipment. All these categories of equipment cost must be reflected in our method of "costing" equipment to the productive process. Following the replacement analysis of Chapter V, we assume, as a first approximation, an equipment operating expense function (in dollars per unit time per unit of equipment) of the form $\phi(kL, t)$ for the kth in an infinite chain of replacements. The variable t is the age of the kth machine in the replacement chain, and is measured from the point in calendar time at which the asset was purchased new, that is, at $(k - 1)L$.

Using Terborgh's linear approximation to $\phi(kL, t)$ allows us to write a simple expression for the current account cost of maintaining a unit of equipment in production. For the moment we assume that the operating cost of equipment is independent of y, x_1, and X_2. With each unit of the stock of equipment, X_2, we associate a current cost — the "flow price" of the equipment — given by

$$w_2 = E + \tfrac{1}{2}(\alpha + \beta)L + W_2/L + rW_2, \qquad (6.1.1)$$

where E is the initial operating cost rate for a new unit of equipment, α is the obsolescence rate, β is the deterioration rate, W_2 is the unit investment cost of equipment, and r is the interest rate, as discussed in Chapter V. Think of (6.1.1) as the cost of maintaining the presence of a unit of equipment in production. That cost includes investment, W_2/L interest, rW_2, and maintenance, servicing and obsolescence, $E + \tfrac{1}{2}(\alpha + \beta)L$, all of which are required as "logistic" support for a unit of equipment. Unless interest payments on the capital investment are met, the firm's creditors foreclose and eliminate the "presence" of equipment. Similarly without the expenditure of maintenance and servicing resources, equipment breaks down and is no longer productively available. Finally, unless the presence of the incumbent equipment is allowed to be continuously challenged by the succession of improved units, via the device of burdening the incumbent equipment with obsolescence charges, its physical presence will not provide economy in production.

The expression for total cost on current account for the process can now be written

$$C = w_1 x_1 + [E + \tfrac{1}{2}(\alpha + \beta)L + W_2/L + rW_2]X_2, \quad (6.1.2)$$

and the problem of choice of technique can be stated as one of minimizing (6.1.2) subject to $y = f(x_1, X_2)$, that is, minimizing

$$\phi = w_1 x_1 + [E + \tfrac{1}{2}(\alpha + \beta)L + W_2/L + rW_2]X_2 \atop - \lambda[f(x_1, X_2) - y], \quad (6.1.3)$$

with respect to x_1, X_2, and L. Setting $\partial\phi/\partial x_1$, $\partial\phi/\partial X_2$, and $\partial\phi/\partial L$ each equal to zero gives the three necessary conditions

$$w_1 - \lambda f_1 = 0, \quad (6.1.4)$$

$$E + \tfrac{1}{2}(\alpha + \beta)L^0 + W_2/L^0 + rW_2 - \lambda f_2 = 0, \quad (6.1.5)$$

$$L^0 = [2W_2/(\alpha + \beta)]^{\frac{1}{2}}, \quad (6.1.6)$$

which together determine L^0, x_1^0, and X_2^0. Note that, as a consequence of our assumptions, the optimal replacement policy L^0 is determined independently of the optimal choice of technique, but technique (x_1^0, X_2^0) is dependent upon replacement policy, since the latter affects the flow cost of the durable input to the process.

Substituting from (6.1.6) into (6.1.5) and combining with (6.1.4) gives the marginal productivity conditions (assuming an optimal replacement policy),

$$\frac{w_1}{f_1} = \frac{E + [2W_2(\alpha + \beta)]^{\frac{1}{2}} + rW_2}{f_2} = \lambda, \quad (6.1.7)$$

where λ is marginal current cost. The input equilibrium will be as shown in the familiar isoproduct-isocost diagram of

Fig. 3–1 except that the slope of an isocost contour is now

$$\frac{w_1}{E + [2W_2(\alpha + \beta)]^{\frac{1}{2}} + rW_2}.$$

In this case *ceteris paribus* increases in either the obsolescence rate (α) or the deterioration rate (β), of equipment, as well as increases in unit investment cost (W_2) or the discount rate (r), will cause a substitution of the current input for the capital input, that is, the firm will elect to operate more intensively on current account and less intensively on capital account.

The assumption that the operating cost function ϕ is independent of the variables appearing in the production function is very unlikely to prove realistic even as a first approximation in actual production processes. Equipment operating cost is almost certain to be positively related to the rate of output, or, most directly, to one or more of the current inputs, in particular the current input that provides the source of energy for the equipment. It is a fundamental physical principle that the rate at which mechanical work is performed by a unit of machinery (for example, a compressor for pumping natural gas), and therefore the intensity of utilization of the equipment, is directly dependent upon the energy supplied to the process. Consequently, a machine's total exposure to mechanical work as of a given time is measured by the machine's cumulative consumption of energy (fuel) up to that time. The operating cost rate (including maintenance and servicing outlays) would tend therefore to be an increasing function of cumulative energy (fuel) consumption or, more generally, an increasing function of both age and the average rate of energy consumption. By this argument the operating cost function would be written $\phi(x_1, kL, t)$ and the expression for w_2 would be

$$w_2 = r \sum_{k=0}^{\infty} e^{-rkL} \left\{ \int_0^L \phi(x_1, kL, t) e^{-rt} \, dt + W_2 \right\}, \qquad (6.1.8)$$

assuming zero salvage value.

A linear approximation to (6.1.8) can be obtained if we assume that the operating cost rate rises in proportion to the cumulative consumption of the current input. That is, if β' is the amount by which the operating cost rate, for the entire stock of equipment, rises per unit increase in the consumption of the current input, then $\beta'x_1$ is the annual increase in the operating cost rate, while $\beta'x_1L$ is the total rise in such costs after L years of equipment service. Therefore, the average annual operating cost rate would be $\beta'x_1L/2$. This term now replaces $\beta LX_2/2$ in equation (6.1.2); thus, the average annual rate of equipment deterioration is proportional to the cumulative consumption of the current input (a measure of the total exposure of the stock of equipment to wear) instead of the total stock of equipment. We will continue to assume, however, that the non-age-variable component of operating cost is proportional to the stock of equipment so that the initial equipment in the chain shows an operating cost function of the form $EX_2 + \frac{1}{2}(\beta'x_1L)$ (see equation [6.1.2]).

In place of equation (6.1.2), the expression for total current account cost is

$$C = (w_1 + \beta'L/2)x_1 + [E + \alpha L/2 + W_2/L + rW_2]X_2. \quad (6.1.9)$$

This expression associates two unit costs with the consumption of input No. 1 — its purchase price, w_1, and the rise in equipment operating costs due to deterioration resulting from the consumption of this input in the presence of durable equipment. The "cost" of the current input to the process is now $(w_1 + \beta'L/2)x_1$.

Minimizing (6.1.9) subject to the constraint $y = f(x_1, X_2)$, we form the Lagrange expression

$$\psi = (w_1 + \beta'L/2)x_1 + [E + \alpha L/2 + W_2/L + rW_2]X_2 \\ - \lambda[f(x_1, X_2) - y]. \quad (6.1.10)$$

Setting $\partial\psi/\partial x_1$, $\partial\psi/\partial X_2$, and $\partial\psi/\partial L$ equal to zero gives

$$w_1 + \beta'L/2 - \lambda f_1 = 0, \quad (6.1.11)$$

$$E + \alpha L/2 + W_2/L + rW_2 - \lambda f_2 = 0. \quad (6.1.12)$$

$$L = \left(\frac{2W_2X_2}{\alpha X_2 + \beta' x_1} \right)^{\frac{1}{2}}. \qquad (6.1.13)$$

These conditions illustrate the organic interdependence between choice of technique (including investment) and replacement policy.[1] Optimal input policy and optimal replacement policy are determined simultaneously in the firm's long-run production plan. By substitution from (6.1.13) we obtain the marginal productivity conditions

$$\frac{w_1 + \beta' \left(\frac{W_2 X_2}{2(\alpha X_2 + \beta' x_1)} \right)^{\frac{1}{2}}}{f_1} = \frac{E + \left(\frac{(2\alpha X_2 + \beta' x_1)^2 W_2}{2(\alpha X_2 + \beta' x_1) X_2} \right)^{\frac{1}{2}} + rW_2}{f_2} = \lambda, \qquad (6.1.14)$$

which apply whenever the equilibrium occurs at an interior point. The firm's minimum cost input equilibrium for such

---

[1] Entirely analogous results are obtained from an analysis of the interdependence between choice of technique and optimal inventory policy. To illustrate, consider the simplest kind of static inventory model. Suppose $y = f(x_1, x_2)$, where x_1 is a storable current input and x_2 is a nonstorable current input. Assume there is a procurement cost, C_P, associated with each order for the storable input. If a stock of X_1 units of this input is ordered every θ years, then annual procurement cost is C_P/θ, where $x_1\theta = X_1$. If the storage cost is C_S per unit stored per unit time, average annual inventory cost is $C_S X_1/2 = C_S x_1 \theta/2$. Hence, if w_1 is the purchase price of input number 1 and w_2 is the price of input number 2, total annual cost is

$$C = w_1 x_1 + \frac{C_S x_1 \theta}{2} + \frac{C_P}{\theta} + w_2 x_2.$$

Minimizing cost subject to the production constraint with respect to the decision variables x_1, x_2, and θ gives

$$w_1 + \frac{C_S \theta}{2} - \lambda f_1 = 0$$
$$w_2 - \lambda f_2 = 0$$
$$\theta = (2C_P/C_S x_1)^{\frac{1}{2}}$$

The similarity between these conditions and (6.1.11)–(6.1.13) and the analogy between replacement theory and inventory reinvestment will be evident. In the one model, reinvestment in equipment occurs every L years, while in the other reinvestment in inventory occurs every θ years. In each case the investment "period" is given by a square root formula.

an interior solution is shown graphically in Fig. 6–1. The isocost lines are defined by equations (6.1.9) and (6.1.13), that is, cost minimization over replacement policy is presupposed. As indicated in the diagram, the isocost curves

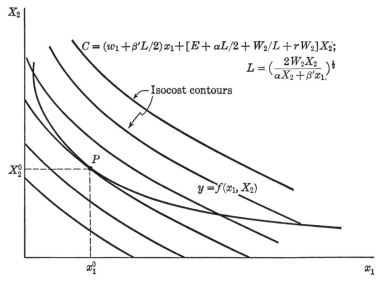

Fig. 6–1. Neoclassical choice of technique under optimal replacement policy.

are convex to the origin [2] as are the neoclassical isoproduct contours.

THE RESPONSE TO CHANGES IN OUTPUT REQUIREMENTS

An interesting application of this analysis is to explore the firm's response to a discontinuous once-for-all change in the output requirement parameter. In so doing it is possible to develop an explicit statement, composed of a set of planning rules, of the firm's short- and long-run response to such a

---

[2] The reader may verify the following derivatives:
$C_1 = w_1 + \frac{1}{2}\beta'L > 0$, $C_2 = E + \frac{1}{2}\alpha L + W_2/L + rW_2 > 0$, $C_{11} = \frac{1}{2}\beta'L_1 < 0$, $C_{22} = \frac{1}{2}\beta'L_2/L_1 < 0$, $C_{12} = \frac{1}{2}\beta'L_2 > 0$, where $C_1 = \partial C/\partial x_1$, $C_2 = \partial C/\partial X_2$, $L_1 = \partial L/\partial x_1$, $L_2 = \partial L/\partial X_2$, $C_{12} = \partial^2 C/\partial x_1\partial X_2$, etc., and therefore $\partial X_2/\partial x_1 < 0$, $\partial^2 X_2/\partial x_1{}^2 > 0$, unambiguously.

change in output requirements. The result is an explicit formulation of these ingenious Marshallian concepts, which continue to represent the heart of partial equilibrium theory. Indeed, under our assumption of an economic as opposed to a fixed replacement policy, it is possible to define the length of the "short-run" adjustment period for the individual firm (the optimal life of the incumbent equipment). "How long is the short-run?" becomes an economic rather than a technical (as under fixed replacement policies) question.

Consider a firm in initial long-run equilibrium, as defined by equations (6.1.11)–(6.1.13), with an investment in $X_2{}^0$ units of the durable input which is being replaced every L^0 years, and consuming $x_1{}^0$ units per year of the current input. Suppose the incumbent equipment has been in use for U years and that suddenly there is an unexpected two-stage increase in output requirements. At the first stage output requirements rise temporarily from y to y_s for a period equal to the life of the incumbent equipment at time U. This is followed by a permanent further increase in requirements from y_s to y'. We shall assume that the firm's optimal response is to meet this new set of output requirements by operating the incumbent equipment more intensively for a (short-run) period of L_0 years, at the end of which time the firm reinvests in an optimal long-run stock of equipment, which in turn is to be replaced optimally thereafter. More specifically, the firm is assumed to minimize current account cost through its choice of (1) the short-run rate of consumption of the current input, x_s, the stock of capital being held fixed at $X_2{}^0$, (2) the remaining economic life of the incumbent equipment, L_0, (3) the (long-run) stock of equipment, X_2', to install at the end of this short-run operating period, (4) the (long-run) rate of consumption of the current input, x_1', and (5) the economic life of the new equipment and all replacements thereafter, L'. Under these assumptions the operating cost function for the incumbent equipment, using our linear approximation, is $EX_2{}^0 + \beta' x_s U + \beta' x_s t$, which states that the equipment has an initial non-age-variable operating cost of $EX_2{}^0$, and total costs will have risen to $EX_2{}^0 + \beta' x_s U$ after U years of service. Hence, the expression for the total current account cost of the enterprise is

$$C^0 = w_1 x_s (1 - e^{-rL_0}) + r \int_0^{L_0} (EX_2{}^0 + \beta' x_s U + \beta' x_s t) e^{-rt}\, dt$$
$$+ e^{-rL_0} C'. \qquad (6.1.15)$$

The first term on the right is the discounted flow cost of the current input over the short-run period. The second term is the discounted current operating cost of the incumbent equipment over its remaining economic life, and C' is the current account total cost of operating the process in all future replacement periods beginning with the first replacement for the incumbent equipment. Using the linear approximation for C' (see equation [6.1.9]) gives

$$C' = \left(w_1 + \frac{\beta' L'}{2}\right) x_1' + \left(E - \alpha L_0 + \frac{\alpha L'}{2} + \frac{W_2}{L'} + rW_2\right) X_2'.$$
$$(6.1.16)$$

The firm's optimal short- and long-run response to the given change in output requirements is obtained by minimizing (6.1.15), with respect to x_s, L_0, x_1', X_2', and L', subject to the short- and long-run production constraints

$$\left.\begin{array}{l} y_s = f(x_s, X_2{}^0), \\ y' = f(x_1', X_2'). \end{array}\right\} \qquad (6.1.17)$$

The Lagrange expression to be minimized is

$$\psi = w_1 x_s (1 - e^{-rL_0}) + \left\{ (EX_2{}^0 + \beta' x_s U)(1 - e^{-rL_0}) \right.$$

$$+ \frac{\beta' x_s}{r} \left[1 - (1 + rL_0)e^{-rL_0}\right]\right\}$$

$$+ e^{-rL_0} \left\{ \left(w_1 + \frac{\beta' L'}{2}\right) x_1' \right.$$ $(6.1.18)$

$$+ \left(E - \alpha L_0 + \frac{\alpha L'}{2} + \frac{W_2}{L'} + rW_2\right) X_2'\right\}$$

$$-- \lambda_s [f(x_s, X_2{}^0) - y'] - \lambda'[f(x_1', X_2') - y'],$$

where λ_s and λ' are Lagrange multipliers (they are respectively marginal short- and long-run current cost). Setting each of the derivatives $\partial\psi/\partial x_s$, $\partial\psi/\partial L_0$, $\partial\psi/\partial x_1'$, $\partial\psi/\partial X_2'$, and $\partial\psi/\partial L'$ equal to zero gives the following necessary conditions for a local (interior) extreme value of C subject to the indicated constraints:

$$\frac{w_1 + \beta'U + \dfrac{\beta'}{r}\left[1 - \dfrac{rL_0 e^{-rL_0}}{1 - e^{-rL_0}}\right]}{f_1(x_s, X_2^0)} = \frac{\lambda_s}{1 - e^{-rL_0}} \quad (6.1.19)$$

$$w_1 x_s + EX_2^0 + \beta' x_s U + \beta' x_s L_0 - \alpha X_2'/r = C' \quad (6.1.20)$$

$$\frac{w_1 + \beta'L'/2}{f_1(x_1', X_2')} = \frac{E - \alpha L_0 + \alpha L'/2 + W_2/L' + rW_2}{f_2(x_1', X_2')} = \lambda' e^{rL_0}$$

$$(6.1.21)$$

$$L' = \left(\frac{2W_2 X_2'}{\alpha X_2' + \beta' x_1'}\right)^{\frac{1}{2}}. \quad (6.1.22)$$

Since we are considering only a two-input process, x_s is determined by the first constraint in (6.1.17), given the short-run level of output to be produced. The short-run marginal productivity condition (6.1.19) then determines short-run marginal cost, λ_s, given L_0. Equation (6.1.20) says that the incumbent equipment is continued in service until the total avoidable cost (out-of-pocket plus obsolescence) of keeping the equipment another year is equal to the total discounted current account cost of operating the process in long-run equilibrium. Equations (6.1.19), (6.1.20), and the second constraint in (6.1.17) apply essentially to the determination of the firm's short-run equilibrium response including the optimal length of the "short-run." Equation (6.1.21) states that at the end of the life of the incumbent equipment, the firm should reinvest in new equipment and adjust its consumption of the current input until the marginal current account cost of the durable input (the current account unit cost of the good divided by its marginal physical productivity) is equal to the marginal current account cost of the flow input (the unit cost divided by marginal physical productivity). Equation (6.1.22) gives the economic life of the optimal stock of new equipment to be installed, after L_0 years. Equations (6.1.21) and (6.1.22) constitute the firm's long-run production-investment planning rules, and together they define the firm's minimum cost schedule as a function of y_s and y', given the firm's initial long-run equilibrium stock of capital, X_2^0.

OUTPUT EQUILIBRIUM AND THE RESPONSE TO CHANGES IN DEMAND

So far, our concern has been entirely with cost minimization under a given output constraint. What happens to the decision rules (6.1.11)–(6.1.13) and (6.1.19)–(6.1.22) if we follow a profit maximization criterion? In determining the firm's initial long-run production-investment program, if $R(y)$ is the firm's current account total revenue and $MR(y)$ is current account marginal revenue, then we simply add

$$MR(y) = \lambda \qquad (6.1.23)$$

to the conditions (6.1.11)–(6.1.13) to obtain the planning rules for profit maximization. Each input is adjusted until its discounted marginal revenue productivity is equal to the marginal cost of that input. The condition (6.1.13) for determining economic life remains unaltered by this addition. On the assumption that price-output policy is to remain unchanged in the future, the separability of choice of technique (x_1^0, X_2^0, L^0) and choice of optimal firm output (y^0) is valid for the capital-using firm, just as in the neoclassical flow theory of cost and production.

Does a similar theorem hold for the response of the capital-using firm to changes in product demand? That is, can we minimize over choice of technique, thereby defining a minimum cost-output function which leads to the same optimal output solution $(MC = MR)$ as direct profit maximization? The answer is "no," if we are to view the firm's response as one in which there is first a "short-run" followed by a "long-run" adjustment in price-output policy. To show this, suppose we begin with a firm in initial long-run equilibrium, (x_1^0, X_2^0, L^0, y^0), as defined by (6.1.11)–(6.1.13) and (6.1.23). Now let there be a permanent increase in demand such as to cause a rise in the total revenue function from R to R'. If y_s is the short-run optimal rate of output and y' the firm's new long-run rate of output, then the firm's discounted total current revenue is $(1 - e^{-rL_0})R'(y_s) + e^{-rL_0}R'(y')$. Current profit is then

$$\pi = (1 - e^{-rL_0})R'(y_s) + e^{-rL_0}R'(y') - C^0, \qquad (6.1.24)$$

where C^0 is given by (6.1.15), $y_s = f(x_s, X_2^0)$, and $y' = f(x_1', X_2')$.

Maximizing (6.1.24) with respect to x_s, x_1', X_2', L_0, and L' gives the following set of planning rules:

$$MR'(y_s) = \lambda_s, \qquad (6.1.25)$$

$$R'(y_s) - [w_1 x_s + EX_2^0 + \beta' x_s U + \beta' x_s L_0 - \alpha X_2'/r] \\ = R'(y') - C', \qquad (6.1.26)$$

$$MR'(y') = \lambda', \qquad (6.1.27)$$

$$L' = \left(\frac{2W_2 X_2'}{\beta' x_1' + \alpha X_2'}\right)^{\frac{1}{2}}, \qquad (6.1.28)$$

where $MR'(y_s)$ and $MR'(y')$ are the short- and long-run marginal revenue functions respectively, and λ_s and λ' are given by the equations (6.1.19) and (6.1.21). From a comparison of (6.1.25)–(6.1.28) with (6.1.19)–(6.1.22) it is evident that the problem of cost minimization is not separable from that of profit maximization. This is due to the discrepancy in the conditions (6.1.20) and (6.1.26) pertaining to the economic life of incumbent equipment in the two models. If price policy is to be subject to review and change at the time the incumbent equipment is replaced, then the conditions for the replacement of such equipment must necessarily involve a comparison of profit alternatives rather than a comparison of cost alternatives [unless $MR'(y_s) = MR'(y')$]. Stated in another way, we cannot solve (6.1.25)–(6.1.28) for y_s, y', x_s, x_1', X_2', L_0, and L', and get the same solution that we would get from (6.1.19)–(6.1.22) using the previous solution values for y_s and y' as the values for the output constraints in (6.1.17). We would get the same solution except for the condition (6.1.26). These results simply reinforce our earlier, less comprehensive, discussion in section 7 of Chapter V.

To see the difference in the results which are obtained if price policy is treated independently of replacement policy, suppose that when revenue rises from R to R' the firm simply selects a new output level y' (and corresponding price policy) which is then permanently maintained without an intervening temporary output response. Then current account profit becomes

$$\pi = R'(y') - C^0 \tag{6.1.29}$$

where C^0 is given by (6.1.15), with $y' = f(x_s, X_2^0) = f(x_1', X_2')$. Maximizing (6.1.29) with respect to y', x_s, x_1', X_2', L^0, and L' gives

$$MR'(y') = \lambda_s = \lambda' \tag{6.1.30}$$

in addition to the conditions (6.1.19)–(6.1.22). It follows that when price policy and replacement policy are independent, the firm can maximize profit by first minimizing cost according to the conditions (6.1.19)–(6.1.22), thereby determining a minimum marginal cost function $\lambda_s = \lambda'$, and then separately determining the value of output which satisfies (6.1.30).

2. The Output and Input Markets

An analysis of the output market in a competitive industry under variable replacement policies follows that of the output market under fixed replacement policies discussed in section 5.1, with the single exception that the life of equipment and therefore the length of the short-run operating responses of firms and the industry is a decision variable determined by an equation set such as (6.1.25)–(6.1.28). Referring to Fig. 3–9 again, if there is an increase in demand from DD to $D'D'$ in an industry whose equipment is subject to economic replacement policies, each firm (following the Marshallian hypothesis) will adjust output to a level y_s by increasing its employment of current inputs. The resulting short-run industry response is to move from P to Q. Each firm continues to operate at this point of temporary equilibrium for a period of L_0 years given by the solution to the equations (6.1.25)–(6.1.28). If at the time demand increases, different firms in the industry have incumbent equipment of different ages, that is; U in (6.1.25) and (6.1.26) varies among different firms, then L_0 will not be the same for all firms. Those firms who operate the longest in temporary equilibrium will be those whose incumbent equipment was new ($U = 0$) at the time of the increase in demand. Eventually all firms will reinvest in X_2' units of equipment and the industry will move from the temporary equilibrium at Q to the "permanent" equilibrium at S in Fig. 3–9. Consequently, $S_v S_v$ in Fig. 3–9 becomes the long-run supply curve of the industry.

The individual firm's long-run demand for current and capital inputs is obtained from (6.1.11)–(6.1.13) and (6.1.23) in the form of the following marginal productivity demand functions:

$$x_1{}^0 = d_1(w_1, W_2, r, \alpha, \beta'), \tag{6.2.1}$$

$$X_2{}^0 = D_2(w_1, W_2, r, \alpha, \beta'). \tag{6.2.2}$$

In the case of pure competition, $\mathrm{MR}(y) = p$ in (6.1.23), and the above demand equations will contain the parameter p also. In addition to the stock demand function (6.2.2), the firm has a long-run flow (replacement) demand for the durable input given by

$$x_2{}^0 = \frac{X_2{}^0}{L} = \frac{X_2{}^0}{[2W_2 X_2{}^0 / (\alpha X_2{}^0 + \beta' x_1{}^0)]^{\frac{1}{2}}}$$

$$= \left[\frac{(\alpha X_2{}^0 + \beta' x_1{}^0) X_2{}^0}{2W_2} \right]^{\frac{1}{2}}$$

or, from (6.2.1) and (6.2.2), this flow demand function can be written

$$x_2{}^0 = d_2(w_1, W_2, r, \alpha, \beta') = \left[\frac{(\alpha D_2 + \beta' d_1) D_2}{2W_2} \right]^{\frac{1}{2}}. \tag{6.2.3}$$

The aggregate industry input demand functions are obtained by summing over all individual demands.

Nothing new or novel is involved in the analysis of the market for a current input to an industry employing capital equipment subject to economic replacement policy. We shall therefore omit any such discussion and proceed directly to the more interesting market for a durable equipment input.

THE MARKET FOR DURABLE INPUT

Figure 6–2 represents the stock-flow conditions of supply and demand operating in the market for a typical capital input. The diagram on the left shows the existing asset market while the one on the right depicts the flow supply

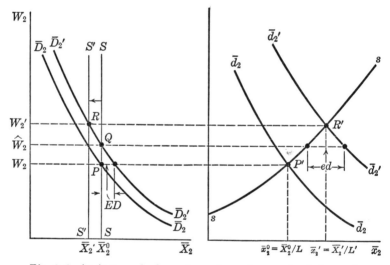

Fig. 6–2. An increase in demand causing a decrease in stock supply of a durable input.

and demand conditions operating in the market. $\overline{D}_2\overline{D}_2$ is the aggregate industry new asset demand for the capital good to maintain in stock. SS is the aggregate quantity of the new asset in existence. $\overline{d}_2\overline{d}_2$ is the total industry replacement flow demand for the good obtained by summation over all individual replacement demands of the form (6.2.3). Finally, ss is the producing industry flow supply of new units of the capital good to the market. This supply curve indicates that at higher selling prices the producing industry is willing to produce more units of the capital good per unit time. Following the analytical sequence of section 2, Chapter IV, the analysis will first proceed by ignoring the effect of the used equipment market. Then we shall turn briefly to a simultaneous treatment of price determination in the new and used equipment markets for the case of equipment with variable life.

Initially the industry is in equilibrium at P and at P' in the existing new asset and flow supply and demand markets, with the consuming industry satisfied to hold $\overline{X}_2{}^0$ units at the price W_2, and to replace this stock at a rate $\overline{x}_2{}^0 = \overline{X}_2{}^0/L$ units per year just equal to the rate at which the producing industry is willing to construct new units of the capital good. Now suppose there is a general rise in the demand for the product of this capital good, an increase in the rate of technological change, α, a general decline in interest rates, or any other change in environmental conditions which might cause an increase in the demand for the capital good. It is clear from equation (6.2.3) that whatever the cause of an increase in the asset demand for a capital input, there must also be an attendant increase in the replacement demand for the asset. In general an increase in the "demand" for a capital good implies an increase in the physical quantity of the good which it is desired to hold, *and* an increase in the consumption (replacement) rate of the good. *The asset and flow demand functions cannot shift independently.*

Suppose the assumed increase in the demand for the capital good takes the form shown in Fig. 6–2 in which $\overline{D}_2\overline{D}_2$ rises to $\overline{D}_2'\overline{D}_2'$ and $\overline{d}_2\overline{d}_2$ rises to $\overline{d}_2'\overline{d}_2'$. In this illustration we assume that the shift in replacement demand is relatively larger than the shift in asset demand. At the previous equilibrium price, W_2, firms attempt to acquire additional holdings of the capital good, thereby generating an excess stock demand, ED, in the existing asset market. Since there is no net inflow of capital goods into the market, this added demand impinges directly upon the existing stock, causing price to rise immediately to $\hat{W}_2$, thereby establishing a temporary equilibrium at Q in the existing asset market. This equilibrium cannot, however, persist, since at the price $\hat{W}_2$ the producing industry desires to produce new capital goods at a smaller annual rate than the consuming industry desires to replace such goods. At the price $\hat{W}_2$ an excess flow demand, *ed*, develops which causes a net *decline* in the existing stock as firms, through replacement policy, proceed to reinvest at lower levels. This reduction of the existing stock supply of the asset causes price to rise until it reaches W_2', at which price the industry is satisfied to hold a stock of capital equipment $\overline{X}_2'$, just equal to the quantity in existence, and the producing industry is satisfied to build new capital units at the rate $\overline{x}_2' = \overline{X}_2'/L'$, just equal to the replacement demand rate. In the new equilibrium at R and R' the stock $\overline{X}_2'$ turns over or is replaced every L' years. The net effect of the assumed increase in the stock-flow pattern of demand for the capital good is to decrease the stock held in production, increase the consumption rate of this stock, raise the unit investment cost of equipment, and raise total annual replacement investment outlays.

If the pattern of increase in initial demand were such that the asset demand increased relatively more than the replacement demand, the results would be as shown in Fig. 6–3. The initial equilibrium is at P and P' and the final long-run equilibrium is at R and R' in the two markets. In this case the increase in demand for the capital input increases both the stock of equipment held and the replacement rate of equipment.

THE MARKET FOR NEW AND USED DURABLE INPUT

In extending this model of the pricing process for new assets to include the market for used durable input, the analysis follows a close parallel to that in Chapter IV concerning the market for a durable input with fixed life. Again we imagine an aggregate industry asset demand for the good,

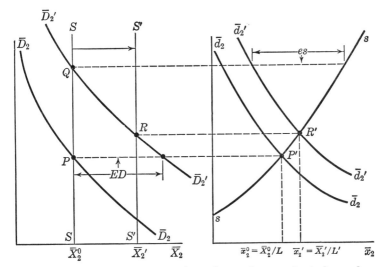

Fig. 6–3. *An increase in demand causing an increase in stock supply of a durable input.*

$\overline{D}(W_2)$, obtained by summing over all individual firm stock demand functions. If S_i is the existing predetermined stock of durable goods of age i, then the net new asset demand is $\overline{D}(W_2) - S_1 - S_2 - \cdots - S_{L^0-1}$, as in the case of durable goods with fixed life. The difference in the present case is that equipment life, L^0, instead of being fixed technologically, is determined by cost-minimizing replacement policy. We assume a perfectly competitive market for new and used equipment, and that the equipment has only one specific use to the large number of identical firms who employ the equipment in production. Hence, all firms will follow the same replacement policies. If there is no technological change in equipment, and a unit of equipment exhibits an operating cost function which increases monotonically with age, $\phi(t)$, then a firm with a new unit of equipment selling for W_2 will retain that unit in production for $L = L^0$ years such that the expression for the annual rental value of the equipment,

$$\overline{R} = r \sum_{k=0}^{\infty} e^{-rkL} \left\{ \int_0^L \phi(t)e^{-rt}\,dt + W_2 \right\}, \qquad (6.2.4)$$

is minimized. Competition and arbitrage in the used equipment market will guarantee this by setting a price $W_2{}^U$ on a unit of equipment of age U such that each firm is indifferent between employing that used unit and a new unit selling for W_2.

What are the conditions for determining $W_2{}^U$ such that each firm is indifferent between new and used equipment? The conditions are that the annual rental value of new equipment be equal to the annual rental value of equipment in each age class; thus,

$$\overline{R} = r \sum_{k=0}^{\infty} e^{-rkL^0} \left\{ \int_0^{L^0} \phi(t)e^{-rt}\,dt + W_2 \right\} = \overline{R}_U$$

$$= r \sum_{k=0}^{\infty} e^{-rk(L^0-U)} \left\{ \int_0^{L^0-U} \phi(U+t)e^{-rt}\,dt + W_2{}^U \right\}, \qquad (6.2.5)$$

$$U = 1, 2, \cdots, L-1.$$

The expression for $\overline{R}_U$ represents the alternative of buying equipment of age U and reinvesting every $L-U$ years instead of buying new equipment and reinvesting every L years.

Given W_2 suppose the price of equipment in each age class is in equilibrium with the exception of equipment three years old, which we assume to be selling below equilibrium. Then we would have $\overline{R} = \overline{R}_U > R_3$, $U = 1, 2, 4, \cdots, L-1$. Three-year-old equipment would be undervalued and firms would offer for sale their equipment in all other age classes, at the same time placing bids to buy three-year-old equipment. The result would be to raise $W_2{}^3$ until $\overline{R} = \overline{R}_U$, for all U.

It will be recalled from our analysis of durable goods with fixed life, and requiring no upkeep, that the condition for indifference between new and used equipment was $W_2{}^U = (L-U)W_2/L$. This condition was derived intuitively and by ignoring interest discounting. The relationship between this earlier condition and the more general conditions in (6.2.5) can be seen by rewriting (6.2.5) in the form

$$\overline{R} = \frac{r}{1-e^{-rL^0}} \left\{ \int_0^{L^0} \phi(t)e^{-rt}\,dt + W_2 \right\} = \overline{R}_U$$

$$= \frac{r}{1-e^{-r(L^0-U)}} \left\{ \int_0^{L^0-U} \phi(U+t)e^{-rt}\,dt + W_2{}^U \right\}. \qquad (6.2.5')$$

By using the approximation $e^{-rL^0} \cong 1 - rL^0$ and $e^{-r(L^0-U)}$ $\cong 1 - r(L^0 - U)$, and solving for $W_2{}^U$, we get

$$W_2{}^U = \frac{L^0 - U}{L^0} \left\{ \int_0^{L^0} \phi(t)e^{-rt}\, dt + W_2 \right\}$$
$$- \int_0^{L^0-U} \phi(U + t)e^{-rt}\, dt, \qquad (6.2.6)$$

which reduces to $(L^0 - U)W_2/L^0$ when $\phi \equiv 0$.

Given the price of new equipment, W_2, we can use the expression (6.2.5) or its rough approximation (6.2.6) to obtain the perfectly elastic demand curves for used equipment in each age class. The resulting analysis of the new and used equipment market follows closely that of Figs. 4–2(a) through 4–2(d). There is one new element, however; the original increase in demand which raises the long-run equilibrium price to $W_2{}''''$, as demonstrated in these figures, will cause a decrease in the economic life of equipment in accordance with the criterion (6.2.4). If analyzed in detail, these repercussions would complicate the new and used asset pricing model of Chapter IV, but they do not alter the fundamental stock-flow market pricing process.

APPENDIX TO CHAPTER VI

1. Equipment Life as a Parameter in the Production Function

Throughout Chapter VI we have assumed that the two-input production function, $y = f(x_1, X_2)$ or $F(y, x_1, X_2) = 0$, was independent of equipment life, L. Intuitively it would seem possible that there might exist some technological situations in which the production function should be written $y = f(x_1, X_2, L)$ or $F(y, x_1, X_2, L) = 0$, that is, given the stock of equipment, the age of the equipment might influence the consumption of current input required to meet any level of output.

One type of process which can exhibit such a production function is the queuing process discussed in section 8 of Chapter II. To develop such a production function from the truck maintenance model, we have only to assume that the truck malfunction rate, λ, is an increasing function of equipment age as well as output. Suppose the relationship is linear. Then equation (2.8.5) would now be written

$$\lambda = \alpha y + \alpha' L. \tag{6A.1}$$

Upon introducing this change, the production function (2.8.9) becomes

$$F(y,x_1,X_2,L) = \frac{\alpha y + \alpha' L}{\beta x_1 - \alpha y - \alpha' L} + \frac{y}{m} - X_2 = 0. \tag{6A.2}$$

This production function has an interesting property: it permits us to *deduce* a maintenance cost function of a form similar to the operating expense function whose existence (and independence of the production function) was postulated in Chapters V and VI. By solving for x_1 in (6A.2), we can write an expression for the annual rate of outlay for maintenance labor, $M(y,X_2,L)$, as follows:

$$M(y,X_2,L) = w_1 x_1 = \frac{w_1}{\beta}\left(1 + \frac{1}{X_2 - \dfrac{y}{m}}\right)(\alpha y + \alpha' L). \tag{6A.3}$$

Hence, for a given stock of trucks we get maintenance cost as an increasing function of output (equipment utilization), y, and an increasing (linear) function of equipment age, L. We could also determine the effect of technological improvements in trucking equipment if we knew their impact upon truck mileage, m, and/or the parameters α and β.

Where the production function has a form such as (6A.2), and therefore the operating expense function has a form such as (6A.3), the problem of choice of technique is one of minimizing the cost function

$$C = r \sum_{k=0}^{\infty} e^{-rkL}\left\{\int_0^L M(y,X_2,t)e^{-rt}\,dt + WX_2\right\} \tag{6A.4}$$

with respect to the stock of equipment, X_2, for given y.

2. A Generalization of the Choice of Optimal Production — Investment Technique

The analysis of Chapters III, IV, and VI dealing with choice of technique under various assumptions concerning the durability and replaceability of equipment is readily generalized to the case of n current and m capital inputs. The expression for total cost on current account can be written

$$
C = \sum_{i=1}^{n} w_i x_i
$$
$$
+ r \sum_{j=n+1}^{n+m} \left[\sum_{k=0}^{\infty} e^{-rkL_j} \left\{ \int_0^{L_j} \phi_j(x_1, \cdots, x_n, kL_j, t) e^{-rt} \, dt \right. \right.
$$
$$
\left. \left. + W_j \right\} \right] X_j. \tag{6A.5}
$$

w_i is the price and x_i the quantity consumed of the ith current input, $i = 1, 2, \cdots, n$. $\phi_j(x_1, \cdots, x_n, kL_j, t)$ is the operating cost function and W_j the unit capital cost of the jth equipment input, $j = n + 1, \cdots, n + m$. The firm's problem is to minimize (6A.5) with respect to x_i, X_j, and L_j, subject to

$$
y = f(x_1, \cdots, x_n; X_{n+1}, \cdots, X_{n+m}). \tag{6A.6}
$$

Necessary conditions for an extreme value of (6A.5) subject to (6A.6) are

$$
w_i + r \sum_{j=n+1}^{n+m} \left[\sum_{k=0}^{\infty} e^{-rkL_j} \int_0^{L_j} \frac{\partial \phi_j(x_1, \cdots, x_n, kL_j, t)}{\partial x_i} e^{-rt} \, dt \right] X_j
$$
$$
- \lambda f_i = 0, \qquad i = 1, \cdots, n. \tag{6A.7}
$$

$$
r \left[\sum_{k=0}^{\infty} e^{-rkL_j} \left\{ \int_0^{L_j} \phi_j(x_1, \cdots, x_n, kL_j, t) e^{-rt} \, dt + W_j \right\} \right] - \lambda f_j = 0,
$$
$$
j = n + 1, \cdots, n + m. \tag{6A.8}
$$

$$
r \left[-\sum_{k=0}^{\infty} rk e^{-rkL_j} \left\{ \int_0^{L_j} \phi_j(x_1, \cdots, x_n, kL_j, t) e^{-rt} \, dt + W_j \right\} \right.
$$
$$
+ \sum_{k=0}^{\infty} e^{-rkL_j} \left\{ \int_0^{L_j} \frac{\partial \phi_j(x_1, \cdots, x_n, kL_j, t)}{\partial L_j} e^{-rt} \, dt \right. \tag{6A.9}
$$
$$
\left. \left. + \phi_j(x_1, \cdots, x_n, kL_j, L_j) e^{-rL_j} \right\} \right] X_j = 0,
$$
$$
j = n + 1, \cdots, n + m.
$$

The cost equation (6A.5) is a generalization of the special cost functions contained in (3.3.2), (4.1.1), (6.1.2), and (6.1.9). If for any j the equipment is of infinite durability and requires no upkeep, we simply set $\phi_j \equiv 0$ and let $L_j \to \infty$ in (6A.5). If we also have $i = n = 1$ and $j = m = 1$, then (6A.5) assumes the form (3.3.2). If for any j replacement must be at fixed intervals, with $\phi_j \equiv 0$, then L_j is fixed in (6A.5), while if $j = m = 1$, the latter further reduces to (4.1.1). Similarly, (6A.5) reduces to (6.1.2) or (6.1.9) depending upon the special linear form of ϕ_j. The equilibrium conditions (6A.7) and (6A.8) include all of the special cases (3.3.4)–(3.3.5), (4.1.2), (6.1.4)–(6.1.5), and (6.1.11)–(6.1.12), while (6A.9) pertaining to replacement policy embraces the special square root forms (6.1.6) and (6.1.13).

If the $n + 2m + 1$ equilibrium equations in the system (6A.6)–(6A.9) have a unique interior solution, we can imagine solving for (1) n current input demand functions, (2) m capital stock input demand functions, (3) m capital equipment lives, and (4) the marginal cost function, as follows:

$$x_i{}^0 = d_i(w_1, \cdots, w_n; W_{n+1}, \cdots, W_{n+m}; r; y),$$
$$i = 1, \cdots, n \tag{6A.10}$$

$$X_j{}^0 = D_j(w_1, \cdots, w_n; W_{n+1}, \cdots, W_{n+m}; r; y),$$
$$j = n + 1, \cdots, m \tag{6A.11}$$

$$L_j{}^0 = L_j{}^0(w_1, \cdots, w_n; W_{n+1}, \cdots, W_{n+m}; r; y),$$
$$j = n + 1, \cdots, m \tag{6A.12}$$

$$\lambda^0 = \lambda^0(w_1, \cdots, w_n; W_{n+1}, \cdots, W_{n+m}; r; y). \tag{6A.13}$$

If the flow (replacement) demand for the jth equipment input is $x_j{}^0 = X_j{}^0 / L_j{}^0$, then from (6A.11) and (6A.12), we deduce the following m replacement flow demand functions

$$x_j{}^0 = d_j(w_1, \cdots, w_n; W_{n+1}, \cdots, W_{n+m}; r; y).$$
$$j = n + 1, \cdots, m \tag{6A.14}$$

Chapter VII

Capital Rationing and Investment Theory

1. The Rationing of Funds

The term "capital rationing" will be used to refer to the existence of some upper limit to the quantity of funds or finance that will be advanced by a lender to an individual enterprise independently of the rate of interest that the borrower is prepared to pay. Under static conditions this limit places a constraint on the total stock of assets that can be acquired by the firm. Such limits may be set by lenders as a means of minimizing or bounding their risk. We shall not be concerned with a rational analysis of such lender behavior, but rather with the effect of such limits on the firm's choice of production-investment technique and scale of operations.

That such lender-imposed limits exist is a commonplace fact and one finds frequent references to the phenomenon throughout the literature of economics. As the Lutzes have observed,

If there is no limit to the volume of additional loan funds which the entrepreneur can obtain, he will go on borrowing up to the point where the last unit of funds borrowed makes no further addition to his "net profit prospects," or to his estimated net worth. If the entrepreneur is "rationed" by the lender, he may not be able to obtain enough funds to allow him to reach this point; it may often happen in practice that an entrepreneur has access only to bank credit, and the bank will not lend him more than a certain sum no matter how high an interest rate he is prepared to offer.[1]

The rationing of funds seems to be a fact of life and may well have a very strategic role to play in the theory of the individual firm in purely competitive markets. In view of the dominance of constant and increasing returns to scale in the production functions of Chapter II, it is clear that we cannot rely upon internal technical diseconomies to provide limits to the expansion of the firm in pure competition. Furthermore, the "divisibility" controversy of some years past seems to have ended on the note that (1) there is nothing in the nature of production processes to guarantee constant returns to scale and (2) there are compelling reasons to believe that internal economies are of widespread incidence in production.[2] This leaves only credit rationing and Kalecki's [3] principle of increasing risk as factors limiting the size of purely competitive firms. These are related factors, in that it is increasing risk that causes the lender to ration the supply of credit to any single borrower. However, the lender's limit is likely to be much lower than that self-imposed by the borrower. The borrower, precisely because

[1] Lutz and Lutz, *Theory of Investment of the Firm*, p. 200. Also see A. G. Hart, "Anticipations, Uncertainty and Dynamic Planning," *Studies in Business Administration*, XI (1940), 39–49, for a discussion of capital rationing.

[2] See T. M. Whitin and M. H. Peston, "Random Variations, Risk, and Returns to Scale," *Quarterly Journal of Economics*, LXVII (November 1954), 603–604, for a bibliography and summary of this controversy. Also see pp. 604–606, and pp. 611–612 for a discussion of several examples of production processes which exhibit technical economies of scale, and for evidence that there are economies of large-scale management.

[3] M. Kalecki, "The Principle of Increasing Risk," *Essays in the Theory of Economic Fluctuations* (London: Unwin, 1939). Doubt has been cast upon the principle of increasing risk as a size-limiting factor by Whitin and Peston in "Random Variations ... ," pp. 607–608. They argue that in many circumstances risk decreases with size.

he is an experienced specialist in the productive activities for which he desires finance, may see substantially less risk in such ventures than the lender who may be totally ignorant of technological and market conditions affecting the venture. Furthermore, the lender not only assumes the increasing risk associated with expanded operations in a given activity (which the "rational" borrower himself will try to avoid by diversification) and the possibility of errors of judgment by the borrower, he also assumes the further risk of the borrower's death and fortuitous occurrences beyond the control of the borrower which the latter may not discount at a very high rate.

2. The Balance Sheet and the Firm's Money Capital Requirements

Before the effects of a constraint on the firm's money capital requirements can be analyzed, it is necessary first to determine the character and extent of these requirements in the execution of the firm's program of input purchases and product sales.

We shall distinguish two broad categories of money capital requirements — fixed capital and working capital. Fixed capital is required to finance the purchase of durable goods, while working capital is required to bridge the gap (if such exists) between outlays to suppliers for current input deliveries and the receipt of the proceeds from the sale of product. In general business practice, working capital is required to finance (1) credit advances to suppliers (which can be and usually are negative, since suppliers may not require payment for some period after effecting delivery), (2) inventories of storable current inputs, (3) inventories of goods-in-process, (4) inventories of product, (5) credit advances to buyers, and (6) the fulfillment of liquidity motives. In our analysis it will be assumed that inventory investment and idle cash balances are zero so that all working capital requirements are in the form of credit advances or "book" credit. Inventory investment does not differ in principle from investment in durable goods in that both represent investments in physical goods which are recoverable through production and/or sale. In our model, money capital is required for the purpose of making credit advances to suppliers and customers, and for financing the physical means of production. In the absence of liquidity motives for holding idle cash, these are the two primary sources of the firm's demand for money capital. Credit advances are interesting because they can serve as a substitute for money in the economic system and as a source of finance to the individual business enterprise.

In the terminology of accounting our assumptions amount to saying that all of the firm's current assets are in the form of accounts receivable (credit advances to customers), all other assets are in the form of fixed assets, and all current liabilities are in the form of accounts payable (credit advances by suppliers to the firm). If we let CA be current assets, CL be current liabilities, FA be fixed assets, and K be the external capital requirements of the firm (either equity, short term, or long term capital), then the balance sheet of our firm appears as follows:

Assets	Liabilities
CA	CL
FA	K

The firm's capital requirements are thus

$$K = CA - CL + FA, \qquad (7.2.1)$$

where $CA - CL$ is the firm's "short-term" working capital requirements.

By definition $CA \gtreqless 0$ and $CL \gtreqless 0$. Current assets would be zero if payment was received for products the moment they are produced, and negative if payment was received prior to their production. Similarly, current liabilities are zero if payments for inputs are simultaneous with delivery, and negative if payment is prior to delivery.[4] Generally, we will

---

[4] The accountant would classify a negative asset as a liability and a negative liability as an asset.

assume that both current assets and current liabilities are positive. Normally firms advance some credit to customers and receive some advances from suppliers.

One would expect, *a priori*, that current assets are some increasing function of gross sales in the uniproduct firm. In the multiproduct firm the contribution of each product to total current assets would be an increasing function of the gross receipts from that product. The sum over all such functions would provide total current assets. Where the firm sells a single product in an imperfect market, and credit advances are deliberately used as a selling device, one would expect the current assets function, beyond some level of sales, to become convex from below. We will adhere to the simple assumption that current assets are proportional to gross sales, or

$$CA = \tau R(y) \qquad (7.2.2)$$

for a single product, where τ is a constant (the ratio of current assets to sales). The parameter τ has the dimensions "time," and represents the constant (or average) lag between the production of output and the receipt of payment for it. If the firm were to shut down production, receipts of $R(y)$ dollars per unit time would continue for a period of τ units of time. Any time there is an increase or decrease in sales, there is a corresponding increase or decrease in current assets following a lag of τ time units. This is illustrated by the numerical example, where τ is three months, as follows:

Month	Monthly Sales	Current Assets
1	100	300
2	100	300
3	100	300
4	200	400
5	200	500
6	200	600
7	200	600
8	200	600

In months 1 through 3 the firm is in a stationary state with sales of 100 per month, and current assets steady at 300. In month 4, sales double to a rate of 200 per month. However, the flow of payments in month 4 is for the sales of month 1, or 100, with the result that all of the additional sales of 100 in month 4 is added to accounts receivable or current assets. Similarly, in months 5 and 6, current assets in the form of accounts receivable continue to climb at the rate of 100 per month. In month 7, payments of 200 are received from the sales of 200 in month 4, and current assets remain unchanged at 600. Current assets and monthly sales have stabilized at a new stationary equilibrium.

The same phenomenon applies to current liabilities. We assume that the current liabilities generated by each current input requirement is proportional to the total expenditure rate on that input. If there is only one current input which is consumed at the rate of x_1 units, then current liabilities are

$$CL = \tau_1 w_1 x_1, \qquad (7.2.3)$$

where τ_1 is the constant (or average) lag between the delivery of the input and the execution of payment for it. If there are n current inputs, then

$$CL = \sum_{i=1}^{n} \tau_i w_i x_i, \qquad (7.2.4)$$

where τ_i is the lag between delivery and payment for the ith current input.

From (7.2.2) and (7.2.4) it follows that the firm's working capital requirements are

$$CA - CL = \tau R(y) - \sum_{i=1}^{n} \tau_i w_i x_i. \qquad (7.2.5)$$

Since CA and CL are normally positive, $CA - CL$ may be positive, negative, or zero. If negative it means that the firm advances less credit to buyers than is advanced to the firm by suppliers (accounts receivable are smaller than accounts payable). Hence, book credit may be a source rather than a use of money capital for physical investment in the firm. The major classes of nonbanking enterprises that typically exhibit negative working capital requirements are the electric and gas utilities where it is not uncommon for current assets to stand at 60–70 percent of current liabilities.

If there are n current inputs and m capital inputs to production, the firm's total requirements for outside capital can be written

$$K = \tau R(y) - \sum_{i=1}^{n} \tau_i w_i x_i + \sum_{j=n+1}^{n+m} W_j X_j, \qquad (7.2.6)$$

where $FA = \sum_{j=n+1}^{n+m} W_j X_j$ represents the firm's total fixed capital requirements.

In the two-input case ($n = 1$, $m = 1$) with $y = f(x_1, X_2)$, the capital requirements function (7.2.6) becomes

$$K = \tau R[f(x_1, X_2)] - \tau_1 w_1 x_1 + W_2 X_2. \qquad (7.2.7)$$

An illustrative set of isocapital or investment possibility contours is shown in Fig. 7–1. The contours for $\tau = 0$, $\tau_1 > 0$, slope up to the right since an increase in the consumption of the current input increases output, which in turn causes an immediate increase in sales receipts (customers pay cash), but current input suppliers do not have to be paid until after a lag of τ_1 time units. This generates an increase in working capital which can be used to finance a larger stock of fixed assets without altering the requirements for external capital. Similarly, the contours for $\tau > 0$, $\tau_1 > 0$ may slope up to the right over some region if marginal working capital needs become negative. In general, the slope of an isocapital contour is given by

$$\frac{\partial X_2}{\partial x_1} = -\frac{\tau R' f_1 - \tau_1 w_1}{\tau R' f_2 + W_2},$$

which is positive when the numerator is negative. But $\tau R' f_1 - \tau_1 w_1$ is simply the marginal working capital requirements per unit expansion in the consumption of the current input. If there are no values of x_1 and X_2 for which marginal work-

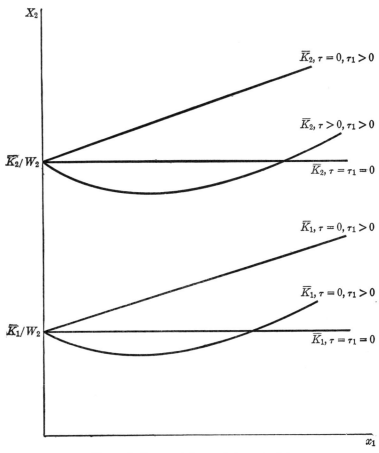

Fig. 7–1. Forms of the capital constraint.

ing capital requirements are negative, then the isocapital contours will decline continuously to the right.

3. Long-Term Capital Rationing and the Theory of the Firm

As an illustration of the effect of capital rationing in providing a determinate theory of the scale of operations of the firm in pure competition, consider the two-input productive process with one current and one capital input. Assume, furthermore, that $\tau = \tau_1 = 0$ in (7.2.7) and that the firm has a "ration" of money capital available which cannot exceed $\overline{K}$ units. The rational firm seeking to choose that input-output technique which minimizes total cost, will want to minimize

$$C = w_1 x_1 + w_2 X_2 \qquad (7.3.1)$$

subject to

$$y = f(x_1, X_2), \qquad (7.3.2)$$

and

$$\overline{K} \geq W_2 X_2, \qquad (7.3.3)$$

where w_2 is the "rental" or flow cost of the capital input.

The expansion path, that is, the optimal values $x_1{}^0$, $X_2{}^0$ corresponding to various outputs, for such a firm is given by SPL' on the isoproduct map of Fig. 7–2. In the absence of capital rationing the expansion path or scale line would

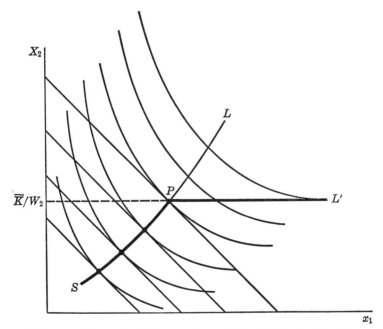

Fig. 7–2. Choice of technique under capital rationing: two inputs.

be SPL, where P is the point at which the constraint $\overline{K}$ becomes effective. Below P the capital constraint is ineffective with $\overline{K} > W_2X_2$, while above P, technique is determined entirely by (7.3.2) and the condition $\overline{K} = W_2X_2$. The constrained long-run average cost curve corresponding to SPL' is $RP'T$ in Fig. 7–3, where LAC corresponds to the (increas-

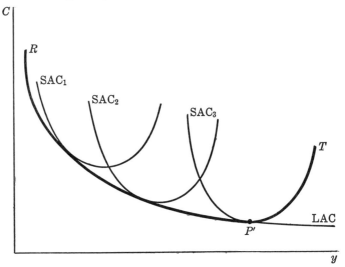

Fig. 7–3. *Short and long-run average costs under capital rationing.*

ing returns) expansion path SPL in the absence of capital rationing. Since the constrained long-run average cost curve, $RP'T$, is U-shaped, the rationing of capital can provide a limit to the scale of plant that will be built under pure competition.

In the three-input case with one current and two capital inputs, the problem is to minimize [5]

$$C = w_1x_1 + w_2X_2 + w_3X_3 \qquad (7.3.4)$$

[5] See H. Makower and William J. Baumol, "The Analogy Between Producer and Consumer Equilibrium Analysis, "*Economica*, XVII (February 1950), pp. 63–80, for a discussion of the theory of production under a capital constraint. The Makower-Baumol analysis differs from ours in that we have explicitly distinguished stock and flow inputs. Such a distinction is essential, I believe, to a proper analysis of capital rationing.

subject to

$$y = f(x_1, X_2, X_3), \qquad (7.3.5)$$

and

$$\overline{K} \geq W_2 X_2 + W_3 X_3. \qquad (7.3.6)$$

In Lagrange form the problem is to minimize

$$\psi = w_1 x_1 + w_2 X_2 + w_3 X_3 - \lambda [f(x_1, X_2, X_3) - y] \\ - \mu [W_2 X_2 + W_3 X_3 - \overline{K}], \qquad (7.3.7)$$

giving the following necessary conditions

$$w_1 - \lambda f_1 = 0, \qquad (7.3.8)$$

$$w_2 - \lambda f_2 - \mu W_2 = 0, \qquad (7.3.9)$$

$$w_3 - \lambda f_3 - \mu W_3 = 0. \qquad (7.3.10)$$

The Lagrange multiplier μ is zero wherever the "greater than" sign holds in (7.3.6). Equations (7.3.5)–(7.3.6) and (7.3.8)–(7.3.10) simultaneously determine

$$x_1{}^0 = h_1(w_1, w_2, w_3, \overline{K}, y), \qquad (7.3.11)$$

$$X_2{}^0 = H_2(w_1, w_2, w_3, \overline{K}, y), \qquad (7.3.12)$$

$$X_3{}^0 = H_3(w_1, w_2, w_3, \overline{K}, y), \qquad (7.3.13)$$

$$\lambda^0 = \lambda(w_1, w_2, w_3, \overline{K}, y), \qquad (7.3.14)$$

$$\mu^0 = \mu(w_1, w_2, w_3, \overline{K}, y). \qquad (7.3.15)$$

where the Lagrange multipliers λ and μ are respectively the marginal cost of output and of money capital.[6]

The solution is demonstrated graphically in the three dimensional diagram of Fig. 7–4. The curve AQB in the input space represents the intersection of the production constraint surface $y = f(x_1, X_2, X_3)$ and the money capital constraint plane $\overline{K} = W_2 X_2 + W_3 X_3$. The line AQB is the locus of all input combinations which produce y units of output and

---

[6] The interpretation of μ as the marginal profitability of capital goes back to the interesting early paper by Oscar Lange, "The Place of Interest in the Theory of Production," *Review of Economic Studies*, III (June 1936).

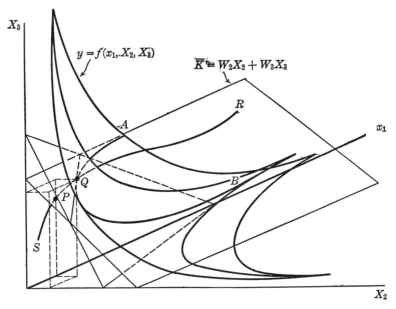

X_3

$y = f(x_1, X_2, X_3)$

$\overline{K} = W_2X_2 + W_3X_3$

R

x_1

A

Q

B

P

S

X_2

Fig. 7–4. Choice of technique under capital rationing: three inputs.

which simultaneously exhausts the capital budget $\overline{K}$. Along AQB we have $\mu > 0$, $\lambda > 0$. At Q we have tangency of the lowest isocost plane with the composite constraint set AQB. The line $SPQR$, where PQR lies in the constraint plane $\overline{K} = W_2X_2 + W_3X_3$, is the expansion path or scale line under a ration of K dollars of capital. Below outputs corresponding to P the minimum cost input combination requires less than $\overline{K}$ dollars of investment capital. Hence SP lies below the money capital constraint plane. Along SP we have $\mu = 0$.

4. Capital Rationing and Profit Maximization

The expression for discounted current annual profit in the two-input case can be written

$$\pi = pf(x_1, X_2)e^{-r\tau} - w_1x_1e^{-r\tau_1} - w_2X_2, \qquad (7.4.1)$$

where product selling price, p, is assumed to be independent of sales. If the firm's objective is profit maximization, then the problem becomes one of maximizing (7.4.1) with respect to x_1 and X_2 subject to a capital constraint of the form

$$\overline{K} \geq \tau p f(x_1, X_2) - \tau_1 w_1 x_1 + W_2 X_2. \qquad (7.4.2)$$

In a region in which maximization occurs at the boundary of the constraint set (7.4.2), necessary conditions for a constrained maximization of (7.4.1) can be written

$$p f_1 e^{-r\tau} - w_1 e^{-r\tau_1} - \mu[\tau p f_1 - \tau_1 w_1] = 0, \qquad (7.4.3)$$

$$p f_2 e^{-r\tau} - w_2 - \mu[\tau p f_2 + W_2] = 0, \qquad (7.4.4)$$

where μ is a Lagrange multiplier representing the marginal profitability of capital $\partial\pi/\partial K$. μ is an increasing, decreasing, or constant function of K according as the production function shows increasing, decreasing, or constant returns to scale. Hence, if constant or increasing returns predominate in industrial production processes, the marginal profitability of capital or marginal rate of net return on capital will be a nondecreasing function of total capital investment.

A possible solution described by the equilibrium conditions (7.4.2)–(7.4.4) is illustrated by P_0 in Fig. 7–5(a). Note that working capital requirements are nonnegative in this solution. In the case in which working capital requirements become negative for sufficiently large x_1, there will exist no finite solution for the purely competitive firm whose production function shows nondecreasing returns to scale. This is illustrated in Fig. 7–5(b).

If the firm sells its product in an imperfect market, and faces a total revenue function $R(y)$, then profit is

$$\pi = R[f(x_1, X_2)]e^{-r\tau} - w_1 x_1 e^{-r\tau_1} - w_2 X_2, \qquad (7.4.1')$$

and the capital constraint becomes

$$\overline{K} \geq \tau R[f(x_1, X_2)] - \tau_1 w_1 x_1 + W_2 X_2. \qquad (7.4.2')$$

The conditions for maximizing (7.4.1') subject to (7.4.2') are the same as (7.4.3) and (7.4.4) with marginal revenue,

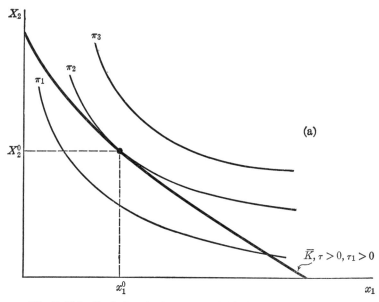

Fig. 7–5(a). *Capital rationing as a scale limit in pure competition.*

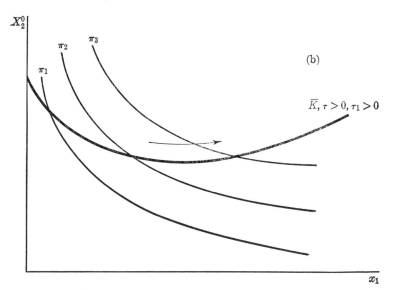

Fig. 7–5(b). *Capital rationing as an ineffective limit with negative working capital.*

$\partial R/\partial y$, now replacing the price, p. Figure 7–6 illustrates the equilibrium under imperfect competition with various assumptions concerning the capital constraint function (7.4.2′). If $\tau > 0$ and $\tau_1 > 0$ so that the firm advances some credit to customers and receives some credit from suppliers, then the capital constraint curve may be represented by K_1K_1 or $K_1'K_1'$. If the capital constraint is represented by K_1K_1, the size of the firm is limited by the capital available to it. If

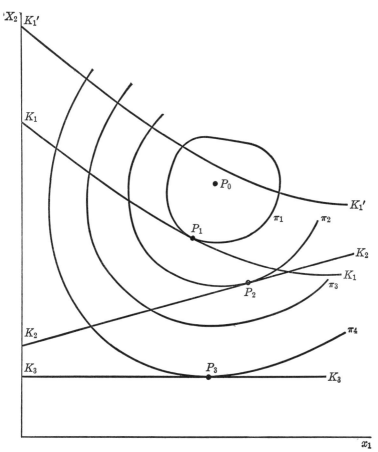

Fig. 7–6. *Profit maximization under capital rationing.*

the capital constraint curve lies above the point of unconstrained profit maximization, P_0, as illustrated by $K_1'K_1'$, the equilibrium is at P_0 where the output of the firm is limited by demand considerations (we assume nondecreasing returns to scale in production). In the latter case the "greater than" sign holds in (7.4.2'). If $\tau = 0$ in (7.4.2'), working capital requirements are always negative. As a result, any increase in the consumption of the current input increases the availability of capital (in the form of book credit) to the firm, and causes an increase in the quantity of fixed assets that can be acquired. Hence the constraint line has a positive slope as shown by K_2K_2 in Fig. 7–6 and the resulting equilibrium choice of technique is at P_2. Finally, if $\tau = \tau_1 = 0$, the only requirement for capital is for fixed investment. The capital constraint line is therefore horizontal as shown by K_3K_3, and the equilibrium is at P_3.

It is worth noting that in the profit maximization models just described we cannot define a cost curve independent of demand parameters. For example, if $\tau \neq 0$, the capital constraint function (7.4.2) includes p as a parameter. If we then minimize a cost function of the form (7.3.1) subject to (7.3.2) and (7.4.2), the result is a minimum cost function that depends upon the price of the product. Similarly, in the imperfect competition case, the firm's cost curve will depend upon the demand curve since sales affect current assets which in turn influence the firm's investment possibility function.

Chapter VIII

Engineering Economy Practice

1. The Study and Literature of Engineering Economy

E. L. Grant defines an economy study "as a comparison between alternatives in which the differences between the alternatives are expressed so far as practicable in money terms. Where technical considerations are somehow involved, such a comparison may be called an engineering economy study." [1] Informally, engineering economy considerations are probably as old as the engineering profession itself. It is not, however, until the present century that the study has crystallized into a distinct body of formalized thought. The first engineer must have discovered that there are different ways, using different materials, of accomplishing any engineering task, and that some criterion must be established for selecting among alternatives. The early practicing engineer, who was frequently without any business or economic training, found it natural to use profit maximization or cost or investment minimization as a choice criterion.

[1] E. L. Grant, *Principles of Engineering Economy*, 3rd ed. (New York: Ronald Press, 1950), p. 3.

Considerations of economy have had impact upon every engineering field. Railway, bridge, and building engineering were among the first engineering specialties to develop a literature on the economic problems peculiar to these areas.[2] One of the early systematic engineering treatises in a specialized field of engineering is a work by Waddell on bridge economics.[3] At about the same time a few textbooks in engineering economy began to appear.[4] More recently, mechanical, electrical, petroleum, and especially chemical, engineering have shown a rapidly increasing awareness of the role of economic criteria in engineering operations.

These developments seem to have taken place completely outside the main stream of economic analysis, without any connections with the body of economic thought on the theory of production. Consequently, the engineer's solution is not formally that of the economist, though, as will be demonstrated in later sections, the engineer's solution is essentially equivalent to that of neoclassical production theory. This independence of engineering economics from general economic theory is somewhat curious, inasmuch as the study of agricultural economics (the counterpart of engineering economics in agriculture) has always maintained close ties with the economics profession. Agricultural production economics has developed using the jargon and conceptual framework of the Walras-Wicksteed theory of production, while engineering production economics has evolved a jargon and conceptual framework entirely of its own making. A similar paucity of attention has been given

[2] See, for example, A. M. Wellington, *The Economic Theory of the Location of Railways* (New York: John Wiley, 1887).

[3] J. A. L. Waddell, *Economics of Bridgework* (New York: John Wiley, 1921). Waddell was something of a patron saint of engineering economics. He tried unsuccessfully to persuade the Society for the Promotion of Engineering Education to sponsor the preparation of an elaborate treatise on "The Economics of Engineering," drawing upon economic design and operating problems in all the various engineering fields. For a quotation of his statement before the Society, see *Economics of Bridgework*, pp. 3–4. The Society has since formed an Engineering Economy Division which publishes *The Engineering Economist*.

[4] The first engineering economy textbook seems to be the one by J. C. L. Fish, *Engineering Economics* (New York: McGraw-Hill, 1915).

to the subject of engineering economics by economists. The unfortunate results of this state of autarky have been that (1) engineering economics is almost entirely problem- or "case"-oriented with little recourse to the use of theoretical constructs or the development of general principles, and (2) the economic theory of production (until very recently) has evolved in an empirical vacuum except for the outstanding contributions of agricultural economists to applied production theory. In recent years the contemporaneous development of linear programming techniques and interest in empirical production research has almost exclusively identified linear programming with applied research. It does not seem to be recognized that a modified production function theory of cost has wide application in engineering processes both as a description of behavior and as a normative tool of analysis.

2. *Economic Balance Solutions and the Theory of Investment and Production*

The extent of the engineering economist's use of theory is contained in the concept of "economic balance." Engineers have observed the repeated occurrence of certain important regularities in a wide class of engineering design problems. In such problems it is found that one or more key design variables affect the total (or average total) cost of the system. Specifically, it is found that certain categories of cost, notably the "fixed" investment costs, tend to rise, while other costs, the "variable" operating costs, tend to fall with the design variable or variables. The problem, as seen by the practicing engineer, is to balance these opposing movements in cost to achieve a minimum cost design. The result might be termed an "economic balance theory" of production planning. A representative statement of the theory of "economic balance" is that by Schweyer:

A study of the costs in design of equipment and processing operations will show in most cases that there are certain costs that increase whereas others decrease when the costs can be related to some common variable. Since the total cost is the sum of all costs, these relationships immediately suggest the possibility that an optimum region exists where operations at values of this common variable will produce the lowest total costs. Economic balance is the design of equipment or the selection of operation conditions whereby the increasing costs are balanced by the decreasing costs to give the greatest economic return. There are numerous types of economic balance: in design, in operation, in calculation of recovery of minerals, in yields for chemical reactions, etc. Charts can be made up to visualize the manner in which the costs vary to determine optimum results and to illustrate the manner in which the costs vary. In many cases the individual cost items may be expressed by a mathematical relation, all such equations can be added, and the sum (or total cost) can be differentiated with respect to the common variable.[5]

A typical economic balance problem is illustrated in Fig. 8–1. "Fixed" costs are shown rising linearly, while variable costs are shown falling in a nonlinear fashion with the common "design" variable. The design variable is usually a physical measure of the capital equipment input to the process, — for example, insulation thickness, pipe size, conductor size, number of evaporators, pump capacity, and so forth. Indeed, the economist can frequently find valuable clues to the proper physical measurement of capital goods by studying these "design" variables. The economic balance or minimum cost point occurs where the rate of rise in the investment costs is equal to, or just "balanced" by, the rate of decline in the variable costs.

Mathematically, the typical engineer's solution can be easily related to the cost and production functions of economic theory. Consider two inputs, a current input, x_1, and a capital input, X_2, and write the production function, $y = f(x_1, X_2)$ in the inverse form

$$x_1 = g(y, X_2). \qquad (8.2.1)$$

If w_1 is the unit cost of the current input, and w_2 is the unit flow cost, including interest and "depreciation," of the capi-

---

[5] Herbert E. Schweyer, *Process Engineering Economics*, p. 208.

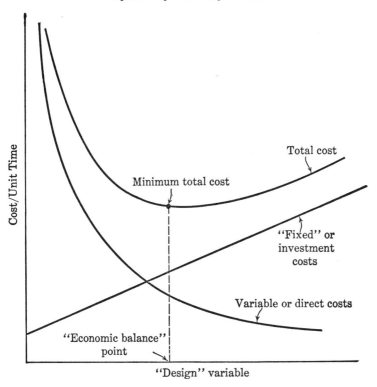

Fig. 8–1. Economic balance in engineering design.

tal input, then total cost is

$$C = w_1x_1 + w_2X_2. \qquad (8.2.2)$$

Substituting from (8.2.1) gives

$$C = w_1g(y,X_2) + w_2X_2. \qquad (8.2.3)$$

The term $w_1g(y,X_2)$ corresponds to the variable cost curve of Fig. 8–1, while w_2X_2 corresponds to the investment cost curve. Total cost is the sum of these two component costs. The point of "economic balance" occurs where $\partial C/\partial X_2 = 0$, or where

$$- w_1(\partial g/\partial X_2) = w_2. \qquad (8.2.4)$$

The engineer's solution is where "marginal" variable cost is equal to "marginal" investment cost, the marginal or incremental variations being computed with respect to the capital input, X_2.[6] This solution is equivalent to that of production theory, which equates the ratios of the marginal physical productivity of each input to the unit cost of the input. The major theoretical shortcoming of the engineer's solution, as will be evident in the examples of the sections to follow, is that it fails to provide a conceptual distinction between engineering data and economic data. As a result, the stage is not properly set to permit the engineer to explore readily the consequences of changes in design technology or changes in the unit costs of inputs. Such concepts as "marginal product" and "input substitution," are very rarely employed by the engineer because he has no formal concept of a production function beyond knowledge of the law of diminishing returns. On the other hand, the engineer's solution has a practical advantage, which he might consider of some importance. In many design problems there are numerous miscellaneous costs such as installation, cleaning, service and operating labor costs which are incurred for inputs other than the substitutive inputs to the process. Since these miscellaneous inputs usually vary with the design variable or the capital input, they are readily incorporated directly into a cost function similar to (8.2.3). It may be for this reason that the engineer declines to push his theory further than drawing a simple distinction between "costs that rise" and "costs that fall" with a common engineering variable. The engineer's form of the cost function (8.2.3) could be written

$$C = C_D(X_2) + C_F(X_2), \qquad (8.2.5)$$

where $C_D(X_2)$ represents all direct operating costs that vary (decline) with X_2, and $C_F(X_2)$ is all "fixed" costs that vary (rise) with X_2.

Figures 8–2(a) and 8–2(b) illustrate graphically the rela-

[6] W. D. Harbert in "Economic Process Operations," *Industrial and Engineering Chemistry*, XXXIX (August 1947), 940, has extended the economic balance method to profit maximization over a multiplicity of engineering variables.

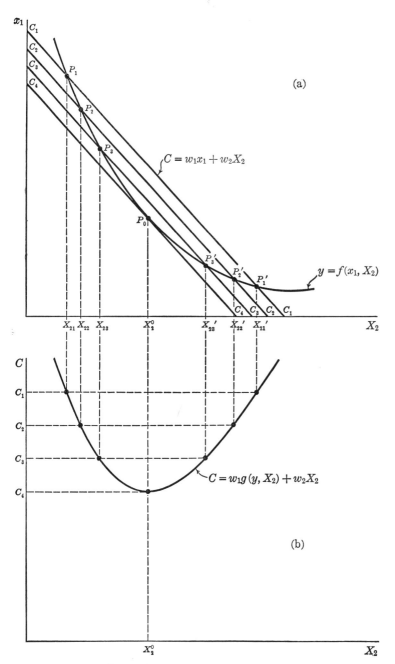

Fig. 8–2. Economic balance and the theory of production.

tionship between the isoproduct analysis of production theory and the engineer's "economic balance" analysis. Figure 8–2(a) shows an isoproduct contour and isocost lines for total outlays of C_1, C_2, C_3, and C_4 dollars per unit time. With an outlay C_1 there are two input combinations, P_1 and P_1', that will produce the required rate of output. P_1 requires X_{21}, and P_1' requires X_{21}' units of the capital input. Therefore, in the "economic balance" diagram of Fig. 8–2(b) the cost C_1 is associated with both X_{21} and X_{21}' units of capital. Similarly, with an outlay of C_2, the required output can be produced with either X_{22} or X_{22}' units of capital. The minimum cost way to produce the given output level is with an investment X_2^0 at a total cost C_4. The resulting curve in Fig. 8–2(b) forms the data of the engineer's least-cost solution.

In describing the typical engineer's solution to a production design problem, we have assumed that the criterion was to minimize total cost with respect to certain design variables. As an indication of the lack of integration of principles and methods in engineering economics one often encounters another, but equivalent, criterion, which is the minimization of total cost per unit of output with respect to the design variables.[7] Of course this is equivalent to minimizing total cost over the input space if optimization is under a constraint on total output.

3. Economic Conductor Size

Two simple examples of the engineer's solution to certain classical design problems will be given to illustrate the procedures used and their relationship to the marginal analysis.

Perhaps the most interesting example, especially to economists with antiquarian interests, is the problem of determining the most economical size of electrical conductor. The problem should be of historical interest to economic theorists since it was first formulated and solved by Lord Kelvin at

---

[7] See, for example, Schweyer, pp. 248–251, 258, 273, and *passim*.

the remarkably early date of 1881.[8] This is just seven years following the first edition of Walras' *Elements*, setting forth the rudiments of production theory; nineteen years before the fourth edition, in which for the first time (with clarity) Walras stated his marginal productivity theory;[9] and thirteen years prior to Wicksteed's famous criticism of the Ricardian theory of rent in which he set forth the marginal productivity theory.[10] Hence, the Walras-Wicksteed theory of production was being formulated at the same time that Lord Kelvin was making one of the first industrial applications of production theory. It will be evident in what follows that Lord Kelvin's solution employs the empirical law of energy loss in electrical conductors used in the derivation of the production function for electrical energy transmission in Chapter II.

Kelvin's derivation [11] proceeded by first writing an expression for energy loss per year in a conductor of sectional area A and carrying a direct current I. This energy loss is kI^2/A, where k is a constant depending upon the resistivity of the conductor material and, in Kelvin's derivation, on the proportion of the year that the conductor is to carry the current, I. If C_e is the unit cost of the lost energy, then the annual cost of energy lost in transmission per unit length of the line is kI^2C_e/A. If C_c is the cost of a cubic unit of the conductor metal, and r is the rate of interest (Kelvin assumed 5 percent), then, according to Kelvin, "the cost of possessing it (the conductor)" is rC_cA. The annual cost of interest and energy lost per unit of line length is then

$$C' = rC_cA + kI^2C_e/A. \qquad (8.3.1)$$

[8] William Thomson, "On the Economy of Metal in Conductors of Electricity," *Report of the British Association for the Advancement of Science*, sec. A., September 2, 1881, pp. 526–528.

[9] See Leon Walras, *Elements of Pure Economics*, trans. William Jaffe (Chicago: Richard D. Irwin, 1954), pp. 384–385, and especially the illuminating notes by Jaffe, pp. 549–554 and 604–605, on the development of Walras' thought on the marginal productivity theory.

[10] Philip Wicksteed, *An Essay on the Coordination of the Laws of Distribution* (London: Macmillan, 1894).

[11] Thomson, "On the Economy of Metal in Conductors of Electricity."

The value of A that minimizes C is that for which

$$rC_c - (kI^2C_e/A^2) = 0 \qquad (8.3.2)$$

or

$$rC_cA = kI^2C_e/A. \qquad (8.3.3)$$

Equation (8.3.3) is the form of the solution that Kelvin considered most important to verbalize to his fellow scientists. In the opening sentence of his paper he writes, "The most economical size of the copper conductor for the electric transmission of energy, whether for electric light or for the performance of mechanical work, would be found by comparing the annual interest of the money value of the copper with the money value of the energy lost annually in the heat generated in it by the electric current." [12] More specifically, the solution provides that value of A "which makes the two constituents of the loss equal." [13] In pointing out the implications of this solution, Kelvin further remarked that, ". . . contrary to a very prevalent impression and belief the gauge to be chosen for the conductor does not depend on the length of it through which the energy is to be transmitted. It depends solely on the strength of the current to be used, supposing the cost of the metal and of a unit of energy to be determined." [14]

Equation (8.3.1) corresponds to (8.2.5), the general form of the cost function normally used by the engineer, with A the "design" variable in this application as well as a measure of the capital input to the transmission process. The solution (8.3.2) is a marginal cost solution which states that the optimal A is where the marginal cost of conductor metal is equal to the marginal cost of electrical energy lost, both margins being calculated relative to the conductor area. This marginal solution is of course generally applicable to the economic balance problems of the engineer, whereas the solution (8.3.3), emphasized verbally by Kelvin and all electrical engineers since, depends on the special properties of

[12] Thomson, "On the Economy of Metal in Conductors of Electricity," p. 526.
[13] *Ibid.*, p. 527.
[14] *Ibid.*

this application (one cost is directly proportional to A, the other is inversely proportional to A).

Kelvin's solution, with certain refinements to take into account other factors, is used regularly by engineers in transmission-line analysis.[15] Indeed, Kelvin himself illustrated his solution by computing the conductor size for a proposed line 300 British statute miles long. As he stated,[16] this line could serve Montreal, Boston, New York, or Philadelphia from a Niagara Falls power-generating station, the construction of which had been proposed three years earlier by Werner Siemens.

It is instructive to contrast the engineer's solution to this problem with that of the marginal productivity theory. The production function for the transmission of direct current is the same as that derived in Chapter II (2.4.6), for alternating current, namely,

$$X_2(x_1 - y) - Ky^2 = 0, \qquad (8.3.4)$$

with $K = 4L^2\rho d/E_0^2 \cos^2 \phi = 4L^2\rho d/E_0^2$, since $\phi = 0$ for direct current. The cost function is

$$C = C_e x_1 + rC_c LA \qquad (8.3.5)$$

where $X_2 = 2dLA$. Solving for x_1 in (8.3.4) and substituting in (8.3.5) gives

$$
\begin{aligned}
C &= C_e\left(y + \frac{Ky^2}{X_2}\right) + \frac{rC_c}{2d} X_2 \\
&= C_e\left(y + \frac{2\rho LI^2}{A}\right) + rC_c LA,
\end{aligned}
\qquad (8.3.6)
$$

[15] See Alfred H. Lovell, *Generating Stations* (New York: McGraw-Hill, 1951), chap. v, *passim*. Also, see J. G. Tarboux, "Most Economical Conductor," *Electrical World*, XCIII (March 1929), 592–593, which publishes two decision maps for computing optimal conductor size for various line loads, load factors, and line length (for alternating current lines more than 100 miles long, line length begins to affect conductor size to a significant extent). These computing maps assume a cost of 0.00045 dollars per kilowatt-hour of lost energy, and an interest charge of 8 percent.

[16] Thomson, p. 528. In particular, see his presidential address before sec. A (Mathematical and Physical Science) of the same meetings, "On the Sources of Energy in Nature Available to Man for the Production of

for a line of length L. The expression (8.3.6) is the specific form assumed by (8.2.3) in the conductor application, that is, we have simply used the production function to eliminate the current input in a cost function of the form (8.2.2). Notice, however, that (8.3.6) is not quite the same as the engineer's cost equation (8.3.1). The difference is the extra term $C_e y$ in (8.3.6), which represents the cost of energy actually delivered in the process. Since this cost has no bearing on the determination of optimal conductor size, minimizing (8.3.6) gives the same solution as minimizing (8.3.1). The engineer's solution is correct since that portion of total cost excluded from his criterion function is independent of the "design" variable. However, the engineer's solution does not permit a direct determination of minimum total cost as a function of output as does the theory of production. After determining the optimal value of A, (8.3.6) provides the minimum total cost curve, which in turn is useful in price and output decisions. Since the engineer is normally not concerned with price and output decisions, but only with choice of technique, it is perhaps not surprising to find (8.3.1), the sum of conductor cost and the cost of lost energy, being minimized rather than over-all cost. The engineer simply chooses a surrogate criterion satisfactory for his immediate objectives.

4. Economic Thickness of Insulation

A standard problem encountered by the mechanical engineer is that of determining the most economical amount of insulation to use on steam pipes, in the walls of buildings, in the walls of refrigeration units, and so forth.[17] The en-

---

Mechanical Effect," *Report of the British Association for the Advancement of Science*, sec. A, September 2, 1881, pp. 516–518.

[17] The elements of the problem and its solution are discussed in all the mechanical engineering handbooks. Some of the handbooks include a computing chart reprinted from L. B. McMillan, "Heat-Insulation Practice in the Modern Steam-Generating Plant," *Mechanical Engineering*, LI (May 1929), 353. This, and an earlier article by McMillan, "Heat Transfer through Insulation in the Moderate and High Temperature Fields: A Statement of Existing Data," *Transactions of the American Society of Mechanical Engineers*, XLIX (1926), 1269–1317, are standard references on the subject.

gineer solves this problem by determining the insulation thickness which "balances" the discounted annual investment cost of the insulation against the cost of the heat saved by the insulation. The solution parallels exactly that of the conductor problem in the previous section.

For example, the heat lost per unit time from a steam pipe is [18]

$$\frac{T_0 - T_i}{K + t/kS},$$

where t is the thickness of insulation around the pipe (see Chapter II, p. 38, for the definition of the constants in this expression). If the cost of a unit of heat is C_h, then the cost of the lost heat is

$$\frac{C_h(T_0 - T_i)}{K + t/kS}.$$

If insulation costs C_i per cubic unit, then the investment cost of tS cubic units of insulation is $C_i tS$, and the annual cost is $rC_i tS$, where r is the interest rate. The total cost expression corresponding to (8.2.5) is

$$C = rC_i St + \frac{C_h(T_0 - T_i)}{K + t/kS}, \qquad (8.4.1)$$

which the engineer proceeds to minimize with respect to t, giving [19]

$$rC_i S - \frac{C_h(T_0 - T_i)kS}{(kKS + t)^2} = 0, \quad \text{or} \quad t = \left(\frac{C_h(T_0 - T_i)k}{rC_i}\right)^{\frac{1}{2}} - kKS.$$
$$(8.4.2)$$

The most economical thickness of insulation is determined by the condition that the annual cost (rent) of an additional unit of insulation is equal to the annual cost of the heat

---

[18] The expression is only approximate for a pipe, though it is exact for a flat surface such as a refrigerator wall. See McMillan, "Heat Transfer through Insulation . . .," pp. 1300–05, and the mathematical appendix.

[19] See McMillan, note 18 above.

saved by that additional unit of insulation. Again, this procedure gives the same solution as the marginal productivity theory.

5. Other Applications

The list of applications of economic balance techniques in the literature of engineering economics is very long. Except for the two previous examples we shall not attempt a detailed exposition of this literature. However, a brief survey of the kinds of problems treated would seem to be in order as a means of conveying the breadth and character of production theory as it finds application in the engineering process industries.[20]

In addition to the insulation and conductor size problems, there are several other classical economic balance problems, among them, economic balance in heat transfer, distillation (mass transfer) and evaporation. The chemical, petroleum, and power-generating industries are continually faced with the problem of dissipating the heat generated by various engineering processes. This is accomplished by the use of heat-transfer equipment which circulates cooling water (or a similar substance) around the equipment generating the undesired heat. Given the amount and thermodynamic characteristics of the material to be cooled, and the inlet temperature of the cooling water, the engineer designs the heat-transfer equipment to be installed by determining the most economical outlet temperature for the cooling water. The higher this temperature the lower the amount of water required and the lower the cost of cooling water. But at higher temperatures the area of the heat-exchange surface must be greater. A minimum cost design balances the annual cost of water against the annual cost of heat-exchange equipment. In terms of production theory, the inputs of water and equipment are substitutes.

---

[20] A comprehensive summary of economic balance applications is contained in Schweyer, *Process Engineering Economics*, chaps viii, ix, and x. I have relied heavily on this work and the many references it contains in studying the engineering economy literature.

In distillation processes the design variable is the "reflux ratio." In this problem the investment cost of the distillation tower at first falls and then rises with the reflux ratio, while direct costs (heat) rise with the reflux ratio.[21] In this example there is a minimum investment point as well as a minimum total cost point.

In evaporation processes the design variable is the number of evaporator effects to be used. The larger the number of effects (evaporating surface) the greater the investment cost but the lower the direct steam cost.[22] In this case the current input, steam, and the capital input, evaporator effects, are substitutes in the production of any given output rate.

Many economic balance problems arise in the chemical process industries, and chemical engineers have long been sensitive to the existence of such problems, and ingenious in obtaining solutions. In simple batch chemical operations there is a problem of determining optimal batch size. If the cycle time (residence time + changeover time) for the batch is fixed, then operating cost and the cost of charging and discharging the reactor vary directly with the number of batches per year, which in turn is given by the ratio of output per year to output per batch. Hence, these direct costs vary inversely with batch size, while reactor investment cost is an increasing function of batch size. Reactor vessel equipment and operating inputs are substitutes in this example. The analysis is similar in batch operations where the residence time is a variable, since residence time can usually be expressed approximately in terms of the batch size.

Economic balance considerations also arise in filter press

---

[21] See McAdams, "Economic Balance," in C. Tyler, *Chemical Engineering Economics*, pp. 134–140, for a distillation process analysis. Also see W. D. Harbert, "Economic Distillation Design," *Petroleum Refiner*, XXVII (April 1948), 106, which provides a two-dimensional mapping of a three-variable engineering input-output function for distillation processes.

[22] See C. F. Bonilla, "Design of Multiple-effect Evaporators for Minimum Area or Minimum Cost," *Transactions American Institute of Chemical Engineers*, XLI (1945), 529.

operations. The filtering process leads to the accumulation of "filtering cake" and a decline in the filtering rate. The process is terminated after a time and the press is cleaned by washing. Fewer washings are necessary on larger presses, and vice versa, with the result that filtering press capacity and cleaning inputs are substitutes in producing any given output. The engineer, however, solves the problem in terms of filtering cycle time. Annual investment costs rise with filtering time while operating costs fall. A balancing of these two costs determines optimal cycle time.[23]

These and many more similar examples illustrate the wide range of application of the theory of production. The solutions almost invariably determine the same optimal technique, or input mix, as would be obtained by application of the marginal productivity analysis. The literature of these applications is rich with empirical production functions, provided that the appropriate transformations are applied, and provides strong direct verification of the hypothesis that firms follow optimal policies in the choice of best static long-run production technique.

6. Economic Balance and Multistage Operations

Many engineering design problems can be analyzed to a sufficient degree of generality by considering only two inputs, that is, one "design" variable. Where more than two inputs are involved, and therefore two or more design variables, the engineer simply extends the above method to the multivariable case.[24] However, in many multistage processes in which the various individual processes are operated in series, such as the electric generation process discussed in Chapter II,[25] the question arises as to whether an over-all optimization is achieved by solving a stagewise sequence of simple two-variable economic balance problems. The answer is in the affirmative only if the intermediate inputs (outputs)

[23] See W. H. Walker, W. K. Lewis, W. H. McAdams, and E. R. Gilliland, *Principles of Chemical Engineering*, 3rd ed. (New York: McGraw-Hill, 1937), chap. xi, especially pp. 358–364.

[24] See, for example, Schweyer, pp. 226–233.

[25] Chapter II, sec. 5, above.

are priced at their marginal cost efficiency prices. However, these efficiency prices cannot be determined from an independent minimum cost design of each stage. The entire multistage system must be solved to obtain the efficiency prices.

To see this, consider a three-stage system in which each process requires two inputs. The first stage requires the two inputs x_1 and x_2, and produces the output $x_5 = h(x_1,x_2)$. Stage two uses the two inputs x_3 and x_5 and produces $x_6 = g(x_3,x_5)$. Stage three uses x_4 and x_6, and produces the final product $y = f(x_4,x_6)$.[26] The price of the ith input is w_i. We consider two problems. The first minimizes the total cost of the inputs to each stage subject to a constraint on the output of each stage, while the second minimizes the total cost of inputs to the system, subject to a constraint on final output.

I: (i) Minimize $C_1 = w_1x_1 + w_2x_2$,
         subject to $x_5 = h(x_1,x_2) = $ constant.
         Conditions: $w_1/h_1 = w_2/h_2 = \lambda_1$

    (ii) Minimize $C_2 = w_3x_3 + w_5x_5$,
         subject to $x_6 = g(x_3,x_5) = $ constant.
         Conditions: $w_3/g_3 = w_5/g_5 = \lambda_2$

   (iii) Minimize $C_3 = w_4x_4 + w_6x_6$,
         subject to $y = f(x_4,x_6) = $ constant.
         Conditions: $w_4/f_4 = w_6/f_6 = \lambda_3$

II: Minimize $C = w_1x_1 + w_2x_2 + w_3x_3 + w_4x_4$,
         subject to $y = f(x_4,x_6) = $ constant,
                           with $x_5 = h(x_1,x_2)$
                           and $x_6 = g(x_3,x_5)$

         Conditions: $w_1/h_1 = w_2/h_2 = \lambda_1 = \lambda_2g_5 = w_3g_5/g_3$
                     $w_3/g_3 = \lambda_1/g_5 = \lambda_2 = \lambda_3f_6 = w_4f_6/f_4$

If $\lambda_1 = w_5$ and $\lambda_2 = w_6$, then

$$w_1/h_1 = w_2/h_2 = \lambda_1; \quad w_3/g_3 = w_5/g_5 = \lambda_2; \quad w_4/f_4 = w_6/f_6 = \lambda_3.$$

[26] The technology of our process is a special case of the problem discussed by W. Leontief, "Introduction to a Theory of the Internal Structure of Functional Relationships," *Econometrica*, XV (October 1947), 361–373.

Hence, provided that each intermediate input is priced at its marginal cost of production in the previous stage, problems I and II are equivalent. The engineer is assured of an overall minimum cost design if each process is designed to minimize its net contribution to total cost, *and* the intermediate inputs are priced at their marginal costs. But each stage solved independently produces that stage's marginal cost as a function of its output. Thus, the efficiency price of the intermediate output x_5 is $w_5 = \lambda_1(w_1, w_2, x_5)$. Similarly, $w_6 = \lambda_2(w_3, w_5, x_6)$, and the three stages must be considered simultaneously in order to get x_5, x_6, λ_1, and λ_2. The engineer would not be correct in designing each stage at minimum cost, unless he is able to make an accurate estimation of the marginal costs of all intermediate outputs.

Chapter IX

A Theory of the Pay-off Criteria
of Business Practice

1. Introduction

The most popular investment decision rule in business practice is undoubtedly the short pay-off requirement. Typically, under this scheme, the upper echelons of management specify that no investment outlay will be undertaken unless it is expected to generate profits that will return the investment within a certain period of time, say three, five, or ten years.[1] Since business practice is largely written in the language of the pay-off period, while investment theory is cast in the language of discounted marginal productivity analysis, the two systems are not directly comparable without translation. In this chapter we will attempt to develop a theory of investment allocation among competing project alternatives, and interpret this theory in terms of the pay-off period rules of business practice. It will be shown that

---

[1] See G. Terborgh, *Dynamic Equipment Policy*, pp. 189–194, for a discussion of several industrial surveys of investment behavior showing the prevalence, and providing frequency distributions, of pay-off periods in practice.

the discounted marginal productivity conditions of investment theory can be alternatively stated in terms of the proper set of pay-off period rules. Also, it will be indicated that certain aspects of the pay-off period rules of business practice are consistent with the requirements of rational investment theory.

2. A Pay-off Period Theory of Investment

As a first attempt toward the formulation of a theory of pay-off decision rules, consider a firm faced with n alternative investment projects. We assume each project uses capital goods of infinite durability and is of infinite duration. The ith project yields a discounted expected profit flow, $\pi_i(K_i)$, with $\pi' > 0$, $\pi'' < 0$, where K_i is the investment expenditure on the ith project. The profit function presumes that optimal production and price policies are followed for each allocation, K_i.[2] We may define a profit function not only for each new project that might be undertaken by the firm, but also for the expansion or "replacement" of each project already under operation. If the jth project involves replacement of a presently operating facility with a new one, the profit on the contemplated new facility $\pi_j(K_j)$ must be reckoned net of the profit that would have been earned with the old facility. Similarly the investment, K_j, for that project is net of any disinvestment receipts (resale or salvage value) from the old facility. In this way our analysis embraces both the new and the established firm. Now suppose the enterprise has a fixed amount of capital, $\overline{K}$, to distribute among the n projects. The rules for best allocation are determined by maximizing

$$\pi = \sum_{i=1}^{n} \pi_i(K_i), \qquad (9.2.1)$$

[2] If the ith project requires one current and one capital input, the profit function might appear as follows

$$\pi_i = R_i[f_i(x_{1i}, X_{2i})] - w_{1i}x_{1i} - w_{2i}X_{2i}$$

where $R_i[f_i(x_{1i}, X_{2i})]$ is the expected revenue function and w_{2i} is the unit rental of the durable input. Capital investment in the ith project is $K_i = W_{2i}X_{2i}$, where W_{2i} is unit investment cost of the durable input to project i.

subject to

$$\overline{K} \geq \sum_{i=1}^{n} K_i. \tag{9.2.2}$$

From the Kuhn-Tucker theorem, necessary conditions for a relative maximum of total profits are

$$\frac{\partial \pi_i}{\partial K_i} \begin{cases} < \mu, & K_i = 0 \\ = \mu, & K_i \geq 0 \end{cases} \quad i = 1, 2, \cdots, n. \tag{9.2.3}$$

where $\mu = \partial \pi / \partial \overline{K}$ is the marginal profitability of capital. Now suppose we define a version of the pay-off period as follows: The marginal pay-off period on the ith project is the period of time required for an increment of net profit from an increment of investment in the ith project to "return" the additional investment. Hence, we define

$$\phi_i = \frac{1}{\partial \pi_i / \partial K_i}, \tag{9.2.4}$$

where ϕ_i is the marginal pay-off period on the ith project. Similarly, we define the equilibrium pay-off period, associated with the marginal profitability of capital to the firm,

$$\phi^* = \frac{1}{\partial \pi / \partial \overline{K}} = \frac{1}{\mu}. \tag{9.2.5}$$

From (9.2.4) and (9.2.5) the conditions (9.2.3) can be written in the following pay-off form:

$$\phi_i \begin{cases} > \phi^*, & K_i = 0 \\ = \phi^*, & K_i \geq 0 \end{cases} \quad i = 1, 2, \cdots, n. \tag{9.2.6}$$

The decision rules in (9.2.6) state that an investment project will not be undertaken if its pay-off period exceeds the minimum specified cut-off period, ϕ^*. All projects whose marginal pay-offs (at zero investment levels) are below ϕ^* are expanded until the pay-off on the last unit of investment is equal to ϕ^*. We have assumed no limit to the expansion of investment in any project. If such limits exist, then investment is expanded in each project until this investment limit is reached or the marginal pay-off is ϕ^*, whichever occurs first. Think of top management specifying the standard pay-off criterion, ϕ^*, then requiring all investments whose pay-offs exceed ϕ^* to be rejected. The process can be considered as quasi-dynamic in the sense that management might review their investment program at regular intervals, say once each year, budgeting the expenditure of capital made available by the year's operations, and specifying a new ϕ^* in the light of new conditions.

How should management determine ϕ^*? The marginalist will immediately recognize that ϕ^* must equal the reciprocal of the cost of capital to the firm if a full profit equilibrium is to be established. $\overline{K}$ will then be the supply of capital available to the firm at that price. If the marginal cost supply of funds curve, $C(K)$, is upward-sloping, the cost of capital (and its reciprocal) cannot be specified independently of $\overline{K}$. The equilibrium $\overline{K}$ is determined by the intersection of the firm's marginal profitability of capital curve and the supply of funds curve as shown in Fig. 9–1(a). In this case we think of management seeking a ϕ^* rule by trial and error, prior examination of the investment projects, or emulation of successful competitors. In principle, ϕ^* is a function of all the parameters of the supply and demand for funds curves shown in Fig. 9–1(a). If the cost of capital is a constant, C_K, to the firm, and the firm is unrationed with unlimited access to the market for funds, management should set $\phi^* = 1/C_K$, and proceed to raise whatever amount of capital is necessary to satisfy this condition. This case is demonstrated in Fig. 9–1(b). If the cost of capital is constant, and the firm is small or otherwise faces limited credit worthiness, lenders may ration funds at a level $\overline{K}$ below what the firm would otherwise desire. In this case $1/\phi^*$ cannot be established without knowledge of the marginal profitability of capital schedule. Here we have capital rationing proper. The case is illustrated in Fig. 9–1(c).

Under the purest of competition the firm can either lend or borrow at the market rate, r, which is the firm's cost of capital. Hence, the decision rules for any such firm are very

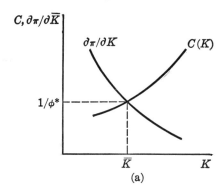

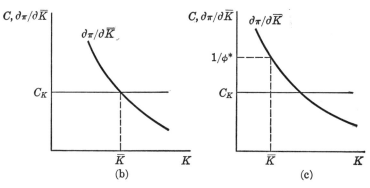

Fig. 9-1. *The cost of capital in investment allocation.*

simple. The equilibrium pay-off standard is $\phi^* = 1/r$ (for example, the pay-off is twenty years at a 5 percent interest rate). All firms expand investment in any project as long as $\phi_i < 1/r$. In equilibrium (assuming no investment bounds on any project) all projects show marginal pay-offs equal to the reciprocal of the interest rate.

Our analysis provides a simple transformation of marginalist theory to permit rational investment planning rules to be stated in the language of a pay-off concept. The theory can be readily extended or modified to permit simultaneous determination of best input-output policy, replacement policy, or to allow for finite horizons. Finite horizons may be more realistic since in practice new products are continually being introduced while old products are modified or abandoned. The corollary investment projects are for finite periods equal to the expected lives of the products. Capital expenditures typically seem to be planned with such finite horizons in mind. If we let the profit function, $\pi_i(K_i,t)$, be variable with time over the life of the project, T_i, then the criterion function becomes

$$\pi = \sum_{i=1}^{n} \frac{r}{1 - e^{-rT_i}} \int_0^{T_i} \pi_i(K_i,t)e^{-rt} \, dt. \qquad (9.2.7)$$

Necessary conditions for maximizing (9.2.7) subject to (9.2.2) are

$$\frac{r}{1 - e^{-rT_i}} \int_0^{T_i} \frac{\partial \pi_i(K_i,t)}{\partial K_i} \, e^{-rt} \, dt \begin{cases} < \mu, \ K_i = 0 \\ = \mu, \ K_i \geq 0 \end{cases} \quad i = 1, 2, \cdots, n.$$
$$(9.2.8)$$

If $\phi^* = 1/\mu$ and ϕ_i is the reciprocal of the expression for discounted marginal profitability on the left of (9.2.8), then the latter conditions can be stated in the pay-off form (9.2.6). In this case $\overline{K}$ and $T_1, T_2, \cdots, T_n$ are parameters of μ and therefore the equilibrium pay-off function ϕ^*.

3. The Pay-off Period in Business Practice

Is the pay-off concept of the above theory the same as the pay-off concept of business practice? Unfortunately the pay-off period, as it finds application in business investment policy, does not bear such a simple relationship with marginalist theory.

THE COMPUTATION OF PAY-OFF PERIODS

The pay-off concept in the foregoing theory is based upon profit net of *all* costs including capital cost (or "depreciation" as it is referred to in accounting practice). The pay-off period of business practice is computed in a variety of ways. For example, Terborgh lists no less than ten different methods (including several minor variations) of computing the pay-off period in practice.[3] There are cases in practice in which the pay-off is computed net of depreciation in a manner conforming to our definition of ϕ_i, but by far the most popular computation of the pay-off period is to divide some measure of the net investment in a project by the net cash flow of that project. By net cash flow we mean profit net of all current out-of-pocket costs but not capital or depreciation cost. Where the investment project involves the replacement of a facility, the net increase in cash flow, due to the savings effected by the new facility, is used to compute the pay-off period. This pay-off concept provides a direct measure of the *speed with which the capital outlay on a project is recovered* from the cash flow generated, whether the investment involves replacement or expansion. Such a concept seems to have enormous intuitive significance to the business investment policymaker. The concept places obvious emphasis on the ability of an investment to generate liquidity — to convert the fixed initial capital outlay back into liquid capital. It must be viewed against the backdrop of business emphasis on (a) liquidity, (b) the uncertainty of many, if not most, capital ventures, and (c) capital rationing, either externally imposed, or internally imposed by managerial insistence on financing capital outlays out of depreciation allowances and retained earnings only.

The trade literature of the machinery and engineering process industries is rich with information on pay-off practice. In order to demonstrate the typical pay-off computation recommended by investment practitioners, we shall cite the examples and arguments of the chief industrial engineer of the Republic Steel Corporation appearing over twenty-five years ago,

To bring out these conditions (*i.e.*, the factors affecting replacement) we will consider a machine operated by six men, normally running 5,000 hours a year, and producing 25 units per hour with 2 percent rejections, with the material costing $4 per unit. . . .

[3] G. Terborgh, appendix to chap. xii, pp. 269–271.

Table 1. Cost per operating hour

	Present equipment	Example I	Example II
Material loss	25 × $4 × .02 = $2.00	25 × $4 × .02 = $2.00	25 × $4 × .02 × 10 = $20.00
Labor	6 men × .50 = 3.00	2 men × .50 = 1.00	12 men × .50 = 6.00
Repairs	.50	.75	1.50
Supplies	.10	.10	.50
Power	2.00	1.50	3.00
Total cost	7.60	5.35	31.00
Hours operated	5,000	5,000	500
Units produced	125,000	125,000	125,000
Gross savings		(7.60 − 5.35) × 5000 = $11,250	7.60 × 5000 − 31.00 × 500 = $22,500
Gross return on investment		$\dfrac{\$11,250}{\$15,000}$ = 75 percent	$\dfrac{\$22,500}{\$45,000}$ = 50 percent

In Example I, we propose to replace this machine with another unit costing $15,000, which will have no greater rate of production nor any change in rejections, but which can be operated with two men in place of six, at a reduced power cost and somewhat increased repair cost.[4]

The data for example I are shown in Table 1. The author goes on to explain that

This machine, by showing a 75 percent gross return on the investment, will pay for itself during the second year, and ordinarily would be considered with favor.[5]

In a second alternative example, also shown in Table 1, the machine costs $45,000. The number of men is doubled per machine, and repairs, supplies, and power are also increased per hour, but the rate of production is ten times that of the old equipment.

This machine will pay for itself in two years, and the investment probably would be considered with favor also.

We are now confronted by this situation. Two new machines have been considered to do the work. One will give a gross return of 75 percent; the other, 50 percent. At first thought the 75 percent return proposal, which costs the least to install, would appear to be the more desirable. However, the other machine, although it costs more, also saves more money. The problem . . . then becomes a determination of the *additional return on the additional investment*.[6]

The author then presents the appropriate calculations which are reproduced in Table 2.

The figures indicate that there will be a gross return of 37½ percent on the additional investment. In other words, *the additional investment would be returned in somewhat less than three years*. Under normal business conditions this would be considered satisfactory, and in all likelihood the more costly machine with its 50

---

[4] E. M. Richards, "To Buy or Not to Buy Equipment," *Factory Management and Maintenance*, XCI (December 1933), 499.

[5] *Ibid.*, p. 499.

[6] *Ibid.*, p. 500. Italics mine.

Table 2

	Gross saving	Installation cost
Example II	$22,500	$45,000
Example I	11,250	15,000
Difference	11,250	30,000
Gross return of additional saving on additional installation cost	$\dfrac{11,250}{30,000} = 37\frac{1}{2}$ percent	

Source: E. M. Richards, "To Buy or Not to Buy Equipment." Reprinted by specific permission of *Factory Management and Maintenance*, December 1933. Copyright by the McGraw-Hill Publishing Co., Inc.

percent return on the investment would be chosen in the place of the one with the 75 percent return.[7]

Observe that in both examples the writer computes the savings on operating account or the additional cash flow generated by the contemplated purchase. This sum is then divided by the investment outlay to obtain the (cash flow) return on the investment gross of depreciation. The pay-off is then the reciprocal of this cash flow rate of return. In this example the writer uses the reciprocal concepts of the pay-off period and the return on the investment interchangeably when discussing the investment problem. Most writers in the trade literature work primarily with the pay-off concept. Note also that the writer is suggesting the use of marginal pay-off criteria. In the example, investment is pushed to the greater level required by the larger machine because the last increment of cash flow ($11,250 in Table II) pays for the last increment of investment ($30,000) in a "sufficiently short" period of time.

A THEORY OF THE CASH-FLOW PAY-OFF PERIOD

Suppose we adopt the typical pay-off concept of business practice, that is, the period of time required for the last

[7] *Ibid.*, p. 500. Italics mine.

increment of cash flow to pay for the last increment of investment in a project. We shall call this the (marginal) cash-flow pay-off period. Our objective is to write a theory of the cash-flow pay-off period from our general approach to production-investment theory.

Again we will assume that the firm is confronted with n alternative investment projects. The ith project has an expected annual profit flow, π_i, and annual cash flow, Q_i, over an infinite horizon. If the quantity of durable capital input to project i is X_{2i}, with unit investment cost W_{2i} and given life L_i, then the annual rate of capital cost or depreciation on the ith investment is

$$r \sum_{k=0}^{\infty} W_{2i} X_{2i} e^{-rkL_i} = \frac{rW_{2i}X_{2i}}{1 - e^{-rL_i}}.$$

Since cash flow is profit plus depreciation, we have

$$\pi_i = Q_i - \frac{rW_{2i}X_{2i}}{1 - e^{-rL_i}}. \tag{9.3.1}$$

Assuming a capital constraint of the form (9.2.2), with $K_i = W_{2i}X_{2i}$, the marginal conditions for maximizing $\sum_{i=1}^{n} \pi_i$ subject to (9.2.2) are

$$\left. \begin{array}{l} \dfrac{\partial \pi_i}{\partial x_{1i}} \leq 0 \\[1.2em] \dfrac{\partial \pi_i}{\partial X_{2i}} \leq \mu W_{2i} \end{array} \right\} \quad i = 1, 2, \cdots, n. \qquad \begin{array}{l} (9.3.2) \\[1.2em] (9.3.3) \end{array}$$

Our main interest is in the condition (9.3.3), which we will interpret in terms of the cash-flow pay-off period, θ_i, given by

$$\theta_i = \frac{W_{2i}}{\partial Q_i / \partial X_{2i}} = \frac{W_{2i}}{\partial \pi_i / \partial X_{2i} + rW_{2i}/(1 - e^{-rL_i})},$$
$$i = 1, 2, \cdots, n. \qquad (9.3.4)$$

We define the equilibrium pay-off period,

$$\theta_i{}^* = \frac{1}{\mu + r/(1 - e^{-rL_i})}, \quad i = 1, 2, \cdots, n. \quad (9.3.5)$$

that is, the reciprocal of the pay-off period is the marginal profitability of the last dollar's worth of available capital plus the annual depreciation on the last dollar's worth of investment in the capital good. Hence, from (9.3.4) and (9.3.5), the marginal condition (9.3.3) can be written

$$\theta_i \geq \theta_i{}^*, \quad i = 1, 2, \cdots, n. \quad (9.3.6)$$

Only those projects are undertaken that promise to yield cash-flow pay-offs that are below the equilibrium pay-off $\theta_i{}^*$. Each project operated at a positive investment level is expanded until the cash flow generated by the last unit of investment in that project promises to return the investment in $\theta_i{}^*$ years. Note in the expression (9.3.6) that the equilibrium pay-off period, $\theta_i{}^*$, which serves as the standard for measuring the profit-worthiness of investment projects, *is different for each project*. In (9.2.6), however, the equilibrium pay-off, ϕ^*, was the same for all projects. Our investment decision rules are seen to lose some of their simplicity when we abandon the net profit — in favor of the cash-flow — concept of the pay-off period.

Since the pay-off requirements of business practice vary substantially from one industry to another and from one type of equipment to another, it is important that we determine the parameters of $\theta_i{}^*$ and the qualitative effects of changes in these parameters on $\theta_i{}^*$. Such an investigation is potentially rich in empirically verifiable theorems concerning rational pay-off behavior.

First, we will introduce certain approximations into the expression (9.3.5) for pay-off requirements. These approximations are intended to bring the model closer to business practice as well as to simplify the analysis. The term $r/(1 - e^{-rL_i})$ in (9.3.5) represents depreciation per dollar of investment in the ith project. Under the straight-line depreciation method of business practice, this term is simply $1/L_i$, which is equivalent to introducing the approximation $e^{-rL_i} \cong 1 - rL_i$.[8] If we further assume that L_i is a decision variable determined by a square root formula of the form (9.2.6) in Chapter IV, then $L_i = [2W_{2i}/(\alpha_i + \beta_i)]^{\frac{1}{2}}$, where α_i and β_i are the linear obsolescence and deterioration rates of the capital input to the ith project. With these approximations, (9.3.5) becomes

$$\theta_i^* = \frac{1}{\mu + [2W_{2i}/(\alpha_i + \beta_i)]^{-\frac{1}{2}}}, \quad i = 1, 2, \cdots, n. \quad (9.3.7)$$

We observe next that (9.3.2), (9.3.3) and the constraint $\overline{K} \geq \sum_{i=1}^{n} W_{2i}X_{2i}$ (assuming equalities to hold everywhere), allows us to solve for μ (and therefore θ_i^*) in terms of all the parameters w_{1i}, W_{2i}, $\alpha_i + \beta_i$, r and $\overline{K}$. Our major interest is in the signs of the derivatives $\partial \theta_i^*/\partial W_{2i}$, $\partial \theta_i^*/\partial \alpha_i$, $\partial \theta_i^*/\partial r$, and $\partial \theta_i^*/\partial \overline{K}$. We assume that the marginal profitability of capital falls if there is a *ceteris paribus* decrease in the rate of obsolescence (technological improvement), or the interest rate, or a *ceteris paribus* increase in the price of the durable good, or the availability of money capital. We assume, in other words, that $\partial \mu/\partial \alpha_i > 0$, $\partial \mu/\partial W_{2i} < 0$, $\partial \mu/\partial r > 0$, and $\partial \mu/\partial \overline{K} < 0$. Using the signs of these derivatives and differentiating (9.3.7) we obtain the following results:

$$\left. \begin{aligned}
\frac{\partial \theta_i^*}{\partial W_{2i}} &= - (\theta_i^*)^2 \left[\frac{\partial \mu}{\partial W_{2i}} - \frac{1}{2W_{2i}} \left(\frac{\alpha_i + \beta_i}{2W_{2i}} \right)^{\frac{1}{2}} \right] > 0, \\
\frac{\partial \theta_i^*}{\partial \alpha_i} &= - (\theta_i^*)^2 \left[\frac{\partial \mu}{\partial \alpha_i} + \frac{1}{2W_{2i}} \left(\frac{2W_{2i}}{\alpha_i + \beta_i} \right)^{\frac{1}{2}} \right] < 0, \\
\frac{\partial \theta_i^*}{\partial r} &= - (\theta_i^*)^2 \frac{\partial \mu}{\partial r} < 0, \\
\frac{\partial \theta_i^*}{\partial \overline{K}} &= - (\theta_i^*)^2 \frac{\partial \mu}{\partial \overline{K}} > 0, \qquad i = 1, 2, \cdots, n.
\end{aligned} \right\} \quad (9.3.8)$$

The first of these conditions states that the standard pay-off requirement for a particular type of durable good is in-

[8] See the discussion of Chapter IV, p. 109, above.

creased if there is an increase in the unit investment cost of the good. If, for example, there is an increase in factory construction cost per square foot, the pay-off rule for new factory buildings should be lengthened. In particular, it is consistent with optimality if in these circumstances firms are observed to lengthen the pay-off period required on new factory outlays. According to the second condition, the greater the rate of technological change in a facility the lower the pay-off period required of investment in the facility. For example, if the equipment for a particular type of machining operation is subject to rapid technological change, then, *ceteris paribus*, the pay-off required of such equipment should be shorter than that required of other machine tool equipment. The third condition states that a general rise in interest rates should decrease the equilibrium pay-offs on all types of investments. The last condition asserts that the greater the money capital available the longer the pay-offs required of all investments undertaken. Given two industries or firms which are alike in other respects, it is consistent with optimality if the one with the greater availability of capital uses longer pay-off investment rules.

4. A Brief Examination of the Pay-off Trade Literature

The trade literature of the past three decades is filled with articles, reports, symposiums, and questionnaire summaries containing information concerning the purchase and utilization of equipment in business practice. A sample of this material has been examined in an attempt to determine whether business investment practice can be consistent with the foregoing theory of the pay-off period. This material, in the form of quotations from the statements of business executives, was selected by surveying the trade literature in search of information as to how pay-off criteria are determined and used in business decision practices. Are the qualitative properties of business decision rules and practices consistent with the qualitative properties of our theory? Specifically, do the pay-off criteria of business practice vary with the same parameters and in the same direction as the pay-off criteria of our theory? If the answers to these questions are in the affirmative in at least some firms and industries, we have evidence which is consistent with the hypothesis that these firms follow one possible set of optimal investment policies. The results of this survey, which is not exhaustive, seem to be consistent with this hypothesis.

One of the earliest sources of empirical information on investment practices is to be found in a three-article survey of equipment policies conducted by the editor of *Manufacturing Industries* in 1927.[9] This journal conducted a questionnaire survey of manufacturers, obtaining answers to several questions. The question most relevant for our purposes is the following: "Has your company a policy against the purchase of new equipment unless the production savings will return the initial investment within a definite period? If so, what is this period?"

In reply to this question, the general manager of the Morton Pottery Company writes:

We do not have a definite policy regarding the purchase of labor saving or cost cutting equipment. I do feel, however, that equipment that will not completely pay for itself within a period of 18 months' to 2 years' time had better be investigated very thoroughly by the *small* industry before purchasing.[10]

The short pay-off indicated here is not unusual, but of special interest is the qualification that it should apply to the *small* industry. One important characteristic of such an industry is the rationing of funds. We have shown that the less capital available to a firm, the shorter will be the pay-off required of all investment projects. Under the capital rationing interpretation, the statement is consistent with one implication of our theory.

---

[9] L. P. Alford, "Representative Policies and Methods for Purchasing New Equipment," *Manufacturing Industries*, XIV (October 1927), 277–282. "Can We Afford New Equipment?," *ibid.*, XV (January 1928), 27–30; "How Is Cost of New Manufacturing Equipment Charged to Product?," *ibid.*, XV (February 1928), 107–110.

[10] *Manufacturing Industries*, XIV, 278. Italics are mine.

A company which was not named emphasizes the role of intangible factors at the margin of the investment decision.

> Of course there are several reasons for buying new productive equipment other than the anticipated reduction in costs, for example: (1) Improvement in quality, (2) Replacement of worn-out equipment, (3) Increase in capacity, (4) Improvement in working conditions. However, when equipment is bought purely on a basis of savings, we ordinarily require a 50 percent return per annum, which means the machine must pay for itself in two years. When there are other contributing factors of a more or less tangible nature, we occasionally ask for an appropriation, when three years of normal production are required for the equipment to pay for itself. Where more than three years are required, some other justification for the investment must be advanced and proved or the purchase will not be made.[11]

This statement suggests a fairly systematic priority ranking of projects according to their expected pay-off periods. The zone of two to three years is one in which the corresponding investments may be undertaken if certain intangible factors are favorable to the decision. Beyond a three-year pay-off it is very unlikely that the investment will be made without special justification. This description of the investment decision process is entirely consistent with our theory.

Another suggestive statement by an unidentified machine tool executive is as follows:

> Developments in machine tools have come so rapidly during recent years that an entire change of policy has become necessary. There are so many factors to be taken into consideration that we are not following a hard and fast rule in the purchase of new equipment. Each case is treated on its own merit and considered upon a basis of conditions surrounding that particular piece of equipment. Roughly speaking, however, if purchasing entirely on the basis of production, such new equipment should show at least a 20 per cent saving.[12]

The extreme flexibility emphasized here seems to be conditioned by exposure to rapid technological progress.

[11] *Manufacturing Industries*, XIV, 278.
[12] *Ibid.*

One of the clearest and most revealing statements in support of our hypothesis is that of the vice-president of the Washburn Manufacturing Company, a metal-working firm that produced standardized products.

For some time we have had a policy of not purchasing new equipment unless we can expect to save the cost of the investment in new equipment through reductions in the cost of operations within the period of approximately two years.

A large percentage of our equipment is special for our particular manufacturing operations, and is constructed in our own machine shops. The constant studies of our operations and costs, . . . has provided us *with enough new ideas to date that we have discovered sufficient outlets for all the money the Company has desired to spend in new equipment*, most of which has returned, or will return, the whole investment in reduced costs in much less than two years.

Whether this condition will continue for a great length of time I cannot say, but think that the time may come in the not far distant future *when it may be necessary to extend the time for the cost of new equipment to be returned in reduced costs of products.*[13]

Several comments are in order. To begin with, the role of technological change in determining the length of the pay-off period could hardly be more clearly emphasized. In this particular case many of the equipment innovations are internal, but the rate of introduction of these new ideas is sufficiently great to render it unnecessary to consider investments with pay-offs in excess of two years (or cash flow returns of less than 50 percent on the investment). Also, the pay-off behavior of this firm is conditioned by what appears to be self-imposed capital rationing. Perhaps "the money the Company has desired to spend" has been restricted to book depreciation allowances plus retained profits. In any case the statement recognizes the effect of capital limitations in shortening the pay-off requirement. More capital, if available, would push the firm to longer pay-offs. When such conditions change, it is clear that the firm is prepared to respond by extending the pay-off time on new

[13] *Ibid.*, p. 282. Italics mine.

investments. The practice of this firm appears to be quite unambiguously consistent with our theory.

These comments and conclusions also apply to the policies of the Standard Conveyor Company.

At the present time we are using three years as a basis, meaning that we are not buying new equipment that won't pay for itself in three years. This is not because three years should be the limit *but because we find it is possible to carry on a conservative program of this character on that basis. When we see no opportunity to purchase new equipment that will pay for itself in three years, I feel that four years is not too long to wait for savings to pay for the equipment.*[14]

Given the circumstances of this firm, there are more than enough three-year pay-off investments for it to undertake, but once the three-year pay-offs are exhausted, the firm is prepared to move to four-year pay-off requirements. This is precisely the way one might proceed to apply our pay-off theory.

Following a similar line of thought is the experience of a Chicago electrical manufacturer who required a one-year pay-off on new investments.

Up to the present time it has been relatively simple to find equipment which will prove itself in under this one-year restriction. *But as time goes on and more and more cost-cutting equipment is installed, the task of meeting this requirement will become more difficult.* This condition is clearly appreciated and the management frankly states that when that point is reached, the limit will be extended from one year to eighteen months, and after that, to two years.[15]

In some instances it appears that businessmen compute the pay-off period *after* deducting depreciation, in accordance with the concept of the pay-off period discussed in section 2 above. This computation was used, for example, by the Warner and Swasey Company as reported by the assistant to the president of the company.[16] Warner and Swasey at

---

[14] *Manufacturing Industries*, XV, 28. Italics mine.

[15] *Ibid.*, p. 29. Italics mine.

[16] H. P. Baily, "Profitable Replacement in an 'Average Lot' Plant," *American Machinist*, LXXV (December 1931), 836–853.

that time produced mainly turret lathes and other special machinery in average lots of 15–20 pieces. When the product is continually changing, this tends to promote very short pay-off periods (as in the automobile industry). But in machine tools the effect does not appear to be quite so pronounced, since the tools used in producing machine tools are highly flexible. The product (say, turret lathes) may be continually modified, but it still takes about the same type of equipment to build it. Only certain jigs may be rendered completely obsolete by such product changes. Warner and Swasey followed the policy of purchasing new equipment that would show a net profit of 20 percent or better after depreciation. This implies a five-year pay-off. However, this policy was not rigidly followed since variations in net profit from 14.8 to 71.2 percent actually occurred in the examples given. Thus, the pay-off period on a sample of investments varied from one and one-half to seven years.

The superintendent of the manufacturing equipment department of the Westinghouse Electric Company reported in 1930 on a replacement program undertaken at their East Pittsburgh plant which brought earnings sufficient to justify the investment in four years. He writes:

My own observation is that four years should be about the length of time necessary to justify replacement of a machine, *especially since changes in machine tools and in the design of products are so rapid that it is necessary to pay for a machine in a shorter time than it was formerly.* I would not, however, leave the impression that all these tools will justify themselves within four years. Although certain of the tools which figured in the survey have paid for themselves in a much shorter time, there *are others which will realize no savings at all except on the maintenance cost.*[17]

The effect of product change in industries using metalworking equipment often manifests itself in a shorter pay-off requirement for specialized equipment than for more flexible general purpose equipment. For example, in one rotary air

[17] J. R. Weaver, "Determining the When and Why of Machine Tool Replacement," *American Machinist*, LXXII (June 1930), 1013. Italics mine.

tool company,[18] a two-year pay-off was required for tools, jigs, and fixtures, while a four-year period was required for machine tools.

A final statement recognizing the impact of technological change and liquidity considerations on the pay-off criterion is the following:

In making any improvements we are constantly confronted with the possibility of obsolescence of the equipment due either to the development of a new machine or to a change in the market demand. For this reason, under normal business conditions, it is felt in many industries that an improvement should pay for itself in three years or less. In severe depression, where the conserving of cash is paramount, companies are inclined to work on the basis that an improvement must pay for itself in one year.[19]

Occasionally the trade literature registers a vehement objection to the widespread prevalence of "short" pay-off criteria, and such behavior is branded as much too conservative.

The practice of expecting all new equipment to pay for itself out of savings in from one to three years, or at the very longest five years, does not have the effect of keeping plants up to date. In fact, it often has exactly the opposite effect.

. . . This practice started about twenty years ago in the automotive industry, but was not generally adopted by other industries until the beginning of 1932, when the extreme curtailment of all capital expenditures became almost imperative. Since then it seems to have become almost universal practice. . . . It is not unusual to find equipment 20–30 years old still in operation because new equipment will require from 7 to 9 years in which to pay for itself. This does not lead to low cost production.

. . . The most reasonable method of deciding on the length of time in which equipment must pay for itself is based on the probable length of time experience has shown it will be profitable to keep that particular equipment in operation. It is as unreasonable and uneconomical to expect equipment that will probably operate

[18] D. S. Linton, "Diversified Replacement in a Small Plant," *American Machinist*, LXXV (December 1931), 946–953.

[19] E. M. Richards, in *Factory Management and Maintenance*, XCL (December 1933), 499.

for 20 years to pay for itself in 3 years as it is to allow 5 years in which to pay for equipment that will probably operate economically for only 3 years.[20]

It would seem that the objective of business investment policy is not "keeping plants up to date," but rather profit maximization. The latter may require some, even considerable, operation with old equipment. It is not certain *a priori* that 20–30-year-old equipment should be replaced by new equipment with 7–9-year pay-offs. These assertions too often confuse cause and effect. The fact that a poor firm or industry is operating with old equipment does not mean that the entity in question owes its poverty to any failure to keep equipment up to date. I doubt that anyone could seriously prescribe new plants and new machines as a solution to the problems of a declining industry. New boxcars can hardly be expected to solve the problems of the American railroad industry. It is inevitable that some products and industries will decline and others grow in an enterprise economy. In declining industries, with short horizons, optimal policy may require a considerable stretching of "normal" equipment life. No matter how ancient a railroad's stock of boxcars, it is entirely possible that its best strategy is to replace none of them, using the capital to buy trailer flatcars instead. One entirely sensible way to describe such conditions is to say that replacement equipment exhibits excessively long pay-off periods. As we have seen from (9.3.6), if two classes of equipment have approximately the same lives, and both have pay-offs below the equilibrium pay-off given by (9.3.5), the one with the shorter pay-off is the more urgent. Actually, investment in both should be pushed until their pay-offs are equal to the equilibrium pay-off. In practice, however, the exact equilibrium pay-off may not be known, in which case there may be an intuitive trial-and-error searching for the equilibrium in which it is most certainly correct to suppose that investments with shorter cash-flow pay-offs should

[20] W. W. Gaylord, "Don't Expect All New Equipment to Pay Out in Three Years," *Factory Management and Maintenance*, XCVIII (February 1940), 52.

be given priority. According to our theory, exceptions occur only if the contemplated investments vary considerably in expected life. Thus, if equipment Number 1 has a life of about 5 years with a one-year pay-off, while equipment Number 2 has a life of 20 years with a four-year pay-off, it is possible that the second investment is more urgent than the first.

In recent years the most ardent protagonist of the anti-pay-off school has been George Terborgh and his associates. Terborgh maintains that the practice of requiring short pay-off periods "betokens a stodgy conservatism, willing to protect its aged mechanical assets by a Chinese wall. For the short pay-off requirement is a barrier of the most formidable character to the replacement of equipment." [21] It is doubtful that Terborgh has proved his case, though he is entirely aware that pay-off period criteria, properly defined, may be consistent with optimality.[22] In my view the "short" pay-off requirement of business practice is a natural consequence of the problem of business planning under uncertainty and within a framework of capital rationing. Investment in practice is not pushed to the margin at which the interest cost of obtaining an additional dollar of finance is equal to the net return on an additional dollar invested. In many cases this is not true because the firm cannot, at any price, obtain sufficient funds to push investment this far. In other cases, the firm, precisely because the expected return is *not certain*, tries to limit its risk by undertaking only those investment projects for which the expectation of gain is very high (that is, the pay-off expectation is very "short"). The amount of capital that a firm feels it can commit for fixed investment in any planning period depends vitally upon risk considerations as well as the contractual capital or interest cost of the funds. This decision, once made, provides a fund of money capital which must be allocated among competing projects. Properly used, the pay-off period can serve as a means of

---

[21] G. Terborgh, pp. 194–195. Also see chap. xii, *passim*, chap. xiv, and the appendix to chap. xii for Terborgh's views and analysis of the pay-off period.
[22] *Ibid.*, pp. 200, 216–220.

ranking projects in accordance with their urgency (profitability). It is correct for the firm to start at the top of this system of priorities and work downward until the available fund of capital is exhausted. If, at the margin, the resulting pay-off is "short" no one should protest.[23] Whether Terborghian or pay-off methods are used, if capital limitations prevent the execution of all profitable investments, the method should not allocate sums to less profitable projects, while more profitable projects go begging. In practice I doubt that it is known beforehand how much capital is "available." The amount of capital invested depends partly upon how attractive the projects appear. In this context it makes sense to start with the more profitable quick recovery investments, and feel outward to the less attractive projects until it is agreed among firm managers that sufficient risk has been incurred pending the generation of additional liquidity within the firm. There is always some probability that all, or an alarmingly large number, of the projects will fail. If no liquid balances have been held in reserve, or no quick pay-off investments undertaken, the firm is confronted with ruin.

[23] Of course the firm may be carrying risk avoidance much too far. For example, the decision to invest only so much money capital may imply a degree of risk aversion which is inconsistent with other aspects of firm behavior. Or, the firm may simply, through ignorance, be avoiding more risk than it would like to avoid. In such circumstances there is a case for protesting the firm's pay-off standards.

Multifacility Production in Theory and Practice

1. Introduction; Multiplant Firm Theory

In Chapters III, IV, and VI we have seen that the irreversibility associated with investment in durable equipment causes the typical firm to acquire more than a single production facility or "plant" in the process of growth and adaptation to changing conditions. Several years ago important extensions in the theory of the firm to multiplant production complexes were made by Patinkin [1] and Leontief.[2] These papers set forth necessary and sufficient conditions for the minimum cost allocation of a firm's total output

_____

[1] Don Patinkin, "Multiple-Plant Firms, Cartels, and Imperfect Competition," *Quarterly Journal of Economics*, LXI (February 1947), 173–205. See also his reply to W. Leontief in the same journal, "Note on the Allocation of Output," pp. 651–657.

[2] Wassily Leontief, "Multiple-Plant Firms: Comment," *Quarterly Journal of Economics*, LXI (August 1947), 650–651.

among any number of producing plants that make up the firm. The Patinkin-Leontief discussion seems to have been responsible for first introducing professional economists to a rigorous analysis of the multiplant firm problem.[3]

Later, Westfield [4] provided a valuable discussion of the problem of loading generating plants distributed along a transmission-line network as an example of the applied theory of multiplant firms. This problem has been a matter of operating concern to power-plant engineers for the past quarter-century, and the methods of solution developed by them have been most ingenious and practical.

Alexander and Spraos [5] have since applied the structure of the theory to shift working, that is, the problem of the minimum cost allocation of output between two work shifts within a plant. This latter contribution suggests that the theory has broader application than is implied by the term "multiple-plant." Actually, the theory has for many years found extensive application in the literature of engineering economics in the form of a general problem of loading parallel facilities or production units in the engineering process industries. For example, in electic utilities there is not only a network plant loading problem but also a problem of distributing plant load among turbine generators in the turbine room and the resulting steam load among boilers in the boiler room. Hence, the title of the present chapter deliberately refers to the "multi*facility* enterprise" as a means of directing attention to the more general character of the allocation problem posed in the multiplant firm literature.

[3] Patinkin, p. 173, cites Henry C. Simons, "Economics 201 Syllabus," University of Chicago Book Store (1944), as having provided the basis for his article. Simons, p. 54, states the equimarginal cost necessary conditions for optimal allocation of output among plants. This condition had, no doubt, been well known long before the Patinkin-Leontief development.

[4] Fred M. Westfield, "Marginal Analysis, Multi-Plant Firms and Business Practice: An Example," *Quarterly Journal of Economics*, LXIX (May 1955), 253–268.

[5] K. J. W. Alexander and John Spraos, "Shift Working: An Application of the Theory of the Firm," *Quarterly Journal of Economics*, LXX (November 1956), 603–612.

2. Conditions for Multifacility Allocation

Turning to the derivation of the Patinkin-Leontief conditions for a minimum cost allocation of output among multiple production facilities, we shall assume that, for whatever reason, the firm has invested in n distinct facilities for manufacturing a homogeneous product. The facilities might be plants, departments, or shifts in the same plant, or units of operating equipment within a given plant concerned with the production of the firm's final product, or an intermediate product. For example, the equipment might be chemical reactors, blast furnaces, boilers, turbine-generators, pumps, and so forth. In general, the facilities are dissimilar in that they exhibit different current account cost functions.

If y_i is the output of the ith facility, and $C_i(y_i)$ the current account cost [6] (for fixed investment in durable goods) of the ith facility, then total cost can be written

$$C = \sum_{i=1}^{n} C_i(y_i). \tag{10.2.1}$$

If the firm's total output requirement is y, then (10.2.1) is to be minimized subject to

$$y = \sum_{i=1}^{n} y_i. \tag{10.2.2}$$

Assuming for the moment that the optimal allocation requires some production in every facility, this is equivalent to

---

[6] Bearing in mind our analysis in Chapter VI of the derivation of such current account cost functions, $C_i(y_i)$ might have the following structure: Assume one current input, x_{1i}, and one capital "facility" input, X_{2i}^0. Current account total cost would then be

$$C_i = w_1 x_{1i} + w_2(x_{1i}, L_i) X_{2i}^0$$

where

$$w_2(x_{1i}, L_i) = r \sum_{k=0}^{\infty} e^{-rkL_i} \left\{ \int_0^{L_i} \phi_i(x_{1i}, kL_i t) e^{-rt} \, dt + W_{2i} \right\}$$

and $y_i = f_i(x_{1i}, X_{2i}^0),$

permitting C_i to be expressed in terms of y_i given X_{2i}^0. Note that with X_{2i}^0 fixed, cost is still variable with x_{1i} and replacement policy L_i, and hence with y_i.

minimizing

$$\psi = \sum_{i=1}^{n} C_i(y_i) - \lambda \left(\sum_{i=1}^{n} y_i - y \right), \qquad (10.2.3)$$

where the Lagrange multiplier λ is greater than zero. Necessary conditions for minimizing (10.2.3) are

$$C_1'(y_1) = C_2'(y_2) = \cdots = C_n'(y_n) = \lambda. \qquad (10.2.4)$$

The constraint (10.2.2), together with the conditions (10.2.4), determines the output of each facility as a function of total output requirements; thus,

$$y_i^0 = h_i(y), \qquad i = 1, 2, \cdots, n. \qquad (10.2.5)$$

The firm's minimum total cost function is then

$$C = \sum_{i=1}^{n} C_i[h_i(y)], \qquad (10.2.6)$$

assuming that a policy of optimal internal allocation of output is always followed. The Lagrange multiplier, λ, is the firm's marginal current account total cost under such a policy, that is, $\lambda = dC/dy$.

Sufficient conditions for a local relative minimum may be written by considering, in the usual way, the principal minors of the bordered Hessian of the cost function which assumes the especially simple form [7]

$$\begin{vmatrix} 0 & 1 & 1 & \cdots & 1 \\ 1 & C_1'' & 0 & \cdots & 0 \\ 1 & 0 & C_2'' & \cdots & 0 \\ \cdot & \cdot & \cdot & \cdot & \cdot \\ \cdot & \cdot & \cdot & \cdot & \cdot \\ \cdot & \cdot & \cdot & \cdot & \cdot \\ 1 & 0 & 0 & \cdots & C_n'' \end{vmatrix},$$

where $C_i'' = d^2 C_i/dy_i^2$. For a relative minimum the principal

[7] See Fred M. Westfield, pp. 256–257.

minors of this determinant must be negative, that is,

$$
\begin{vmatrix} 0 & 1 & 1 \\ 1 & C_1'' & 0 \\ 1 & 0 & C_2'' \end{vmatrix} < 0; \quad \begin{vmatrix} 0 & 1 & 1 & 1 \\ 1 & C_1'' & 0 & 0 \\ 1 & 0 & C_2'' & 0 \\ 1 & 0 & 0 & C_3'' \end{vmatrix} < 0; \text{ etc.,}
$$

or

$$
C_1'' + C_2'' > 0
$$

$$
\left(\frac{1}{C_1''} + \frac{1}{C_2''} + \frac{1}{C_3''} \right) C_1'' C_2'' C_3'' > 0
$$

$$
\vdots \tag{10.2.7}
$$

$$
\left(\frac{1}{C_1''} + \frac{1}{C_2''} + \cdots + \frac{1}{C_n''} \right) C_1'' C_2'' \cdots C_n'' > 0
$$

These conditions must be invariant under any renumbering of the facilities. In particular, the first condition in (10.2.7) must hold for any two of the n facilities. It follows that under an optimal allocation not more than one facility can be operated at declining marginal cost. It also follows that if one facility is operated at declining marginal cost, the rate of decline of marginal cost in that facility must be smaller in absolute value than the rate of rise of the marginal cost of every other facility, that is, if one facility is operated at declining marginal cost, say the first, then $- C_1'' < C_j''$ or $| C_1'' | < C_j''$ for all $j \neq 1$. However, this last result is not as strong as can be deduced from the remaining conditions in (10.2.7). The 2nd, 3rd, up to the nth of these conditions place successively stronger conditions on the rate of decline of the marginal cost of such a facility. If $C_1'' < 0$, then $C_1'' C_2'' \cdots C_n'' < 0$ in the last inequality of (10.2.7). Hence, if that inequality is to be satisfied we must have

$$
\frac{1}{C_1''} + \sum_{j=2}^{n} \frac{1}{C_j''} < 0, \quad \text{or} \quad | C_1'' | < \frac{1}{\displaystyle\sum_{j=2}^{n} \frac{1}{C_j''}},
$$

thus, if one facility is operated at declining marginal cost, the rate of decrease of its marginal cost curve must be smaller in absolute value than the rate of increase of the horizontally summed marginal cost curves of all other facilities. But the horizontally summed marginal cost curves of the other facilities constitute the optimal total marginal cost curve for those $n - 1$ facilities. Therefore, in giving an intuitive interpretation of this condition, think of replacing the marginal cost curves of the other $n - 1$ facilities with their Lagrange multiplier marginal cost curve, call it $\overline{C}'$, which presupposes an efficient internal allocation of output among those $n - 1$ facilities. Now consider facility Number 1 and the constructed composite facility. By a condition of the same form as that of the first in (10.2.7), we must have $C_1'' + \overline{C}'' > 0$ or $|C_1''| < \overline{C}''$.

This argument suggests an important computing procedure for adding previously idle facilities to a producing complex of dissimilar facilities producing the same product. We will assume that all operating facilities are producing at rising marginal cost. The rules are as follows: With an existing complex of n units, always impose conditions (10.2.2), (10.2.4), and (10.2.7) in distributing any given total output load among the units of the complex. Using these conditions, compute the Lagrange "efficiency price" function $\lambda(y)$. Now, if a previously idle facility with cost function $C_{n+1}(y_{n+1})$ is to be added to the existing complex, we impose the conditions

$$
\begin{aligned}
\lambda(y) &= C_{n+1}'(y_{n+1}) \\
y + y_{n+1} &= y_T \\
\lambda'(y) + C_{n+1}''(y_{n+1}) &> 0,
\end{aligned}
\tag{10.2.8}
$$

where y_T is the total output to be allocated between the old n-unit complex and the new facility. The first two conditions require equality between the marginal total cost of the composite producing facilities, and the idle facility to be added, at their respective output distributions, y and y_{n+1}. The last condition adds an $n + 1$th condition to the set in (10.2.7) of exactly similar form. This can be shown by differentiating

$C_1' = C_2' = \cdots = C_n' = \lambda$ to give

$$C_1'' \frac{dy_1}{dy} = C_2'' \frac{dy_2}{dy} = \cdots = C_n'' \frac{dy_n}{dy} = \lambda'.$$

But, $\sum_{i=1}^{n} dy_i/dy = 1$, from (10.2.2). Therefore,

$$\sum_{i=1}^{n} \frac{dy_i}{dy} = \sum_{i=1}^{n} \lambda' \frac{1}{C_i''} = 1, \quad \text{or} \quad \lambda' = 1 \Big/ \sum_{i=1}^{n} \frac{1}{C_i''},$$

and from $\lambda' + C_{n+1}'' > 0$ and the last condition in (10.2.7), we can write $(1/\lambda' + 1/C_{n+1}'')C_1''C_2''\cdots C_n''C_{n+1}'' > 0$. If none of the original n facilities are operated at declining marginal cost over the relevant range, and the marginal condition $\lambda = C_{n+1}'$ requires the added facility to be operated at declining marginal cost, then the rate of decline of the marginal cost of that facility must be smaller in absolute value than the rate of rise of the Lagrange marginal cost function.

Since the total cost function is the sum of the independent facility cost functions, a boundary solution allocation, with one or more facilities allowed to remain idle, is not only possible, but altogether likely. If the possibility of idle facilities is to be entertained, it becomes necessary to pay special heed to the implicit nonnegativity restrictions $y_i \geq 0$, $i = 1, 2, \cdots, n$ when minimizing (10.2.1) subject to (10.2.2). Necessary conditions, corresponding to (10.2.4), are now

$$C_i' \begin{cases} > \lambda, \; y_i = 0 \\ = \lambda, \; y_i \geq 0 \end{cases} \quad i = 1, 2, \cdots, n, \qquad (10.2.9)$$

that is, no facility is held idle if its marginal cost at zero output is smaller than the marginal cost of any facility operating at its optimal positive output, while all operating facilities produce at levels which equate their marginal costs.

The conditions (10.2.7) and (10.2.9) are necessary and sufficient for either boundary or local interior solutions to the problem of multiple facility allocation. Given a feasible solution satisfying these conditions, say $y_1^0, y_2^0, \cdots, y_n^0$, is that solution a minimum minimorum? It is, provided that the "total conditions,"

$$\sum_{i=1}^{n} C_i(y_i^0) \le \sum_{i=1}^{n} C_i(y_i) \qquad (10.2.10)$$

are satisfied, where $y_1, y_2, \cdots, y_n$ is any output set satisfying the feasibility requirement (10.2.2).

3. Graphical Analysis of Two Facilities

The above conditions, and the entire problem of output allocation among producing facilities, can be greatly illucidated by a graphical analysis of the two-facility case.

The two-facility problem is illustrated in terms of the familiar s-shaped total cost curves in Fig. 10–1. In this figure the objective is to determine an output allocation y_1^0, y_2^0 such that $C_1 + C_2$ is as small as possible, and $y = y_1^0 + y_2^0$.

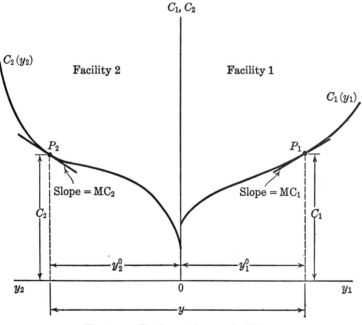

Fig. 10–1. Total costs for two facilities.

A necessary condition for minimum over-all cost is that the slope of $C_1(y_1)$ at P_1 be equal to the slope of $C_2(y_2)$ at P_2 for outputs that add up to y. This is the "slope" method to which reference is made so often in the early engineering literature.

The solution in terms of the usual U-shaped marginal cost curves is shown in Fig. 10–2. An optimal allocation of the

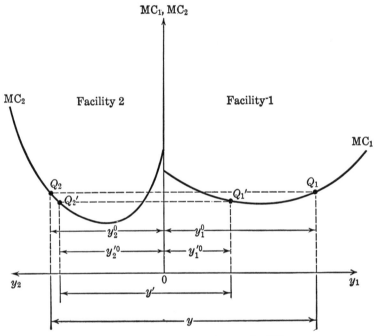

Fig. 10–2. Marginal costs for two facilities.

output y is at Q_1 and Q_2, where $MC_1 = MC_2$ and $y = y_1^0 + y_2^0$. We know from condition (10.2.7) above, that the solution may require one of the two facilities to be operated at declining marginal cost. It is not immediately clear from Fig. 10–1 that there exists output levels that require one facility to be operated at decreasing cost. However, from Fig. 10–2 it is evident that for low enough total output requirements, facility 1 must be operated at declining marginal cost. Thus, if total output requirements are y', facility 1 will be operated at Q_1', while facility 2 will be operated at Q_2'. Note that the slope of MC_1 at Q_1' is less in absolute value than the slope of MC_2 at Q_2', that is, $(dMC_1/dy_1) + (dMC_2/dy_2) > 0$, in satisfaction of condition (10.2.7). In general, a diagram such as Fig. 10–2 is not suitable for providing a graphical analysis of such allocation problems. Where the performance characteristics of the facilities present highly dissimilar marginal cost curves, it may be very difficult to determine those ranges of output in which (1) only one facility is used, (2) both facilities are used with one operated at falling marginal cost, and (3) both facilities are employed at rising marginal costs. In particular, changes in output requirements may necessitate abrupt and discontinuous shifts in the allocation of output between the two facilities, even though the total and marginal cost functions are smooth.

A far more valuable device for graphical organization of the problem, which permits a thorough exploration of optimal allocation strategy, is the isocost-isoproduct contour map. Starting with the general S-shaped total cost curves, we shall determine the allocation regions which are characterized by strictly convex or strictly concave isocost contours as well as the areas in which such curvature properties cannot be stated unambiguously.

(i) Consider first the shape of an isocost contour for values of y_1 and y_2 small enough so that the corresponding values of C_1 and C_2 are on the concave (from below) portion of the cost functions. Over such ranges of y_1 and y_2, the corresponding isocost contours are all convex to the origin.[8] A reduction in the output of either facility requires a more than proportional increase in the output of the other facility if total outlay is to remain unchanged. This is illustrated in

---

[8] Mathematically we have $C = C_1(y_1) + C_2(y_2)$, with

$$\frac{d^2 y_2}{dy_1^2} = -\frac{1}{C_2'}\left[C_1'' + \frac{(C_1')^2 C_2''}{(C_2')^2}\right] > 0$$

if both C_1'' and C_2'' are strictly negative.

Fig. 10–3. For outputs not exceeding the points of inflection, $\bar{y}_1$ in facility 1 and $\bar{y}_2$ in facility 2, the total cost curves are concave from below. The corresponding isocost contours, that is, for $y_1 \leq \bar{y}_1$ and $y_2 \leq \bar{y}_2$, are shown in region I on the diagram on the right.

(ii) At the other extreme consider the range of output

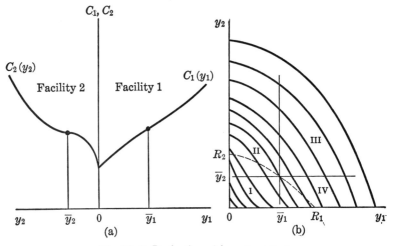

Fig. 10–3. Derivation of isocost contours.

$y_1 > \bar{y}_1$ and $y_2 > \bar{y}_2$, in which the total cost curves are strictly convex to the origin. Over this range the marginal cost curves are strictly rising, and the corresponding isocost contours are concave to the origin as shown in region III of Fig. 10–3(b).

(iii) For those output combinations in which one facility is operated at decreasing, and the other at increasing, marginal cost, the corresponding isocost contours may be either convex or concave. If we let R_1R_2 in regions II and IV be the locus of inflection points in the $y_1 - y_2$ space, then in the area above R_1R_2 the isocost contours are concave and below R_1R_2 the contours are convex.[9] In Fig. 10–3 we have assumed

[9] More specifically, R_1R_2 is defined by the condition,

$$\frac{d^2 y_2}{dy_1^2} = -\frac{1}{C_2{}'}\left[C_1{}'' + \frac{(C_1{}')^2 C_2{}''}{(C_2{}')^2}\right] = 0.$$

that marginal cost in facility 2 both falls and rises more rapidly than the corresponding decline and rise of marginal cost in facility 1.

Three representative isocost contour maps are illustrated in Figs. 10–4, 10–5, and 10–6, along with several possible interior and boundary solutions to the problem of least-cost output allocation. The constraint functions of the form $y_1 + y_2 = \bar{y}$ are shown in these figures as 45° lines. The map of Fig. 10–4 simply repeats the example used in the deriva-

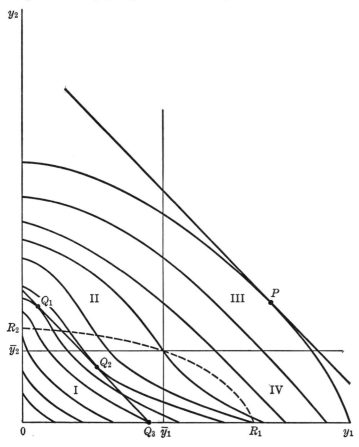

Fig. 10–4. An isocost contour map: I.

tion of Fig. 10–3. Figure 10–5 applies where the marginal cost curves for both facilities fall rapidly at first, and then rise slowly after the minimum points are reached, while Fig. 10–6 represents a case in which the marginal cost curves fall slowly, and then rise rapidly beyond the minimum marginal cost points.

In multiple-facility allocation problems we can probably assume that when required total output is large relative to the output at which the marginal cost in each facility starts to increase, each operating facility will normally produce at

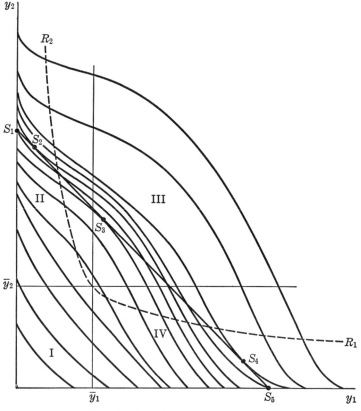

Fig. 10–5. An isocost contour map: II.

rising marginal cost, that is, for large enough output rates the minimum cost solution is expected to occur in region III of the isocost map. Such a typical interior solution is illustrated at P in Fig. 10–4. This solution is obtainable mathematically by application of the marginal cost conditions (10.2.4). A typical boundary solution, obtained by application of the inequality condition in (10.2.9), is shown at B in Fig. 10–6. From the graph it is clear that the slope of the isocost contour at B is smaller algebraically than the unit

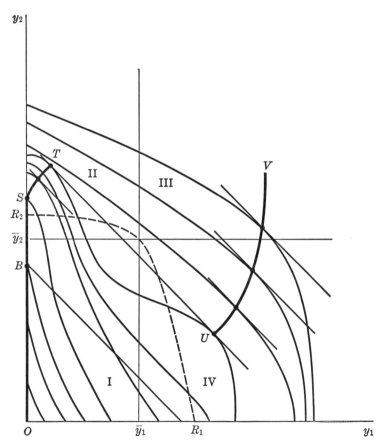

Fig. 10–6. The expansion path for two facilities.

slope of the constraint line or $- [MC_1(0)/MC_2(B)] < -1$.
Hence, $MC(0) > MC_2(B)$, which is the inequality condition
in (10.2.9). Note, in particular, that all solutions below R_1R_2
in Figs. 10–4, 10–5, and 10–6 must necessarily be boundary
solutions since there exist no interior solutions in these
regions that will satisfy the second order conditions (10.2.7).
All solutions in regions of strict isocost convexity must be
boundary solutions.

In Fig. 10–4, points Q_1 and Q_2 satisfy the marginal conditions, while Q_3 satisfies the boundary conditions in (10.2.9).
By application of the second-order conditions (10.2.7) we
can eliminate Q_2, leaving the two candidates for optimality,
Q_1 and Q_3. We can only choose between these alternative
optima, both satisfying the necessary conditions for a minimum, by application of the total conditions (10.2.10). In the
diagram, Q_3 lies on a lower isocost contour than Q_1 and is
therefore preferred to both Q_1 and Q_2. Neither of the two
points satisfying the usual marginal conditions provides a
minimum minimorum.

Another example of multiple solutions is illustrated in
Fig. 10–5. In this case a systematic application of the necessary conditions (10.2.9) yields no less than five solutions,
namely, S_1, S_2, S_3, S_4, and S_5. The marginal conditions generate the solutions S_2, S_3, and S_4, while the boundary conditions give S_1 and S_5. The interior solutions at S_2 and S_4 are
eliminated by the second-order local condition, (10.2.7). By
application of the total conditions to S_1, S_3, and S_5, it is seen
that S_3 lies on a lower isocost contour than either of the
boundary solutions S_1 or S_5.

These examples illustrate a general procedure for lo-
cating a minimum minimorum. First apply the necessary
marginal and boundary conditions. From the set of all such
solutions, reject all subsets that fail to satisfy the local
second-order conditions. Finally, reject all subsets of solutions that do not satisfy the total conditions. Any remaining
solutions (the optimum need not be unique) constitute minimum minimorum solutions.

The expansion path or scale line for a multifacility complex is the set of minimum minimorum solutions generated by considering all possible output loads on the system. The operating expansion path for the two-facility case illustrated in Fig. 10–6 is the heavy line $OSTUV$. The expansion path will always follow one of the two boundaries in region I. It is possible that there might exist several points at which it pays to shift production entirely from one facility to another. Abrupt discontinuities in the expansion path are entirely to be expected whenever one or more facilities present declining marginal cost curves over some range.

The analysis thus far has assumed implicitly that there are only two categories of cost associated with the operation of a facility — fixed costs (which do not affect the allocation) and continuously variable costs. However, in many such problems there exists another important category of cost, namely, avoidable "fixed" costs or costs which are discontinuously variable at zero output. In plants, certain costs such as minimum utility fees, certain maintenance outlays, equipment start-up costs, and administrative operating labor, may have to be incurred in fixed amount per unit time if any output is produced, but can be avoided by a complete shutdown. The engineer may refer to such costs as starting losses or "start-up" costs, emphasizing the incurring of such costs when equipment is activated instead of the avoidance of such costs when equipment is shut down. In the analysis to follow it will be assumed that start-up and shutdown costs are equal, though they need not be equal in practice.

If $V_i(y_i)$ represents the continuously variable cost of operating the ith facility, and a_i is the cost increment that can be avoided by idling the facility, then the total cost function becomes

$$C_i(y_i) = \begin{cases} V_i(y_i) + a_i, & y_i > 0 \\ V_i(0) = 0, & y_i = 0 \end{cases}. \qquad (10.3.1)$$

The isocost contours for the two-facility case are shown in Fig. 10–7. The effect of the avoidable costs a_1 and a_2 is to provide a discontinuity in the isocost contours at each axis.

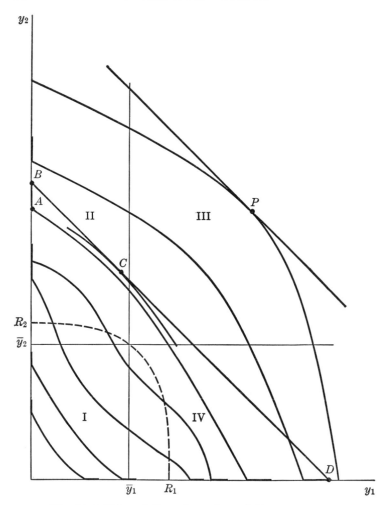

Fig. 10–7. Effect of discontinuously variable start-up costs.

For example, assume that facility 1 is idled and facility 2 is operated at the point B producing $y_2{}^B$ units of output at a cost $V_2(y_2{}^B) + a_2$. Now, if facility 1 is brought into production, a starting cost of a_1 must be incurred. If the operation is to remain on the same total cost contour as at B, the output of facility 2 must fall to a level $y_2{}^A$, such that $V_2(y_2{}^A)$ $+ a_1 + a_2 = V_2(y_2{}^B) + a_2$. This allows the starting cost a_1 to be financed by an equivalent reduction in the operating cost of facility 2.

One important consequence of introducing an avoidable cost element for each facility is that all isocost contours have infinite slopes at the vertical axis and zero slopes at the horizontal axis. Hence, regardless of the curvature or position of the isocost contours, the Kuhn-Tucker conditions will always provide a solution at each boundary. Indeed, in the general n-facility case every corner point of the constraining hyperplane is a candidate for optimality, and must be tested by the total conditions if a minimum minimorum is to be obtained. In terms of Fig. 10–7, if the constraint line is BD, the Kuhn-Tucker conditions provide the two corner solutions B and D, and the interior solution C. The lowest cost solution is, of course, B. At some larger output requirement both facilities may be necessary to produce at minimum cost, as represented by the solution at P. It is evident from the diagram that minimum minimorum corner solutions are more likely when account is taken of avoidable costs, even in regions of strict concavity of isocost. Thus, in Fig. 10–8, the expansion path $OSTUP$ follows the vertical axis well into the region of strict concavity before it becomes optimal to activate facility 1. Marginal cost in facility 2 must be rising rather sharply before it pays to incur the starting costs of facility 1 and operate both facilities simultaneously.

4. Optimal Expansion and Contraction of Facilities

The analysis so far has been concerned with the allocation of a given output among a number of parallel facilities in which investment has already taken place. The problem has therefore been concerned exclusively with short-run decisions, and the minimization of short-run variable costs (including discontinuous variable, or avoidable, costs). We consider now the problem of adding or investing in new facilities and the related problem of idling or discarding old facilities in response to once-for-all increases in demand. It

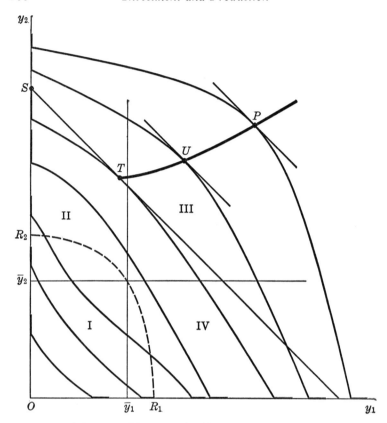

Fig. 10–8. The expansion line with start-up costs.

will be assumed that each facility: (1) is of infinite physical durability, (2) does not experience technological obsolescence, (3) requires no age variable operating outlays, and (4) is subject to increasing returns to scale and therefore declining "long-run" marginal cost. For the case defined by these assumptions it was shown in our discussion of the firm's output equilibrium in Chapter III, section 3, that an increase in output requirements may induce the firm to invest in a new parallel facility. We are now in a position to illustrate graphically the firm's response to such an increase in output requirements. The analysis will include the possibility of idling, abandoning, or placing in "standby" reserve one or more old facilities, as well as adding a new facility, in response to increases in demand. In such circumstances discards or "replacements" are made entirely because of capacity obsolescence generated by growth in demand. That is, the firm may install a small facility at a time when demand is low, which, due to increasing returns, it pays to discard at some later date as a consequence of increases in demand. Hence, obsolescence may arise entirely out of the internal process of adaptation to growth in demand, and need not be due entirely to external improvements in technology.

We can distinguish three routes by which an increase in demand can be satisfied: (1) the new required output can be produced by distributing it optimally among the existing facilities, (2) a new facility can be added and the output distributed between it and the existing facilities with optimal investment in the new facility being simultaneously determined, or (3) a new facility can be added and one or more existing facilities simultaneously discarded or placed in "standby" reserve. We assume zero avoidable fixed cost. Proceeding formally, assume that we have initially n producing facilities, and that each has a monotone increasing short-run marginal cost function. If initial output requirements are y, and none of the n facilities are idle, then the conditions for optimal allocation are $C_i'(y_i) = \lambda$, $i = 1, 2, \cdots, n$, where $y = \sum_{i=1}^{n} y_i$, $y_i > 0$. Now let there be an unanticipated permanent increase in output requirements from y to $\hat{y}$. Suppose further that the "long-run" (all inputs variable) total cost function for a new facility, the $n + 1$th, is $C_{n+1}(y_{n+1})$. This function assumes minimum cost choice of technique at every output level. Since increasing returns are assumed, we have $C_{n+1}''(y_{n+1}) < 0$ at all outputs. If, for all positive combinations $y_1, \cdots, y_n, y_{n+1}$ satisfying $\hat{y} = \sum_{i=1}^{n+1} y_i$, we have $C_i'(y_i) = \lambda < C'_{n+1}(y_{n+1})$, then a new facility will not be added and the optimal allocation is given by $C_i'(y_i) = \lambda \leq C_{n+1}'(0)$, $i = 1, 2, \cdots, n$, and $\hat{y} = \sum_{i=1}^{n} y_i$. If there is at least one positive combination $y_1, \cdots, y_n, y_{n+1}$ satisfying $C_i'(y_i) = \lambda$, for $i = 1, 2, \cdots, n, n + 1$, and $\hat{y} = \sum_{i=1}^{n+1} y_i$, with $\lambda'(\hat{y} - y_{n+1}) + C_{n+1}''(y_{n+1}) > 0$, and if this combination also satisfies the total conditions, then a new facility will be added at the capacity and operating level implied by these conditions. Suppose, finally, that there is at least one nonnegative combination of the y_i satisfying $C_{k+1}'(y_{k+1}) = \cdots = C_n'(y_n) = C_{n+1}'(y_{n+1}) = \lambda \leq [C_1'(0), \cdots, C_k'(0)]$, $\hat{y} = \sum_{i=k+1}^{n+1} y_i$, and the second-order conditions. It follows that the new facility will be added and the first k of the old facilities will be discarded if such a solution is a minimum minimorum.

These alternative responses are illustrated diagrammatically for the case of a single existing facility in Fig. 10–9. The isocost contours are drawn on the assumption that facility 1 is an existing installation with a U-shaped short-run marginal cost function, while facility 2 is a potential new installation with a monotone decreasing long-run marginal cost function. If, initially, output requirements are y^1, then facility 1 is operated at the level indicated by the point P. If output requirements rise to y^2, the optimal response is to operate the existing facility at the new required output rate represented by Q. Suppose, however, that the initial output requirement is y^2, and production takes place at Q. Now let demand rise stepwise from y^2 to y^3. The rational response is to install a new facility of the optimum size for producing $y_2{}^S$ units per year, allocating $y_1{}^S$ units of production to the old facility and $y_2{}^S$ units to the new installation. The annual savings obtained by making the new installation over the alternative of producing the requirements y^3 entirely in the old facility (at S'), is the difference between total cost at S' and the total cost associated with S, that is, $C(S') - C(S)$. As a third alternative, suppose demand rises from y^2 to y^6. In this case the increase in output is so large that it pays to install a new facility, and simultaneously discard (or place in "standby") the existing facility. The effect of increasing returns to scale in lowering production costs in a new facility is such as to render the existing facility entirely obsolete. In such circumstances we

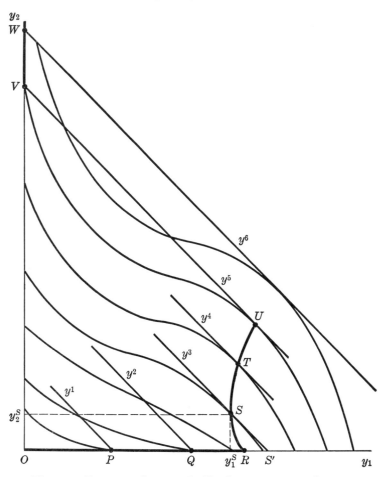

Fig. 10–9. Investment in a new facility in response to an increase in output.

might say that replacement is induced by *scale obsolescence,* a phenomenon due entirely to changes in demand rather than technological improvement in the performance of the capital good itself.

The line $RUVW$ is an *investment expansion* line, and is not to be confused with the operating expansion line of Fig. 10–6.

The movements along the expansion line of Fig. 10–6 are reversible, while a movement along $RUVW$ is not reversible, and only a single movement from a point on OR to one on $RUVW$ is possible. Such a movement implies investment in a new facility, and assumes a once-for-all increase in output. Once such an adjustment has been made, the diagram of Fig. 10–9 can no longer be employed to describe the firm's production responses.

These expansion or contraction responses of the multi-facility firm can be alternatively, and very instructively, exhibited in terms of their impact upon resource consumption and utilization by returning to the constrained minimum cost analysis of Chapter III, section 3. The two-factor production function for a firm operating with a single installed facility of capacity $X_2{}^0$ is

$$y = f^1(x_1{}^1,\ X_2{}^0) + f^2(x_1{}^2,\ X'_2),$$

where f^1 is the production function for the installed facility, f^2 is the (in general, different) production function for a potential new facility, $x_1{}^1$ is the current input to the installed facility, X_2' is the variable potential capacity of an additional facility, and $x_1{}^2$ is the current input to such a facility. Note that we have generalized slightly the analysis of Chapter III by permitting different production functions for old and new facilities. An isoproduct contour map for the output levels y^1, y^2, y^3, relating total current input consumption, $x_1 = x_1{}^1 + x_1{}^2$ and the quantity of additional capital installed, is shown in Fig. 10–10.[10] The isocost contours C_1, C_2, and C_3 are drawn on the assumption that the prices w_1 and w_2 of current and capital inputs are constant. At outputs y^1 and y^2, it does not pay to install an additional facility.[11] At an output y^3 a minimum cost production-investment policy requires an additional facility of capacity X_2', such that $w_1/w_2 = f_1{}^1(x_1{}^1, X_2{}^0)/f_2{}^2(x_1{}^2, X_2') = f_1{}^2(x_1{}^2, X_2')/f_2{}^2(x_1{}^2, X_2')$.

---

[10] These contours are defined by the above production function and the condition $f_1{}^1(x_1{}^1, X_2{}^0) = f_1{}^2(x_1{}^2, X_2')$ for optimal allocation of the current input between two facilities.

[11] Refer to the conditions (3.3.17) in Chapter III.

Hence, an increase in output requirements from y^1 to y^2 causes no increase in investment. The firm moves from P to Q by increasing its consumption of current input only. An increase in output from y^2 to y^3 carries the firm's optimal

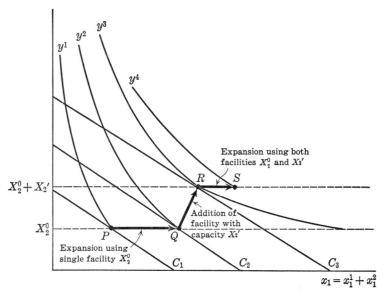

Fig. 10–10. Expansion and the addition of new facilities.

input-output technique beyond the net investment threshold. Investment is increased from X_2^0 to $X_2^0 + X_2'$ by the addition of a new facility, and the new input-output equilibrium is at R. The firm's production function is now

$$y = f^1(x_1^1,X_2^0) + f^2(x_1^2,X_2') + f^3(x_1^3,X_2''),$$

where X_2^0 and X_2' are fixed at historically optimal long-run levels, and X_2'' is the variable potential quantity of additional capital that can be installed. This function and the conditions for best allocation of input number 1 among three facilities defines an isoproduct contour for each output level, such as that for y^4 in Fig. 10–10. Again, expansion takes place along a horizontal line, namely, RS, until a further expansion in investment is required for optimality. The path *PQRS* represents a potential expansion path in the firm's input space.

The process of contraction in a firm with two installed facilities of capacities X_2^0 and X_2', and the resulting impact on the consumption and utilization of current and capital inputs, is demonstrated in Fig. 10–11. We begin with the equilibrium at P in Fig. 10–11(a), and at P' in Fig. 10–11(b). At the point P' we have tangency between an isoinput line, L_1, and the isoproduct curve for y^5 units of output. At this point the minimal current input (also minimal cost) allocation is x_1^{1P} units consumed in facility X_2^0 and x_1^{2P} units consumed in facility X_2'. Since L_1 is a 45°-line it follows that the total consumption of current input at P' is given by the point P'' where L_1 strikes the horizontal axis, i.e., $x_1^P = x_1^{1P} + x_1^{2P}$. If output declines from y^5 to y^4, the new input equilibrium moves to Q' where less of the current input is consumed in each facility. If output continues to fall the firm contracts along the path $P'S'$. At S in Fig. 10–11(a) and S' in Fig. 10–11(b), corresponding to output y^2, facility X_2' is placed in standby, or, in the event that output is expected to remain permanently at y^2 or lower, the surplus capacity is sold or discarded. The withdrawal of X_2' units of capital from production is illustrated by the movement from S to T in Fig. 10–11(a). Any further contraction in output, say to y^1, involves a shift along the paths TU and $T'U'$ in the two diagrams.

5. Applications

Whatever may be the proper relationship between theory and fact in scientific inquiry, it is worth noting that the allocation conditions in the cited economic literature on multiplant firm theory were preceded by at least a quarter-century in the engineering literature. This engineering literature produced papers which (a) stated and proved the marginal conditions for the allocation of output among competing parallel production facilities, (b) stated one important sufficient con-

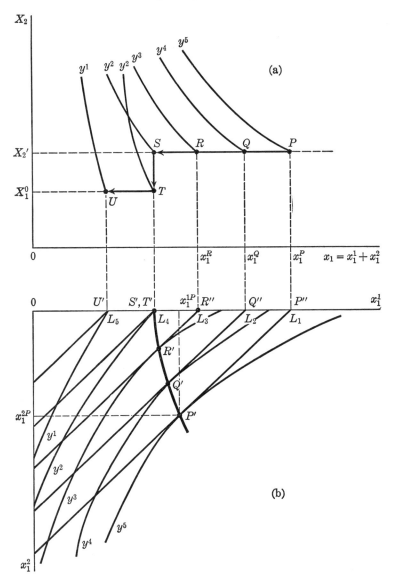

Fig. 10–11. *The contraction process with two facilities.*

dition for a best allocation (monotone increasing marginal cost functions were usually assumed), (c) applied the decision rules to several different types of load distribution problems, and (d) recognized that the allocation rules could be generalized and had application throughout a wide class of engineering decision problems. Consequently, the Patinkin-Leontief theory not only stood on solid empirical ground by 1947; the practitioners themselves had recognized that the solution to these problems could be usefully generalized. For these important reasons the Patinkin-Leontief theory deserves a major role in the economic theory of cost and production.

In many of the multifacility allocation problems confronting the engineer or production manager, each facility has only one primary variable input — for example, fuel, steam, electricity, etc. Therefore total input minimization becomes a surrogate for total cost minimization over parallel equipment complexes. As might be expected from the case orientation of the engineer, he has invariably used the surrogate rather than the more general cost minimization criterion of the economist. The first clear statement of the marginal conditions for an optimal allocation in such problems seems to have been presented in both verbal and graphical form in an article written in 1923 by two engineers concerned with boiler loading:

Whatever the output of each boiler may be, let a tangent be drawn to its performance curve at the point whose abscissa represents the output. The corresponding ordinates then express, to their scale, the inputs to the boilers; the sum of the ordinates the combined input, and the sum of the abscissas the combined output.

The condition which makes the combined input a minimum for a given combined output is that the tangents to the two curves at the respective output points be parallel; that is, that the curves have equal slopes. . . . Under any other condition the input to the boiler whose curve has the greater slope is decreased more by a slight decrease in output than that of the other is increased by the compensating increase in output; so that the result is a net decrease in combined input. Additional progress in the same direction will result in further improvement until the distribution giving equal slopes is reached.[12]

The above authors show no awareness of the applicability of their analysis to a general problem of loading multiunit complexes. It was not until 1929 that an English engineer, Thornton,[13] generalized the analytical conditions verbalized above, pointing out that the problem has general application to fans, turbines, pumps, economizers, and many other types of equipment.[14]

The specific application of multifacility firm theory to the allocation of electrical system loads among generating plants is known to economists through Westfield's excellent paper.[15] The standard character of this application is evidenced by the fact that many years ago engineers were led to the

[12] N. E. Funk and F. C. Ralston, "Boiler-Plant Economics," *American Society of Mechanical Engineers Transactions*, XLV (1923), 633. I do not know, nor am I particularly concerned to determine, whether this is the first statement of the marginal conditions for output allocation in the engineering literature. I suspect it is close.

[13] Brian Thornton, "A Method of Loading Boilers for Maximum Fuel Economy," *Engineering*, CXXVIII (December 1929), 796–797.

[14] Thornton's derivation (note 13 above, p. 796) is as follows: Letting x_1 and x_2 be the outputs of two boilers, and P be the total required output, he writes

$$x_1 + x_2 = P.$$

If y_1 and y_2 are the inputs to the boilers, then the performance characteristics of the boilers determine (production) functions

$$y_1 = f_1(x_1)$$
$$y_2 = f_2(x_2).$$

Hence, if I is total input, the problem is to minimize

$$I = y_1 + y_2 = f_1(x_1) + f_2(x_2).$$

He then writes

$$\frac{dI}{dx} = \frac{df_1(x_1)}{dx} + \frac{df_2(P - x_1)}{dx} = 0$$

and

$$f_1'(x_1) = f_2'(P - x_1),$$

declaring that the last statement gives the general analytical conditions for minimum total input.

[15] Westfield, "Marginal Analysis . . .," note 4 above.

development of a "station-loading slide rule." [16] This device was developed at the Consolidated Edison Company, and, as reported by Steinberg and Smith,

> has clearly demonstrated its utility over a period of years. Its use has permitted improvement in production economy through a closer following of changing conditions; it has provided a faster and simpler means of loading the individual stations by eliminating the need of preparing loading schedules in advance of requirements; it has also been very useful in connection with engineering studies to determine the relative economies that might be expected from new installations when the final answer must be predicated upon the generation expected of the equipment.[17]

The construction and use of station-loading slide rules is discussed in the indicated references and will not be repeated here.

The earliest application of multifacility production theory, as we have indicated, is to boiler-loading with the application to turbine-generators running a close second. These applications are discussed in detail by Steinberg and Smith, including problems of adjusting test input-output curves to reflect operating conditions, problems of discontinuities, and the determination of maximum and minimum equipment operating levels.[18, 19]

[16] H. H. Johnson and M. S. Umbenhauer, "Station Loading Slide Rule," *Power*, LXXXII (November 1938), 62–64. Also by the same authors, "An Effective Loading Device," *Edison Electric Institute Bulletin*, VII (August 1939), 385–389.

[17] Max J. Steinberg and Theodore H. Smith, *Economy Loading of Power Plants and Electric Systems* (New York: John Wiley, 1943), pp. 189–190.

[18] See Steinberg and Smith, chaps. ii and iii, for a discussion of the problem of load division in the boiler and turbine rooms.

[19] In our development of multifacility allocation theory, I have not imposed rigid minimum and maximum capacity limits because I do not believe that the engineers have made an adequate case for the hypothesis of such fixed technical limits. For example, the "maximum steaming rate" of a boiler is an economic and not primarily a technical phenomenon, since the factors usually mentioned that determine the maximum have direct cost implications. Thus, Steinberg and Smith (p. 37) suggest that operating a boiler beyond its "maximum" steaming rate "generally results in excessive maintenance costs and reduces the availability of the boiler for service." Obviously, under such circumstances, maximum capacity limits do not represent fundamental technical constraints on the decision problem, except as crude approximations to boiler maintenance behavior functions.

Steinberg and Smith distinguish three methods of loading power-plant boilers that have been used by engineers; the equal rating method; the equal efficiency method; and the incremental rate method (marginal cost or marginal productivity method). The equal rating method used in the early days of the power industry was probably equivalent to marginal cost loading since, "it was common practice to install a large number of relatively small boilers of uniform design and performance characteristics. For this type of installation the problem of load division did not ordinarily exist, since all the boilers could be uniformly loaded for maximum overall efficiency." [20] As boiler technology changed, however, and the industry grew, power plants developed a broad distribution of different types and sizes of boilers. The practice of loading the boilers in proportion to the manufacturer's rating in boiler horsepower, then came into use. It was recognized that this practice was not optimal, as no allowance was being made for differences in boiler efficiency. It was evident to the practitioners that the more efficient boilers should carry a larger proportion of the load. Hence there arose the practice of loading boilers so that they operated at outputs corresponding to equal efficiencies, or equal *average* productivities. Then came the theory of "incremental loading" in a series of papers in the 1920's and 1930's.[21] Steinberg and Smith [22] compare the three methods of boiler loading and show that the incremental rate method provides the maximum possible combined efficiency curve for a group of dissimilar boilers.

The problem of load division in the turbine room is more difficult than that in the boiler room.[23] Typically, there is a wider choice respecting the number of units to be operated and the sequence in which such units are to be added or idled. Also, turbine units often vary as to type and size more than do boiler units. Finally, turbines are often multivalved

---

[20] Steinberg and Smith, p. 27.
[21] See the Steinberg and Smith, bibliography, pp. 199–200.
[22] Steinberg and Smith, pp. 27–32.
[23] *Ibid.*, p. 68.

units designed for directing the steam to lower stages by by-passing some of the turbine blades. The result is a discontinuity in the input-output curves at the output levels at which an additional valve is opened. Engineers usually handle such discontinuities by smoothing, that is, they work with the "average incremental rate" or average marginal productivity curve.[24]

In the case of turbine-generators there are several nonoptimal methods of loading such units which have been, and continue to be, employed in practice.

(1) The units are sequentially loaded to "capacity" in increasing order of their efficiencies (this method assumes the efficiency curves do not intersect).

(2) The units are sequentially loaded to their most efficient loads, that is, their highest average productivities, and then to capacity in the same order.

(3) The units are loaded in proportion to the manufacturer's "rated capacity."

(4) The units are loaded in proportion to their most efficient load.

(5) The units are loaded optimally at equal incremental rates.

Steinberg and Smith [25] compare these methods using an illustrative three-unit turbine group showing that no method provides a lower combined average productivity curve than the incremental rate method.

We have attempted to show that there exists some empirical foundation for the theory of multifacility production. However, a study of the engineering literature on such applied production problems reveals that in many instances the allocation problem involves more than a single stage of production, with multiple parallel producing units employed at each stage. The steam generation of electricity is a case in point. This literature, therefore, provides the empirical basis for an important generalization of the theory of multifacility production. To these considerations we now turn.

[24] *Ibid.*, pp. 79–89.   [25] *Ibid.*, pp. 89–97.

6. Multistage-Multifacility Production

Since the general problem of multistage-multifacility production arises so clearly in the literature of power-plant economics,[26] we shall continue to use the power-plant example to illustrate the general theory. As indicated in the previous section, engineers consider a power plant to be composed of two primary producing stages. Stage I is composed of a boiler process which converts the chemical energy of fuel into heat energy in the form of steam. This process is performed in the boiler room by firing several boiler units simultaneously. The steam output of the several boiler units in the boiler room is then fed through a steam header to Stage II of the process. Stage II consists of a turbine-generator process which converts heat energy into mechanical energy and thence into electrical energy.[27] The turbine room is typically composed of several turbine-generator units whose combined output is fed directly into the transmission line serving the plant and its customers. Assuming a system with two boilers and two turbine-generators, the process can be represented by the flow diagram of Fig. 10–12. For any given final output

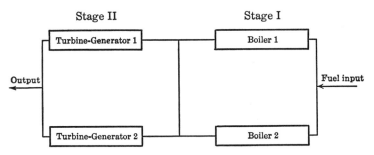

Fig. 10–12. A two-stage, two-facility allocation problem.

[26] For example, see Steinberg and Smith, chaps. ii, iii, iv, and *passim*. This literature does not state the general problem, though it is certainly implied to the careful reader.

[27] Compare our previous discussion of power plant production in sec. 5, Chapter II, in which we considered the turbine and generator processes separately. For short-run analysis these processes are combined by the engineer since there is a turbine associated with each generator and the two form a single producing unit.

requirements, the network flow problem is to allocate this output between the two turbine-generator units of Stage II, and the resulting total steam requirements of Stage II between the two boiler units of Stage I. The solution provided in the engineering literature involves treating the two stages as independent multifacility allocation problems.[28] In general, this solution is not correct, but, as will be demonstrated shortly, it is correct for the special case in which the output of Stage I is the only variable input to the units of Stage II. In general, any stage of a multistage process could use many variable inputs in addition to the output of the previous stage, as in the case of most manufactured items that must pass through various levels of fabrication and assembly in creating the final product.

We shall present the analysis by considering the simple two-stage four-unit process shown in Fig. 10–13(a), placing primary emphasis on conveying an intuitive grasp of the solution. In Fig. 10–13(a), U_{11} and U_{12} are the two producing

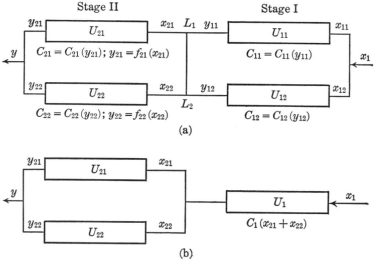

Fig. 10–13. *Reduction of two facilities to their single-facility equivalent.*

[28] Steinberg and Smith, pp. 108–111.

units in Stage I, while U_{21} and U_{22} are the two units in Stage II. The total cost functions in Stage I are $C_{11}(y_{11})$ and $C_{12}(y_{12})$ respectively, and represent the cost of all inputs to the production units U_{11} and U_{12}. In Stage II the cost functions are $C_{21}(y_{21})$ and $C_{22}(y_{22})$. Note carefully that these latter cost functions refer to those variable costs of operating the units of Stage II that are associated with inputs other than x_{21} and x_{22}, since the cost of these intermediate inputs is independently expressed in $C_{11}(y_{11})$ and $C_{12}(y_{12})$. Independently of $C_{21}(y_{21})$ and $C_{22}(y_{22})$, we also require knowledge of the final output-intermediate output transformation functions, $y_{21} = f_{21}(x_{21})$ and $y_{22} = f_{22}(x_{22})$ associated with U_{21} and U_{22}. The total cost function is therefore

$$C = C_{21}(y_{21}) + C_{22}(y_{22}) + C_{11}(y_{11}) + C_{12}(y_{12}) \qquad (10.6.1)$$
$$= C_{21}[f_{21}(x_{21})] + C_{22}[f_{22}(x_{22})] + C_{11}(y_{11}) + C_{12}(y_{12}),$$

which is to be minimized subject to the conservation conditions

$$x_{21} + x_{22} - y_{11} - y_{12} = 0, \qquad (10.6.2)$$

and

$$y - f_{21}(x_{21}) - f_{22}(x_{22}) = 0, \qquad (10.6.3)$$

where y is total final output requirements.

The analysis can be simplified conveniently if we first convert this problem into an equivalent smaller problem by replacing Stage I with a single production unit representing the composite equivalent of the parallel units U_{11} and U_{12}. By considering Stage I as a single stage multifacility production problem, we can define the composite cost function $C_1(x_{21} + x_{22})$ which, for any given total Stage I load $x_{21} + x_{22}$, presupposes a minimum cost allocation of output between U_{11} and U_{12}. $C_1(x_{21} + x_{22})$ is defined by the condition $C_{1j}' \geq \lambda_1, j = 1, 2$, where the given output load $= (x_{21} + x_{22}) = y_{11} + y_{12}$. This is equivalent to replacing the parallel units of Stage I with a single producing unit, U_1, having the total cost function $C_1(x_{21} + x_{22})$. The equivalent system is shown in Fig. 10–13(b). Note that for $C_{11}' = C_{12}' = \lambda_1$, we have

$\lambda_1 = C_1'$ and $\lambda_1' = C_1''$, that is, the composite marginal cost function is the first-stage Lagrange multiplier function.

Our problem now is to minimize

$$C = C_{21}[f_{21}(x_{21})] + C_{22}[f_{22}(x_{22})] + C_1(x_{21} + x_{22}) \quad (10.6.4)$$

subject to

$$y - f_{21}(x_{21}) - f_{22}(x_{22}) = 0. \quad (10.6.5)$$

The necessary conditions for such a constrained minimum can be written

$$C_{21}' + \lambda_1/f_{21}' \geq \lambda_2, \quad C_{22}' + \lambda_1/f_{22}' \geq \lambda_2 \quad (10.6.6)$$

where λ_2 is the marginal cost of final output. Since $C_{11}' \geq \lambda_1$ and $C_{12}' \geq \lambda_1$, these conditions are really four in number when applied to the complete system of Fig. 10–13(a). If the solution is an interior one, then (10.6.6) becomes $C_{21}' + \lambda_1/f_{21}' = C_{22}' + \lambda_1/f_{22}' = \lambda_2$, that is, the marginal cost of producing a unit of final product at either of the output terminals U_{21} or U_{22} must be equal. λ_1 is the internal Lagrange multiplier valuation placed upon the intermediate output. Therefore, λ_1/f_{21}' is the marginal cost of intermediate output in the production of a unit of final output with U_{21}, while C_{21}' is the marginal cost of other inputs in producing such a unit. Since λ_1 depends upon how the first-stage allocation problem is solved, the second-stage allocation cannot be exercised independently of the first-stage allocation.

Assuming both units of each stage are operated at positive outputs, a sufficient condition for a local interior solution is that

$$\begin{vmatrix} 0 & f_{21}' & f_{22}' \\ f_{21}' & \widehat{C}_{21}'' + \lambda_1' - \lambda_2 f_{21}'' & \lambda_1' \\ f_{22}' & \lambda_1' & \widehat{C}_{22}'' + \lambda_1' - \lambda_2 f_{22}'' \end{vmatrix} < 0,$$

or

$$(f_{21}')^2(\widehat{C}_{22}'' + \lambda_1' - \lambda_2 f_{22}'')$$
$$+ (f_{22}')^2(\widehat{C}_{21}'' + \lambda_1' - \lambda_2 f_{21}'') > 2 f_{21}' f_{22}' \lambda_1', \quad (10.6.7)$$

where

$$\left.\begin{array}{l} \hat{C}_{21}'' = \dfrac{d^2 C_{21}}{dx_{21}{}^2} = C_{21}'f_{21}'' + C_{21}''(f_{21}')^2 \\[2mm] \hat{C}_{22}'' = \dfrac{d^2 C_{22}}{dx_{22}{}^2} = C_{22}'f_{22}'' + C_{22}'(f_{22}')^2. \end{array}\right\} \quad (10.6.8)$$

Also, from our definition of $C_1(x_{21} + x_{22})$ as the composite minimum total cost function for Stage I, we have assumed implicitly the sufficient conditions for a local interior solution to the Stage I process considered in isolation, namely,

$$\left(\frac{1}{C_{11}''} + \frac{1}{C_{12}''}\right) C_{11}'' C_{12}'' > 0, \quad (10.6.9)$$

from (10.2.7). In order to interpret the condition (10.6.7) we define $\overline{C}_{11}''$ as the rate of change of the marginal cost of producing a unit of final output via the route U_1 and U_{21}, and $\overline{C}_{12}''$ as the rate of change of the marginal cost of producing final output via U_1 and U_{22}. Hence,

$$\left.\begin{array}{l} \overline{C}_{11}'' = \dfrac{d}{dy_{21}}\left(C_{21}' + \dfrac{\lambda_1}{f_{21}'}\right) = C_{21}'' + \dfrac{\lambda_1'}{(f_{21}')^2} - \dfrac{\lambda_1 f_{21}''}{(f_{21}')^3} \\[3mm] \overline{C}_{12}'' = \dfrac{d}{dy_{22}}\left(C_{22}' + \dfrac{\lambda_1}{f_{22}'}\right) = C_{22}'' + \dfrac{\lambda_1'}{(f_{22}')^2} - \dfrac{\lambda_1 f_{22}''}{(f_{22}')^3}. \end{array}\right\} \quad (10.6.10)$$

But from (10.6.6) (assuming the equality holds), (10.6.8), and (10.6.10) we can write

$$\left.\begin{array}{l} \hat{C}_{21}'' + \lambda_1' - \lambda_2 f_{21}'' = C_{21}''(f_{21}')^2 + \lambda_1' - \dfrac{\lambda_1 f_{21}''}{f_{21}'} \\[2mm] \qquad\qquad = (f_{21}')^2 \overline{C}_{11}'', \\[3mm] \hat{C}_{22}'' + \lambda_1' - \lambda_2 f_{22}'' = C_{22}''(f_{22}')^2 + \lambda_1' - \dfrac{\lambda_1 f_{22}''}{f_{22}'} \\[2mm] \qquad\qquad = (f_{22}')^2 \overline{C}_{12}''. \end{array}\right\} \quad (10.6.11)$$

Therefore, the sufficient condition (10.6.7) becomes

$$\overline{C}_{11}'' + \overline{C}_{21}'' > \frac{2\lambda_1'}{f_{21}'f_{22}'} > 0. \quad (10.6.12)$$

This is the same form as the first condition in (10.2.7) for a single-stage multifacility process, and it is seen that the conditions applying to each unit of a single-stage process apply now to each complete route by which a unit of final output can be produced in the two-stage process. In the present case there are two such "routes"; one is to produce an increment of final output using unit U_{21} and distributing the resulting load on Stage I optimally between U_{11} and U_{12}; the other is to produce such an increment with unit U_{22}, and distribute the consequent Stage I load optimally between U_{11} and U_{12}. Specifically our conditions state that not more than one of these two transformation routes, U_1—U_{21} and U_1—U_{22}, will be operated at declining marginal cost. If one such route is so operated, the rate of decrease of its marginal cost must be smaller in absolute value than the rate of increase in the marginal cost of the other route. The condition (10.6.12) can be written in terms of C_{11}'', C_{12}'', C_{21}'', and C_{22}'' if we substitute from (10.6.10), remembering that $1/\lambda_1' = 1/C_{11}'' + 1/C_{12}''$.

In the special application discussed by Steinberg and Smith [29] it is assumed that the only variable input consumed by boilers is fuel, and the only variable input consumed by turbine-generators is heat energy. If boilers U_{11} and U_{12} consume x_{11} and x_{12} units of fuel respectively, as shown in Fig. 10–13(a); if the Stage I transformation functions are $y_{11} = f_{11}(x_{11})$ and $y_{12} = f_{12}(x_{12})$; and if the price of fuel is w_1; then $C_{11}' = w_1/f_{11}'$ and $C_{12}' = w_1/f_{12}'$, while $C_{21}' = C_{22}' = 0$. (Remember that C_{21} and C_{22} are the Stage II costs associated with inputs other than x_{21} and x_{22}.) Hence, the Stage I conditions become

$$\frac{w_1}{f_{11}'} \geq \lambda_1, \quad \frac{w_1}{f_{12}'} \geq \lambda_1, \qquad (10.6.13)$$

and the conditions (10.6.6) become

$$\frac{\lambda_1}{f_{21}'} \geq \lambda_2, \quad \frac{\lambda_1}{f_{22}'} \geq \lambda_2. \qquad (10.6.14)$$

It is clear in this special case that the marginal conditions on the two stages are independent and separable. If, for ex-

[29] Steinberg and Smith, pp. 108–145.

ample, all four units are operated, the operating rates of the Stage II units can be independently determined by distributing the final output requirements between these units so as to equate their marginal productivities (or marginal costs). The resulting intermediate output requirements are then distributed between the units of Stage I so as to equate their marginal productivities (or marginal costs). Such a procedure could be applied in general to an m-stage process provided that the only variable input to the kth stage is the output of the $k - 1$th stage.

We have assumed in this illustration that either Stage I unit can supply either Stage II unit. Steinberg and Smith,[30] in the steam-generating station application, discuss the case in which the tie line between Stage I and Stage II (L_1L_2 in our Fig. 10–13[a]) is of limited capacity. The solution is then modified in that "whenever independent loading of the turbines and boilers would require the transfer of a quantity of steam in excess of the steam tie capacity, the total station load should be incrementally divided between the sections." [31] By "sections" the authors refer to the producing sections U_{11}—U_{21} and U_{12}—U_{22} in our example, which, under the assumed conditions, are treated as independent "plants."

The above model can be extended to a general m-stage process having n_k parallel production units in the kth stage, where $k = 1, 2, \cdots, m$. We shall close by developing the necessary conditions for optimality in such a process.

Let us first define the following symbols:

x_{ij}, input to jth unit in the ith stage,

$y_{ij} = f_{ij}(x_{ij})$, output of jth unit in the ith stage,

$C_{ij}(y_{ij})$, cost of operating jth unit in the ith stage (not including the cost of intermediate input x_{ij}),

λ_k, Lagrange multiplier marginal cost function for first k composite stages, and

$C_{m-1}\left(\sum_{j=1}^{n_m} x_{ij}\right)$, composite minimum total cost function for first $m - 1$ stages, where $\lambda_{m-1} = C'_{m-1}$, $\lambda'_{m-1} = C''_{m-1}$.

[30] Steinberg and Smith, pp. 120–127.   [31] Steinberg and Smith, p. 121.

The general problem is to minimize

$$C = \sum_{j=1}^{n_m} C_{mj} \left[f_{mj}(x_{mj}) \right] + C_{m-1} \left(\sum_{j=1}^{n_m} x_{mj} \right)$$

subject to

$$y - \sum_{j=1}^{n_m} f_{mj}(x_{mj}) = 0.$$

Necessary conditions are

$$C'_{mj} + \frac{\lambda_{m-1}}{f'_{mj}} \geq \lambda_m, \quad j = 1, 2, \cdots, n_m.$$

By similar treatment of the first $m - 1$ stages, then the first $m - 2$ stages, and so forth, in sequence down to the first, we have

$$\begin{cases} C'_{m-1,\,j_{m-1}} + \dfrac{\lambda_{m-2}}{f'_{m-1,\,j_{m-1}}} \geq \lambda_{m-1}, \quad j_{m-1} = 1, 2, \cdots, n_{m-1} \\[2ex] C'_{m-2,\,j_{m-2}} + \dfrac{\lambda_{m-3}}{f'_{m-2,\,j_{m-2}}} \geq \lambda_{m-2}, \quad j_{m-2} = 1, 2, \cdots, n_{m-2} \\[2ex] \qquad \qquad \vdots \\[1ex] C'_{2j_2} \quad + \dfrac{\lambda_1}{f'_{2j_2}} \quad \geq \quad \lambda_2, \qquad j_2 = 1, 2, \cdots, n_2 \end{cases}$$

where $\qquad\qquad\quad C'_{1j_1} \quad \geq \quad \lambda_1, \qquad j_1 = 1, 2, \cdots, n_1.$

By successive substitution these conditions can be written

$$C'_{mj_m} + \frac{C'_{m-1,\,j_{m-1}}}{f'_{mj_m}} + \frac{C'_{m-2,\,j_{m-2}}}{f'_{mj_m} f'_{m-1,\,j_{m-1}}} + \cdots + \frac{C'_{1j_1}}{f'_{mj_m} \cdots f'_{2j_2}} \geq \lambda_m,$$

$$j_m = 1, 2, \cdots, n_m; \cdots; j_1 = 1, 2, \cdots, n_1.$$

Dynamic Problems in Production-Investment Planning

1. Introduction

Let us review, briefly, the technological concepts underlying most of our study. We imagine individual decision-making units, which we have called "firms," whose input-output decisions are constrained by a convex function relating a portion or all of the stock and flow inputs to a producing process. This function involves both flow and physical stock inputs, because the physical stock of the typical durable input to production directly influences the transformation function of flow inputs into flow outputs. A most important characteristic of such individual durable goods is that they can be assumed to be continuously variable in size with regard to expansionary investment decisions, but cannot be contracted in amount except by shutting down individual physical units. Furthermore, we think of firms typically operating several physical units in parallel. Hence, in the static case the problem contains elements of classical production theory as well as a theory of multifacility production. The new element has been the explicit simultaneous treatment of optimal investment-replacement policy. The term "replacement," is, of course, a hold-over from the earlier literature, since we really conceive of firms as making purchase and discard decisions with regard to capital goods rather than, literally, replacement decisions. The inappropriateness of "replacement" in the literal sense will become especially obvious in the present chapter.

There exists very little literature on the subject matter of this chapter. One paper that bears directly upon the analysis to follow is that by Arrow, Beckmann, and Karlin, "The Optimal Expansion of the Capacity of a Firm." [1] Their formulation of the investment decision problem over time bears similarity to that contained in the analysis to follow in that both approaches recognize the element of irreversibility in capital purchasing decisions. The whole literature of dynamic inventory theory and particularly the papers by Holt, Modigliani, and Muth,[2] and Modigliani and Hohn,[3] on production planning over time is, of course, part of the same class of problems to be treated here.[4]

The strategy of presentation will consist in a step-by-step construction of a theory of production-investment planning, starting with simple finite horizon, single investment models, and proceeding by gradual relaxation of the assumptions to a model with an infinite chain of investments, and, finally, to a continuous investment model.

[1] K. Arrow, S. Karlin, and H. Scarf, *Studies in the Mathematical Theory of Inventory and Production* (Stanford: Stanford University Press, 1958), chap. vii. Also see my article, Vernon L. Smith, "The Theory of Investment and Production," *Quarterly Journal of Economics*, LXXIII (February 1959), 61–87.

[2] C. C. Holt, F. Modigliani, and J. F. Muth, "Derivation of a Linear Decision Rule for Production and Employment," *Management Science*, II (January 1956), 159–177.

[3] F. Modigliani and F. Hohn, "Production Planning Over Time and the Nature of the Expectation and Planning Horizon," *Econometrica*, XXIII (January 1955), 46–66.

[4] See Arrow, Karlin, and Scarf, for an excellent bibliography of recent inventory theory.

2. Two Input, Single-Investment Problems

Consider a process requiring one capital input and one current input. We shall further assume that only a single investment decision is to be made over the planning horizon, and that decision concerns the initial stock of capital to be installed by the firm. Against the background of these general assumptions we shall study three models. The first model assumes a finite horizon, with an undiscounted cost criterion. The second assumes a finite horizon and continuously discounted cost. The third assumes an infinite horizon with discounted cost.

FINITE HORIZON, UNDISCOUNTED COST

Suppose the firm's planning horizon is T years. Assume further that output requirements as a function of time are known with certainty, say, $y(t)$, $0 \le t \le T$. The firm is to choose the level of investment outlay to be made initially, and the rate of consumption of current input at each instant over the horizon. The consumption of the current input at time t is $x_1(t)$, while the quantity of the capital good to be installed is X_2. The process is constrained by a production function of the form $y(t) = f[x_1(t), X_2]$. It is assumed that no output can be produced without some positive amount of each input. If the firm desires to minimize its total current and capital outlays over the interval, $0 \le t \le T$, then the problem is to choose $x_1(t) \ge 0$ and $X_2 \ge 0$ so as to minimize

$$C = \int_0^T w_1 x_1(t) \, dt + W_2 X_2, \qquad (11.2.1)$$

subject to

$$y(t) = f[x_1(t), X_2]. \qquad (11.2.2)$$

An equivalent problem is to minimize

$$\phi = \int_0^T (w_1 x_1(t) - \lambda \{f[x_1(t), X_2] - y(t)\}) \, dt + W_2 X_2 \qquad (11.2.3)$$

with respect to the *extremal* $x_1(t)$ and the scalar *variable* X_2, where λ is a function of w_1, W_2, T, and $y_0{}^T(t)$, to be determined shortly. The function λ plays a role entirely analogous to the Lagrange multiplier of the ordinary theory of relative optima.

Note that the expression for ϕ in (11.2.3) is a special form of the following standard calculus of variations problem: Minimize

$$I = \int_a^b F(x,\dot{x},t) \, dt \qquad (11.2.3')$$

where $x = x(t)$ and $\dot{x} = dx/dt$.[5] The solution to (11.2.3') is the Euler equation $(\partial F/\partial x) - (d/dt)(\partial F/\partial \dot{x}) = 0$ in $x(t)$. We apply this solution directly to (11.2.3) in minimizing ϕ with respect to the extremal $x_1(t)$, and we apply the condition $\partial \phi/\partial X_2 = 0$ in minimizing with respect to the variable X_2. If we let F stand for the integrand in (11.2.3), the conditions for an interior minimum of ϕ are [6]

$$\partial F/\partial x_1 = w_1 - \lambda f_1[x_1(t),X_2] = 0 \qquad (11.2.4)$$

$$\partial \phi/\partial X_2 = - \int_0^T \lambda f_2[x_1(t),X_2] \, dt + W_2 = 0. \qquad (11.2.5)$$

From the production function (11.2.2) and the necessary conditions (11.2.4) and (11.2.5), we determine (if they exist) the optimal consumption path of current input $x_1^0(t)$, the optimal level of investment, X_2^0, and, as a by-product, the

---

[5] See Charles Fox, *An Introduction to the Calculus of Variations* (London: Oxford University Press, 1950), pp. 3–34. Also see chap. iv, *passim*, especially pp. 80–83, and pp. 94–96, for a discussion of constrained extremal problems where the subsidiary equation is of nonintegral type. The problem presented by Fox (in one variable form) is to maximize or minimize $I = \int_{t_1}^{t_2} G(x,\dot{x},t) \, dt$ subject to $S(x,\dot{x},t) = 0$. He then introduces λ, a function of t to be determined, and develops a solution (*ibid.*, p. 96) of the form

$$\frac{\partial G}{\partial x} - \frac{d}{dt}\left(\frac{\partial G}{\partial \dot{x}}\right) - \left\{\lambda \frac{\partial S}{\partial x} - \frac{d}{dt}\left(\lambda \frac{\partial S}{\partial \dot{x}}\right)\right\} = 0.$$

This is equivalent to the solution $(\partial F/\partial x) - (d/dt)(\partial F/\partial \dot{x}) = 0$, with $F = G(x,\dot{x},t) - \lambda S(x,\dot{x},t)$. The well-known Lagrange multiplier shadow price tricks of static theory apply to our class of calculus of variations problems.

[6] Note that the condition (11.2.4) can be obtained by straight scalar optimization since the integral in (11.2.3) does not contain any time derivatives of the extremal. The calculus of variations form of the solution is emphasized because it underlies the class of problems to be discussed, and some of the subsequent problems do not reduce to scalar optimization.

function $\lambda^0 = \lambda[w_1, W_2, T, y_0^T(t)]$ is determined. Specifically, by eliminating λ from (11.2.4) and (11.2.5) we get

$$-\int_0^T \frac{w_1 f_2[x_1(t), X_2]}{f_1[x_1(t), X_2]} \, dt + W_2 = 0. \qquad (11.2.6)$$

The interpretation of this expression is easily clarified. The ratio f_2/f_1 is the amount by which the consumption of input Number 1 is decreased (increased) at time t if the initial installation of capital is increased (decreased) infinitesimally. Then $w_1 f_2/f_1$ is the rate of savings in the cost of the current input per unit increase in the initial stock of capital. Hence, the integral of $w_1 f_2/f_1$ over the interval $0 \leq t \leq T$ is the total savings in current input cost per unit increase in capital investment. Equation (11.2.6) states that investment is expanded, given the time pattern of output requirements, until the total current input cost saved from the last increment of capital equals the cost of that increment of capital. Now, by integrating (11.2.6) in combination with (11.2.2), we determine the optimal values $\bar{x}_1(t)$ and $\bar{X}_2$. With $\bar{x}_1(t)$ and $\bar{X}_2$ determined, (11.2.4) provides the Lagrangian function $\bar{\lambda}$. Hence our solution to (11.2.2), (11.2.4), and (11.2.5) can be written

$$\bar{x}_1(t) = h_1[w_1, W_2, T, y_0^T(t)], \qquad (11.2.7)$$

$$\bar{X}_2 = H_2[w_1, W_2, T, y_0^T(t)], \qquad (11.2.8)$$

$$\bar{\lambda} = \lambda[w_1, W_2, T, y_0^T(t)]. \qquad (11.2.9)$$

The similarity between this solution and the analogous static solution will be evident.[7]

Can we carry the analogy with static theory a step further, and interpret λ as a marginal cost function? The answer is yes. As is evident from equation (11.2.4), when put in the form $\lambda = w_1/f_1[x_1(t), X_2]$, λ *is the discounted instantaneous* (or short-run) *marginal operating cost function.*

The effect of changes in w_1 or W_2 on the consumption of the current input, $\bar{x}_1(t)$, and the level of investment $\bar{X}_2$,

[7] Compare equations (3.3.6)–(3.3.8) in Chapter III, and (4.1.3)–(4.1.5) in Chapter IV.

parallels the effect of similar changes in the analogous static model. An increase in the price of capital relative to the price of current input causes a reduction in investment and increased consumption of current input. A new parameter in the solution equations (11.2.7)–(11.2.9) is the horizon T. What is the effect of a change in the length of the planning horizon on capital investment and the consumption of the current input? By differentiating (11.2.6) and (11.2.2) we obtain:

$$\frac{\partial \overline{X}_2}{\partial T} = - \frac{f_2[x_1(T),X_2]}{f_1[x_1(T),X_2] \displaystyle\int_0^T \left(\frac{f_1{}^2 f_{22} - 2f_1 f_2 f_{12} + f_2{}^2 f_{11}}{f_1{}^3} \right) dt} \cdot \quad (11.2.10)$$

If $f_{12} > 0$, $f_{11} < 0$, and $f_{22} < 0$, it follows that $\partial X_2/\partial T > 0$. Hence, the longer the horizon the greater the level of investment undertaken. With more capital, the rate of consumption of current input is reduced at every operating instant, that is, at each t, $\partial \overline{x}_1/\partial T < 0$.

"OVERCAPACITY" IN DYNAMIC PRODUCTION PLANNING: AN EXAMPLE

With this simple model of production planning over time, some revealing insights into investment dynamics can be obtained by comparing an optimal production plan under a sine-wave cyclical variation in output requirements with the corresponding static optimal production plan in which the requirements are constant and equal to the time average of the dynamic requirements. Under dynamic requirements, it will be shown that optimal firm behavior leads to the installation of more capital than if society consumed the same total output in a uniform stream. In this strict sense, dynamic requirements lead to a form of "overcapacity."

Suppose we assume, for purposes of illustration, that (11.2.2) has the Cobb-Douglas, linear logarithmic form, and that output requirements, $y(t)$, oscillate according to a sine law about a constant (nontrend) level, y_0. If $2\pi/\theta$ is the period of oscillation and γ the amplitude of variation in y, then (11.2.2) can be written in the special form

$$A x_1^\alpha(t) X_2^\beta = y_0 (1 + \gamma \sin \theta t); \quad 0 \le t \le 2\pi n/\theta, \quad -1 \le \gamma \le 1. \tag{11.2.11}$$

If $\gamma > 0$, investment occurs at the midpoint of an upswing in requirements. If $\gamma < 0$, investment occurs at the midpoint of a downswing. We assume, also, that $T = 2\pi n/\theta$, where n is an integer, that is, we make the length of the horizon an integral number of wavelengths. Under these assumptions the equilibrium condition (11.2.6) becomes

$$- \frac{\beta w_1 I}{\alpha} \left(\frac{y_0}{A} \right)^{\frac{1}{\alpha}} X_2^{-\frac{\alpha+\beta}{\alpha}} + W_2 = 0. \tag{11.2.12}$$

Therefore, the optimal level of investment is

$$\overline{X}_2 = \left[\frac{\beta w_1 I}{\alpha W_2} \left(\frac{y_0}{A} \right)^{\frac{1}{\alpha}} \right]^{\frac{\alpha}{\alpha+\beta}} \tag{11.2.13}$$

where $I = \int_0^{2\pi n/\theta} (1 + \gamma \sin \theta t)^{1/\alpha} \, dt$. Consider this solution when $\alpha = \beta = \frac{1}{2}$ (constant returns to scale). Then (11.2.13) becomes

$$\overline{X}_2 = \left(\frac{w_1 y_0^2 I}{W_2 A^2} \right)^{\frac{1}{2}}, \quad \text{with} \quad I = \frac{\pi n}{\theta} (2 + \gamma^2). \tag{11.2.14}$$

From (11.2.11) and (11.2.14), the time path for the consumption of the current input is

$$\overline{x}_1(t) = \left(\frac{W_2 y_0^2}{w_1 A^2 I} \right)^{\frac{1}{2}} (1 + \gamma \sin \theta t)^2. \tag{11.2.15}$$

We will now compare the above solutions with the optimal static production plan where the output rate is constant at y_0, the average level of output in the dynamic case. In the static problem the objective is to minimize total outlay $C = w_1 x_1 T + W_2 X_2$ subject to (11.2.11) with $\gamma = 0$, that is, $A x_1^\alpha X_2^\beta = y_0$. For $\alpha = \beta = \frac{1}{2}$, the optimal employments of the two inputs are

$$x_1{}^0 = \left(\frac{W_2 y_0{}^2}{w_1 A^2 T}\right)^{\frac{1}{2}}, \quad \text{and} \tag{11.2.16}$$

$$X_2{}^0 = \left(\frac{w_1 y_0{}^2 T}{W_2 A^2}\right)^{\frac{1}{2}}, \quad \text{where} \quad T = 2\pi n/\theta. \tag{11.2.17}$$

By substituting from (11.2.16) into (11.2.15) and (11.2.17) into (11.2.14), we can write the dynamic solution in terms of the corresponding static solution, that is,

$$\bar{x}_1(t) = x_1{}^0 \left(1 + \frac{\gamma^2}{2}\right)^{-\frac{1}{2}} (1 + \gamma \sin \theta t)^2 \tag{11.2.18}$$

and

$$\overline{X}_2 = X_2{}^0 \left(1 + \frac{\gamma^2}{2}\right)^{\frac{1}{2}}. \tag{11.2.19}$$

Since $[1 + (\gamma^2/2)] > 1$, these last results allow us to draw two interesting conclusions from this simple dynamic model. (1) The average optimal consumption of the current input in the dynamic model exceeds the corresponding consumption of this input in the static model:

$$\text{ave } [\bar{x}_1(t)] = \frac{x_1{}^0 \theta}{2\pi n} \left(1 + \frac{\gamma^2}{2}\right)^{-\frac{1}{2}} \int_0^{2\pi n/\theta} (1 + \gamma \sin \theta t)^2 \, dt$$

$$= x_1{}^0 \left(1 + \frac{\gamma^2}{2}\right)^{\frac{1}{2}} > x_1{}^0,$$

and (2) the optimal investment in the capital good under dynamic requirements exceeds the level under static requirements, that is, $\overline{X}_2 > X_2{}^0$.[8]

Hence, even under constant returns to scale, if society requires a given average level of output to be produced according to a sine-law variation over time, then more capital

---

[8] The complete lack of ambiguity in these results disappears when a discounted cost criterion is used, as is shown below. These conditions were first developed for the discounted cost case in my article, "Theory of Investment and Production," pp. 80–83. Also see Roger F. Miller, "A Note on the Theory of Investment and Production," *Quarterly Journal of Economics*, LXXIII (November 1959), 672–681.

investment will be needed and more of the current input will be consumed. In a dynamic production planning framework, Chenery has shown that the existence of increasing returns to scale in such industries as gas transmission leads to over-capacity.[9] However, our results show that "overcapacity" may rationally develop under constant returns to scale. The underlying cause is diminishing returns. Owing to diminishing returns, upswings in output requirements lead to more than proportional increases in the consumption of current inputs, while downswings lead to less than proportional decreases in the consumption of current inputs. This asymmetry increases the cost of current inputs and induces the substitution of capital inputs. Hence, increasing returns to scale is not a necessary condition for "overcapacity" to occur in a dynamic framework.

The principle involved is illustrated in Fig. 11–1. Think of $x_1(t)$ being transformed into $y(t)$ through a nonlinear transformation process depending upon how much X_2 is "present" in production. The static minimum cost way to produce y_0 is to use $x_1{}^0$ and $X_2{}^0$, as shown in the diagram. Under dynamic production requirements there is an upward distortion in the time path of x_1 consumption caused by its nonlinear (diminishing returns) transformation into output. If we blindly applied the static solution and held the capital stock at $X_2{}^0$, the time path of x_1 requirements would become $x_1{}^0(1 + \gamma \sin \theta t)^2$ with average value

$$x_1{}^0(1 + \tfrac{1}{2}\gamma^2) > \text{ave}\left[\bar{x}_1(t)\right] = x_1{}^0(1 + \tfrac{1}{2}\gamma^2)^{\frac{1}{2}} > x_1{}^0.$$

But minimum-cost dynamic production scheduling requires us to escape part of this increased consumption of the current input by increasing the stock of capital from $X_2{}^0$ to $\overline{X}_2$, and reducing the average consumption of current input from $x_1{}^0(1 + \tfrac{1}{2}\gamma^2)$ to $x_1{}^0(1 + \tfrac{1}{2}\gamma^2)^{\frac{1}{2}}$.

Clearly we cannot solve the dynamic problem by imposing a static solution based on time averages. Under our assumptions such a procedure would always undercapitalize the

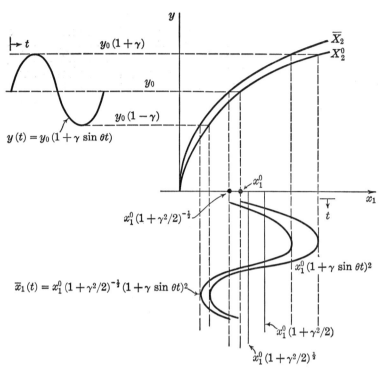

Fig. 11–1. Effect of investment on the current input consumption path.

enterprise, causing excessive consumption of the current input.

FINITE HORIZON, DISCOUNTED COST

If the criterion of action is to minimize the discounted uniform annual equivalent of all outlays over the horizon then the mathematical problem is to minimize

$$\phi = \frac{r}{1 - e^{-rT}} \int_0^T \big[w_1 x_1(t) e^{-rt}$$
$$- \lambda \{ f[x_1(t), X_2] - y(t) \} \big] \, dt + \frac{r W_2 X_2}{1 - e^{-rT}} \qquad (11.2.20)$$

with respect to $x_1(t)$ and X_2. Necessary conditions, corresponding to (11.2.4) and (11.2.5) are

$$w_1 e^{-rt} - \lambda f_1[x_1(t), X_2] = 0, \qquad (11.2.21)$$

$$-\frac{r}{1 - e^{-rT}} \int_0^T \lambda f_2[x_1(t), X_2] \, dt + \frac{rW_2}{1 - e^{-rT}} = 0. \qquad (11.2.22)$$

The Lagrangian, $\lambda[w_1, W_2, r, T, y_0^T(t)]$, is now the *discounted* instantaneous marginal operating cost function. By eliminating λ, these conditions can be put in the form

$$-\frac{r}{1 - e^{-rT}} \int_0^T \frac{w_1 f_2[x_1(t), X_2] e^{-rt}}{f_1[x_1(t), X_2]} \, dt + \frac{rW_2}{1 - e^{-rT}} = 0, \qquad (11.2.23)$$

which requires investment to be expanded until the discounted annual savings in current input is equal to the annual rent of capital.

INFINITE HORIZON, DISCOUNTED COST [10]

If the horizon is infinite, the previous solution applies if we allow T to approach infinity. For example, the condition (11.2.23) becomes

$$-r \int_0^\infty \frac{w_1 f_2[x_1(t), X_2] e^{-rt}}{f_1[x_1(t), X_2]} \, dt + rW_2 = 0. \qquad (11.2.24)$$

Suppose we apply this solution to our earlier "overcapacity" example. It will be shown that the introduction of a discounted cost criterion prevents us from obtaining the unambiguous results of that section. Evaluating the integral in (11.2.24), using the production function and requirements path of (11.2.11) for $\alpha = \beta = \frac{1}{2}$, gives

$$\overline{X}_2 = \left(\frac{w_1 y_0^2 B}{rW_2 A^2}\right)^{\frac{1}{2}} = X_2^0 B^{\frac{1}{2}},$$

where $\qquad\qquad\qquad\qquad\qquad\qquad\qquad\qquad$ (11.2.25)

$$B = 1 + \frac{2r\theta\gamma}{r^2 + \theta^2} + \frac{2\theta^2\gamma^2}{r^2 + 4\theta^2}.$$

[10] See V. L. Smith, "Theory of Investment and Production," pp. 80–83.

The current input consumption path is then

$$
\begin{aligned}
\bar{x}_1(t) &= \left(\frac{r\overline{W}_2 y_0{}^2}{w_1 A^2 B}\right)^{\frac{1}{2}} (1 + \gamma \sin \theta t)^2 \\
&= x_1{}^0 B^{-\frac{1}{2}}(1 + \gamma \sin \theta t)^2.
\end{aligned}
\tag{11.2.26}
$$

If $\gamma > 0$, with investment occurring at the midpoint of the upswing in requirements, then $B > 1$. Hence, $\overline{X}_2 > X_2{}^0$ and ave $[\bar{x}_1(t)] = x_1{}^0 B^{-\frac{1}{2}}[1 + (\gamma^2/2)] \gtreqless x_1{}^0$. However, if $\gamma < 0$, with investment occurring on the downswing, then $B \gtreqless 1$, giving $\overline{X}_2 \gtreqless X_2{}^0$ and ave $[\bar{x}_1(t)] \gtreqless x_1{}^0$. Depending upon the point of the cycle at which the investment occurs, the amount of capital installed and the average consumption of current input may or may not exceed the corresponding static quantities. The effect of discounting is to attach greater weight to the costs incurred in the depressed earlier years of the planning period. In particular, the cost of capital is given greater weight, with the result that if $\gamma < 0$, it is possible that the optimum capital installation under dynamic requirements is less than that under the corresponding static requirements.[11]

The general conclusion can be stated as follows: If society wants a given average level of nonstorable output, y_0, to be produced in a sine-wave pattern over time, it is possible that both more capital and more of the current input will be required than if society consumed y_0 in a constant steady flow. Exceptions may occur when (1) production begins on the downswing of the cycle,[12] and (2) the rate of discount used in the cost criterion function is large relative to the cycle period.[13]

[11] See R. F. Miller, pp. 672–681.

[12] The reader can demonstrate for himself that $B > 1$ unambiguously if production begins anywhere between the midpoint of the upswing and the upper turning point of the requirements path.

[13] When $\gamma < 0$, r and θ must satisfy the condition

$$
\frac{r}{\theta} > -\left[\gamma(r^2 + \theta^2)/r^2 + 4\theta^2\right]
$$

if the dynamic investment level is to be smaller than the static level. See Miller, p. 674.

3. The Two Input, Two Investments Chain

Returning to the finite horizon case, consider a slight extension of the problem discussed in the first two parts of section 2. Assume a finite horizon of T years, with a known dynamic requirements function, $y(t)$, defined over the interval $0 \leq t \leq T$. We divide the interval into two parts of unknown lengths, T_1 and T_2, thus forming two operating periods, I and II, as shown in Fig. 11–2. It is assumed that

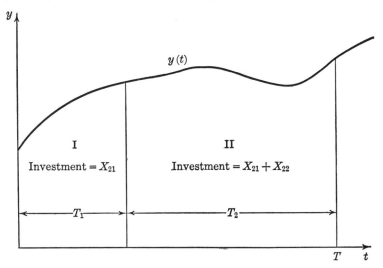

Fig. 11–2. The requirements path for the two-investments chain.

at most two investments are to be made in the interval $0 \leq t \leq T$. The first investment is at $t = 0$, the second at $t = T_1$ to be determined. We wish to determine the following: (1) how much capital to install initially; (2) how much capital to install at T_1; (3) when to install (if at all) the second capital facility, that is, we wish to determine T_1; (4) the optimal instantaneous operating rules in periods I and II; (5) the optimal consumption path for the current input in periods I and II; and (6) rules for discarding either capital facility in period II if such action is optimal. We assume that neither facility is to be idled temporarily over any subinterval. If at any time it pays to withdraw one facility from production, it is assumed that the action is permanent and the facility is discarded at zero salvage value.

Using a discounted cost criterion, the objective is to minimize

$$C = \frac{r}{1 - e^{-rT}} \left\{ \int_0^{T_1} w_1 x_{11}{}^1(t) e^{-rt} \, dt + W_2 X_{21} \right\} \tag{11.3.1}$$

$$+ \frac{r}{1 - e^{-rT}} \left\{ \int_{T_1}^{T} w_1 [x_{11}{}^2(t) + x_{12}{}^2(t)] e^{-rt} \, dt + W_2 X_{22} \, e^{-rT_1} \right\},$$

where X_{21} is the quantity of capital input installed at the beginning of operating period I (facility 1); X_{22} is the amount installed at the beginning of period II (facility 2); $x_{11}{}^1(t)$ is the consumption path of current input by facility 1 in period I; $x_{11}{}^2(t)$ is the consumption path of current input by facility 1 in period II; and $x_{12}{}^2(t)$ is the consumption path of current input by facility 2 in period II. The expression (11.3.1) is to be minimized subject to

$$y(t) = f^1[x_{11}{}^1(t), X_{21}], \quad 0 \le t < T_1, \quad \text{and} \tag{11.3.2}$$

$$y(t) = f^1[x_{11}{}^2(t), X_{21}] + f^2[x_{12}{}^2(t), X_{22}], \quad T_1 \le t \le T. \tag{11.3.3}$$

The functions f^1 and f^2 refer to the production functions for facilities 1 and 2. That is, the production technology ruling at the beginning of period I is $f^1[x_{11}{}^1(t), X_{21}]$, while the production technology available at the beginning of period II is $f^2[x_{12}{}^2(t), X_{22}]$. By time T_1, technological improvements in equipment and operating technique may have rendered f^2 entirely different from f^1. We allow for this by permitting the production function to alter from one investment point to the next.[14]

By introducing two Lagrangian functions, λ_1 and λ_2, one for each of the constraints in (11.3.2) and (11.3.3), a problem

---

[14] A more general way to introduce technological change is to write the second period production function in the form $f^2[x_{12}{}^2(t), X_{22}, T_1]$, that is, the "state of the arts" is a function of the point in calendar time at which the capital equipment of a process is installed. The class of problems under discussion are tedious enough without pursuing maximum generality.

equivalent to the one just stated is to minimize

$$\phi = \frac{r}{1 - e^{-rT}} \left\{ \int_0^{T_1} (w_1 x_{11}{}^1(t)e^{-rt} - \lambda_1\{f^1[x_{11}{}^1(t),X_{21}] - y(t)\}) \, dt \right.$$
$$\left. + W_2 X_{21} \right\} + \frac{r}{1 - e^{-rT}} \left\{ \int_{T_1}^T (w_1[x_{11}{}^2(t) + x_{12}{}^2(t)]e^{-rt} \right.$$
$$- \lambda_2\{f^1[x_{11}{}^2(t),X_{21}] + f^2[x_{12}{}^2(t),X_{22}] - y(t)\}) \, dt$$
$$\left. + W_2 X_{22} e^{-rT_1} \right\}, \tag{11.3.4}$$

with respect to the nonnegative extremals $x_{11}{}^1(t)$, $x_{11}{}^2(t)$, $x_{12}{}^2(t)$, and the nonnegative variables X_{21}, X_{22}, T_1 (since T is fixed, T_2 is determined once we know T_1).

Assuming an interior solution, for the present, the necessary intratemporal conditions for minimum ϕ with respect to the current input consumption paths $x_{11}{}^1(t)$, $x_{11}{}^2(t)$, and $x_{12}{}^2(t)$, in that order, are

$$w_1 e^{-rt} - \lambda_1 f_1{}^1[x_{11}{}^1(t),X_{21}] = 0, \quad 0 \le t < T_1 \tag{11.3.5}$$

$$\left. \begin{aligned} w_1 e^{-rt} - \lambda_2 f_1{}^1[x_{11}{}^2(t),X_{21}] = 0 \\ w_1 e^{-rt} - \lambda_2 f_1{}^2[x_{12}{}^2(t),X_{22}] = 0 \end{aligned} \right\} \quad T_1 \le t \le T \quad \begin{aligned} (11.3.6) \\ (11.3.7) \end{aligned}$$

The intertemporal conditions on the investment levels X_{21} and X_{22} are

$$-\frac{r}{1 - e^{-rT}} \left\{ \int_0^{T_1} \lambda_1 f_2{}^1[x_{11}{}^1(t),X_{21}] \, dt \right. \tag{11.3.8}$$
$$\left. \int_{T_1}^T \lambda_2 f_2{}^1[x_{11}{}^2(t),X_{21}] \, dt - W_2 \right\} = 0,$$

$$-\frac{r}{1 - e^{-rT}} \left\{ \int_{T_1}^T \lambda_2 f_2{}^2[x_{12}{}^2(t),X_{22}] \, dt - W_2 e^{-rT_1} \right\} = 0. \tag{11.3.9}$$

Finally, the optimal timing of the second investment, T_1, must satisfy the condition

$$w_1 x_{11}{}^1(T_1) - w_1[x_{11}{}^2(T_1) + x_{12}{}^2(T_1)] - rW_2 X_{22} = 0 \tag{11.3.10}$$

The conditions (11.3.5)–(11.3.10) contain practically the whole of a marginalist dynamic theory of production and investment. λ_1 in (11.3.5) and (11.3.8) is the discounted marginal operating cost function in period I, namely, $\lambda_1 = w_1 e^{-rt}/f_1^1$ over the interval $0 \leq t < T_1$. λ_2 is the discounted marginal operating cost function in period II. From (11.3.6) and (11.3.7) we have $\lambda_2 = w_1 e^{-rt}/f_1^1 = w_1 e^{-rt}/f_1^2$, for $T_1 \leq t \leq T$, during operating period II, that is, the two facilities are operated at output (and current input) rates that equalize their instantaneous marginal costs (and marginal productivities).

In interpreting equation (11.3.8), note that the first integral under the brackets gives the present value of the period I savings in current input resulting from an incremental increase in the initial investment level X_{21}. Similarly, the second integral gives the value of corresponding period II savings. Therefore (11.3.8) requires the initial investment to be expanded until the discounted annual value of the savings from the last unit of capital equals the unit rent of capital, $rW_2/(1 - e^{-rT})$. Equation (11.3.9) requires the level of additional investment at T_1 to be expanded until the annual discounted value of the savings resulting from the last unit of capital is equal to the unit rent of capital.

The first term in (11.3.10) is the instantaneous operating cost, at T_1, of operating facility 1 alone. The second term is the initial cost of operating facilities 1 and 2 in parallel after the latter has been installed. Therefore, the difference between these terms is the initial net rate of operating cost savings resulting from adding the new facility. The last term in (11.3.10) is the instantaneous interest on the investment in a new facility. Therefore (11.3.10) says to time the installation of a second parallel facility when the rate of operating cost savings equals the instantaneous interest on the investment. In a word, a new facility should be installed whenever the first "year" savings effected by the new unit will pay the first "year" of interest on the new investment.

So far the analysis has assumed an interior solution. Can we replace the strict equalities in (11.3.5)–(11.3.10) with inequality signs and give Kuhn-Tucker interpretations to the surplus fulfillment of one or more of these conditions?

We can,[15] and the resulting conditions will provide rules for an optimal equipment discard policy.

Consider first the conditions (11.3.5)–(11.3.7), which we rewrite in the form

$$w_1 e^{-rt} - \lambda_1 f_1{}^1[x_{11}{}^1(t), X_{21}] \geq 0, \quad 0 \leq t < T_1 \quad (11.3.5')$$

$$\left. \begin{array}{l} w_1 e^{-rt} - \lambda_2 f_1{}^1[x_{11}{}^2(t), X_{21}] \geq 0 \\[2mm] w_1 e^{-rt} - \lambda_2 f_1{}^2[x_{12}{}^2(t), X_{22}] \geq 0 \end{array} \right\} \quad T_1 \leq t \leq T \quad \begin{array}{l} (11.3.6') \\[4mm] (11.3.7') \end{array}$$

If $>$ holds in (11.3.5') for some $t = t_{11}$, $0 \leq t_{11} < T_1$, then $x_{11}{}^1(t_{11}) = 0$, that is, at t_{11} it pays to withdraw the first facility from production. If this occurs in the first operating period it means that output requirements have declined to zero. If $>$ holds in (11.3.6') for some $t = t_{12}$, $T_1 \leq t_{12} \leq T$, then $x_{11}{}^2(t_{12}) = 0$ and at t_{12} the first facility is withdrawn from production in favor of the singular operation of the new facility installed at T_1. Or, if $>$ holds in (11.3.7') for some t_{22}, $T_1 \leq t_{22} \leq T$, then $x_{12}{}^2(t_{22}) = 0$, and at t_{22} the second facility is withdrawn from production leaving the original facility only. Hence, by proper interpretation of the corner solutions implied by (11.3.5')–(11.3.7'), we can obtain all possible equipment discard alternatives contained in the planning interval $0 \leq t \leq T$. Note the strategic role played by the inequalities; they define implicitly the firm's optimal equipment discard policies. Our formulation of the problem allowed explicitly *for equipment purchases only*, namely, at 0 and T_1. The discard points, if they exist, are then evolved by interpretation of the equilibrium condition. Also note that the extension of our analysis to dynamic problems has not destroyed the intuitive usefulness of the Lagrange multipliers; they continue to provide valuable service as shadow price evaluators. In this sense the conditions (11.3.5')–(11.3.7') require each facility to be operated at all times so that the internal instantaneous value of a unit of the current input, for example, $\lambda_1 f_1{}^1[x_{11}{}^1(t), X_{21}]e^{rt}$ in (11.3.5'), does not exceed the external cost, w_1, of acquiring a unit of this input.

[15] See F. Morin, "Note on an Inventory Problem," *Econometrica*, XXIII (October 1955), 448. Also see Arrow, Karlin, and Scarf, p. 63.

Similarly, we can replace "$=$" with "$\geq$" in (11.3.8) and (11.3.9) to obtain more general conditions on the investment levels X_{21} and X_{22}. If "$>$" holds in (11.3.8), then $X_{21} = 0$. This could only obtain if requirements are zero throughout the first operating period, since we assume that no output can be produced without some positive investment. If "$>$" holds in (11.3.9), then $X_{22} = 0$, and the best policy is to employ singly the original facility, $X_{21} > 0$, throughout the planning period. The condition (11.3.10) could also be written with "$\geq$" in place of "$=$". If "$>$" holds, then $T_1 = 0$, and only a single facility is used over the entire period. Hence $X_{22} = 0$ and $T_1 = 0$ have equivalent implications.

What happens if we drop the assumption that neither facility is to be idled temporarily over any subinterval? We can still write conditions on optimal policies, but the problem becomes more cumbersome. Now, if "$>$" holds for some t in any of the conditions (11.3.5')–(11.3.7'), the corresponding facility is discarded only if there is no later $t' > t$ at which the "$=$" in that condition can be satisfied. For example, suppose "$>$" holds in (11.3.6') for some interval $T_1 \leq t_{12} \leq t \leq t_{12}' \leq T$, with the equality holding elsewhere. Then at t_{12}, instead of discarding the equipment, it is placed in standby until t_{12}', at which time it is returned to the operating state.

4. The Two-Input, Multiple Investments Chain

Turning next to a generalization of the two-input problem in production-investment dynamics, our objective is to extend the analysis of the last section to the infinite horizon investment chain. We divide the planning interval, $0 \leq t \leq \infty$, into an infinite sequence of segments of unknown lengths $T_1, T_2, T_3, \cdots$, forming an infinite sequence of operating intervals, as shown in Fig. 11–3. The objective in this case is to minimize the discounted current account cost over all future operating intervals, subject to input-output constraints of the form (11.3.2) and (11.3.3) for each operating interval. By introducing Lagrange multipliers $\lambda_1, \lambda_2, \lambda_3, \cdots$, this constrained minimum problem is equivalent to mini-

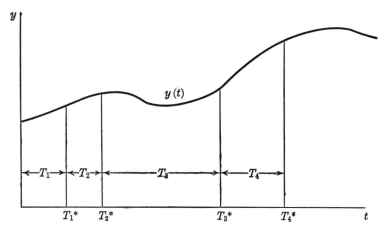

Fig. 11–3. The requirements path for a multiple-investments chain.

mizing the expression

$$\phi = r \sum_{k=1}^{\infty} \left\{ \int_{T_{k-1}^*}^{T_k^*} \left(w_1 \sum_{j=1}^{k} x_{1j}{}^k(t) e^{-rt} \right. \right.$$
$$\left. \left. - \lambda_k \left[\sum_{j=1}^{k} f^i[x_{1j}{}^k(t), X_{2j}] - y(t) \right] \right) dt + W_2 X_{2k} e^{-rT_{k-1}^*} \right\}, \tag{11.4.1}$$

where $T_k^* = \sum_{i=1}^{k} T_i$, and $T_0^* = 0$, with respect to the extremals $x_{j1}{}^k(t)$, the capital stock levels X_{2k}, and the purchasing dates T_k^* $(j \leq k = 1, 2, 3, \cdots)$. The expression (11.4.1) is the infinite dimensional counterpart of (11.3.4). We continue to assume that whenever optimality requires a facility to be idled, that facility is discarded.

With respect to the extremals, necessary conditions for minimizing (11.4.1) are

$$w_1 e^{-rt} - \lambda_k f_1{}^i[x_{1i}{}^k(t), X_{2i}] \geq 0, \quad k = 1, 2, 3, \cdots, \\ i = 1, 2, \cdots, k. \tag{11.4.2}$$

The infinite dimensional conditions on the X_{2k} and T_k are

$$-r \sum_{k=j}^{\infty} \left\{ \int_{T_{k-1}^*}^{T_k^*} \lambda_k f_2{}^i[x_{1j}{}^k, X_{2j}] \, dt \right\} + re^{-rT_{j-1}^*} W_2 \geq 0, \\ j = 1, 2, 3, \cdots \tag{11.4.3}$$

and

$$\sum_{k=j}^{\infty} w_1 \sum_{h=1}^{k} x_{1h}{}^{k}(T_k{}^{*})e^{-rT_k{}^{*}} - \sum_{k=j+1}^{\infty} w_1 \sum_{h=1}^{k} x_{1h}{}^{k}(T_{k-1}{}^{*})e^{-rT_{k-1}{}^{*}}$$

$$- r \sum_{k=j+1}^{\infty} W_2 X_{2k} e^{-rT_{k-1}{}^{*}} \geq 0, \quad j = 1, 2, 3, \cdots \quad (11.4.4)$$

where $T_k{}^{*} = \sum_{i=1}^{k} T_i$ and $T_0{}^{*} = 0$. The intratemporal conditions (11.4.2) require the current input to each facility in all operating periods to have a marginal imputed value which does not exceed the market price of the input. When the equality holds, these conditions also imply that all facilities in any period must be operated at output levels which equate their marginal operating costs (and marginal physical productivities). If, at any instant in any period, the equality contained in (11.4.2) cannot be maintained, the appropriate facility is at that moment idled, and therefore, by assumption, discarded.[16]

The intertemporal conditions (11.4.3) require investment in a new facility at each purchase date to be expanded until the discounted current account cost of all future savings in operating expenses, effected by the last increment of physical investment, is equal to the annual rent of the capital good. The integral in (11.4.3) serves the function of cumulating these discounted savings in each future operating period, which are then summed to obtain the total of such savings. If the rent of capital exceeds these savings for all feasible investment levels (the " > " prevails), then the investment is not undertaken. It is entirely possible that these conditions will signal an end to the investment chain. For example, if optimality requires the nth facility to be the last in the chain, then " > " will hold in (11.4.3) for X_{2k}, $k = n + 1, n + 2, n + 3, \cdots$. The same situation will also be reflected in (11.4.4) if there is no solution for T_{n+1}, that is, if no new facilities are acquired after the nth investment. In general, the conditions (11.4.4) determine the length of the operating intervals $T_1, T_2, T_3, \cdots$, and therefore the pur-

---

[16] The problem of temporary idling can be handled by seeking subintervals over which the appropriate inequalities hold in the conditions (11.4.2).

chase dates, T_1^*, T_2^*, T_3^*, $\cdots$. These conditions require a new parallel facility to be installed whenever the discounted cost of operating the existing complex of parallel facilities is equal to or exceeds the discounted annual operating and capital cost of an additional facility. Each year we imagine the firm comparing the cost of maintaining the *status quo*, that is, continuing to operate the existing equipment complex without benefit of an additional unit, with the cost of adding a new unit, proper account being taken of the savings effected by the latter. The *status quo* is maintained an additional year if the discounted cost of making the addition exceeds that of not making it. Abrupt technological improvements, reflected by a shift in new equipment production functions, are of course favorable to the early purchase of a new unit.

5. *Extensions and More General Models*

DISCUSSION

The solutions of the last section are quite general for the two-input case. To obtain more specific results requires more specific information concerning output requirements, price parameters and technological change. For example, in Fig. 11–4, assuming an infinite horizon, the solution might require a chain of five investment expansions to be made at A, B, C, D, and E. The third new facility might be added at C, even though output requirements have risen only slightly since the second facility was installed at B, because of technological improvements occurring after the second facility was purchased. The investment chain might end at E, after five facilities have been purchased, if output requirements are due to decline to a constant level as shown, and no important technological improvements are in store. At F, t_{15} years after the purchase of the last facility, the declining output level may precipitate the discard of the first facility (or any of the other four facilities depending upon the state of technology at the time each was purchased and the scale of the unit purchased).

Can we generalize our two input results to multiple inputs? The extension is easy if we have multiple *current* inputs, with a single durable input. The solution is identical
with that of (11.4.2)–(11.4.4) except we must add conditions
of the form (11.4.2) for each current input. Such additional
conditions simply require every current input to be con-

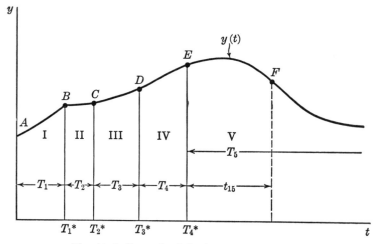

Fig. 11–4. Example of five-investment expansion.

sumed at rates which equalize their marginal costs, that is,
the ratio of the price of each input to the marginal productivity of that input must equal the ratio for every other current
input in each operating period. The case of multiple durable
inputs is not so simple. It is easy to see intuitively that conditions like those of (11.4.3) must surely apply to every type
of durable input to the process. That is, at every purchase
date for each type of equipment, investment is expanded
until the savings on both current and capital account of the
last increment of the capital good are equal to its annual rent.
But to deduce such conditions in a form similar to (11.4.3)
is most formidable since the moment we admit of more than
a single capital good we lose the one-to-one correspondence
between the equipment purchase dates $T_1{}^*, T_2{}^*, T_3{}^*, \cdots,$
and the operating intervals $T_1, T_2, T_3, \cdots$. That is, we must

now distinguish purchase dates for each equipment type. In the general case of n current inputs and m capital inputs, we cannot even write an expression of the form (11.4.1) without knowing how the purchase dates for each capital input are phased with respect to each other. Furthermore, the problem cannot be sidestepped by attempting to by-pass the production function and formulating the investment problem directly in terms of a current account cost function. There still remains the problem of determining such a cost function, and defining the optimal policies which it contains implicitly. The hypothesis of a cost function always presumes a wide class of optimal decisions to have been made. Also, the problem is not solved by formulating it in terms of "capacity" in the sense of output. This is a most nebulous concept, and leaves unanswered the question of the connection between "capacity" and the stocks of equipment in kind which are the direct objects of adjustment in investment decisions.

In the absence of more general solutions it has been demonstrated, I think, that a study of several simple models can sharpen analytical intuition and convey considerable depth of understanding. It is especially rewarding to find so much that is familiar in the solutions that have been developed.

THE SOLUTION WITH MAINTENANCE OUTLAYS

There are, no doubt, many different directions in which the dynamic models we have developed can be extended. One important element that has not been incorporated into the dynamic analysis is the cost of capital equipment maintenance and servicing. It will be assumed that the rate of increase in maintenance costs per unit increase in the consumption of the current input is an increasing function of the cumulative consumption of current input. I have argued elsewhere [17] that equipment maintenance cost can be expected to vary with the equipment's cumulative consump-

---

[17] Smith, "Theory of Investment and Production," pp. 78–80.

tion of fuel or energy.[18] The latter is a direct measure of the total exposure of a machine to wear and tear. If we let $U_1 = U_1(t)$ be the cumulative consumption of the current input up to time t, then $U_1 = \int_0^t x_1(\tau)\, d\tau$. Our assumption is that $dM/dU_1 = m(U_1)$, where dM/dU_1 is the rate at which maintenance and servicing expenditures increase with increases in current input consumption, and $m(U_1)$ is an increasing function. Hence, the time rate of expenditure for maintenance and servicing is $\dot{U}_1 m(U_1)$, where $x_1 = \dot{U}_1 = dU_1/dt$. Both the current rate of equipment utilization and its cumulative utilization contribute to current maintenance outlays.

Suppose we illustrate the effect of maintenance cost considerations on dynamic solutions by means of the model of section 2 above. Total current expenditure, including maintenance and servicing outlays, is now $w_1 \dot{U}_1 + \dot{U}_1 m(U_1)$. Making the change of variable $x_1 = \dot{U}_1$ throughout, the expression corresponding to (11.2.3) to be minimized can be written

$$\phi = \frac{r}{1 - e^{-rT}} \int_0^T \Big(\big[w_1 \dot{U}_1 + \dot{U}_1 m(U_1) \big] e^{-rt}$$

$$- \lambda \{ f(\dot{U}_1, X_2) - y(t) \} \Big)\, dt + \frac{rW_2 X_2}{1 - e^{-rT}}. \qquad (11.5.1)$$

The integral in (11.5.1) is of the form (11.2.3) and is minimized with respect to the extremal $U_1(t)$ if $(\partial F/\partial U_1) - (d/dt)(\partial F/\partial \dot{U}_1) = 0$. In this case the derivative with respect to $\dot{U}_1$ will enter the solution, whereas in our previous analysis the derivative with respect to the time rate of change of the extremal was identically zero. In this model we get a true calculus of variation problem, whereas previously the analysis reduced to ordinary scalar calculus minimization.

---

[18] Also see Vernon L. Smith, "Economic Replacement Policies: An Evaluation," *Management Science*, IV (October 1957), 26–28, for an empirical study of truck-tractor maintenance costs, in which maintenance costs per mile are found to be an increasing function of cumulative mileage. In the present context, it would be argued that a more direct explanatory variable is cumulative fuel consumption rather than cumulative mileage.

Equation (11.5.1) is therefore minimized with respect to $U_1(t)$ if the following differential equation is satisfied

$$\dot{U}_1 \frac{\partial m}{\partial U_1} e^{-rt} - \frac{d}{dt} \{[w_1 + m(U_1)]e^{-rt} - \lambda f_1(\dot{U}_1, X_2)\} = 0.$$

$$(11.5.2)$$

Integrating (11.5.2) and solving for λ gives

$$\lambda(t) = \frac{[w_1 + m(U_1)]e^{-rt} - \int_0^t \dot{U}_1 \frac{\partial m}{\partial U_1} e^{-rt} dt + C_1}{f_1(\dot{U}_1, X_2)}, \quad (11.5.3)$$

where C_1 is an arbitrary constant of integration. Since

$$\int_0^T \dot{U}_1 \frac{\partial m}{\partial U_1} e^{-rt} dt = \int_0^t \dot{U}_1 \frac{\partial m}{\partial U_1} e^{-rt} dt + \int_t^T \dot{U}_1 \frac{\partial m}{\partial U_1} e^{-rt} dt,$$

equation (11.5.3) can be written in the form

$$\lambda(t) = \frac{\int_t^T \dot{U}_1 \frac{\partial m}{\partial U_1} e^{-rt} dt + [w_1 + m(U_1)]e^{-rt} + K_1}{f_1(\dot{U}_1, X_2)}. \quad (11.5.4)$$

If at $t = T$, the termination of the planning interval, we impose the condition $\lambda(T) = [w_1 + m(U_1)]e^{-rT}/f_1(\dot{U}_1, X_2)$, then $K_1 = 0$. The Lagrangian $\lambda(t)$ is again interpreted as discounted marginal operating cost at time t. Equation (11.5.4) says that, in equilibrium, $\lambda(t)$ is the ratio of the discounted cost of employing an additional unit of input Number 1 at time t to the marginal physical productivity of input Number 1 at time t. The discounted cost of employing an additional unit of input Number 1 at time t is composed of three parts. The first part $\int_t^T \dot{U}_1(\partial m/\partial U_1)e^{-rt} dt$, is the additional cost of maintaining the stock of capital over the rest of the planning interval from t to T as a result of consuming an additional unit of input Number 1 at t. The second part, $w_1 e^{-rt}$, is the direct cost of buying the additional input. The third part, $m(U_1)e^{-rt}$, is the additional cost of maintaining the capital in the current period, namely, at t, when an additional unit of current input is consumed at t. (Remember that the consumption of input Number 1 exerts both a current and a cumulative influence on maintenance outlays.)

Finally, by setting $\partial\phi/\partial X_2 = 0$, we get the condition

$$\frac{r}{1 - e^{-rT}} \int_0^T - \lambda(t)f_2(\dot{U}_1, X_2) \, dt + \frac{rW_2}{1 - e^{-rT}} = 0. \quad (11.5.5)$$

Equations (11.5.4) and (11.5.5), together with the constraint $y(t) = f(\dot{U}_1, X_2)$, provide necessary conditions for determining x_1^0, X_2^0, and λ^0 over the interval $0 \leq t \leq T$.

We have written the solution with maintenance outlays for the case of a single investment and finite horizon. The solution is easily extended to a chain of investments over a finite or infinite horizon. Where the Kuhn-Tucker-Euler conditions require a facility to be idled (or discarded), we get $x_1(t) = \dot{U}_1(t) = 0$, and total operating cost $w_1\dot{U}_1 + \dot{U}_1m(U_1)$ drops to zero for the idled facility.

INVENTORY POLICY AND PRODUCTION PLANNING; AN EXTENSION OF THE MODIGLIANI-HOHN MODEL

An alternative extension of our fundamental models is to drop the assumption of a nonstorable product. This introduces the necessity for simultaneous treatment of optimal inventory policy and optimal production-investment technique. We will follow a continuous version of the Modigliani-Hohn [19] model in introducing inventory considerations into our analysis. Modigliani and Hohn assume a given marginal production cost function which depends only on the rate of production at time t. In our analysis the short-run marginal cost function will be a by-product of choosing the best input-output technique over the planning interval. Certain interesting results follow from this construction of the problem.

Following Modigliani and Hohn, we assume a finite planning horizon of T years, and take as our criterion the minimization of undiscounted cumulative cost over this period.

---

[19] *Ibid.* See also F. Morin, p. 448, and Arrow, Karlin, and Scarf, pp. 61–69, for continuous formulations of the Modigliani-Hohn model.

Suppose the amount of product inventory held at time t is $H(t)$. Then if $Y(t)$ is the unknown cumulative production up to t and $S(t)$ is the given cumulative sales up to t, we have $H(t) = H(0) + Y(t) - S(t)$. That is, inventory at t is initial inventory plus the excess of cumulative production over cumulative sales at t. We assume one current and one capital equipment input to the process. We let k be the constant marginal cost of holding a unit of inventory per unit of time.[20]

Cumulative cost over the horizon can now be written

$$C = \int_0^T (w_1 x_1(t) + k[H(0) + Y(t) - S(t)]) \, dt + W_2 X_2. \tag{11.5.6}$$

The problem is to choose $x_1(t)$, X_2, and $Y(t)$ so as to minimize (11.5.6) subject to the production function constraint

$$f[x_1(t), X_2] - \dot{Y}(t) = 0. \tag{11.5.7}$$

Also, we have the important nonnegativity condition on inventory stocks,

$$H(t) = H(0) + Y(t) - S(t) \geq 0, \tag{11.5.8}$$

and the boundary condition requiring no inventory at the end of the planning period,

$$Y(T) = \int_0^T f[x_1(t), X_2] \, dt = S(T) - H(0). \tag{11.5.9}$$

Necessary conditions for such a minimum are

$$w_1 - \lambda f_1[x_1(t), X_2] = 0, \tag{11.5.10}$$

$$\int_0^T -\lambda f_2[x_1(t), X_2] \, dt + W_2 = 0, \tag{11.5.11}$$

and

$$k - \frac{d}{dt}(\lambda) \geq 0. \tag{11.5.12}$$

[20] I am following tradition in making this assumption. A more satisfactory treatment of inventory costs in "long-run" planning would recognize the obvious fact that a substantial portion of inventory costs is fixed investment in warehouse space.

It is assumed that equalities hold in (11.5.10) and (11.5.11), since inequalities here are not of substantive interest in the two-input case if some of both inputs are required to produce any positive output. λ is the short-run or operating marginal cost function, assumed given by Modigliani and Hohn.

The new center of interest is the Euler condition (11.5.12). Integrating this condition from t to $t + \theta$, where $0 \leq t + \theta \leq T$, gives

$$\int_t^{t+\theta} k \ dt - \lambda(t + \theta) + \lambda(t) \geq 0,$$

or

$$k\theta + \lambda(t) \geq \lambda(t + \theta). \tag{11.5.13}$$

The left side of (11.5.13) is the marginal cost of producing a unit at time t and holding it in inventory until time $t + \theta$. The right side of (11.5.13) is the marginal cost of producing a unit at $t + \theta$. Hence, (11.5.13) states that the marginal cost of producing a unit at any given time must not exceed the cost of producing it at an earlier time and holding it until the given time.

If the inequality in (11.5.13) holds over some interval $t_1 \leq t + \theta \leq t_2$, then in that interval it costs more to produce a unit at t and hold it until any subsequent time, than to produce the unit at the later time. Therefore, at any t in this interval, we should make $Y(t)$ as small as possible subject to the condition (11.5.8). If inventories are zero at the opening of the interval, that is, $H(t_1) = H(0) + Y(t_1) - S(t_1) = 0$, then the smallest we can make $Y(t)$ is $Y(t) = S(t) - H(0)$, and current sales are satisfied out of current production in the interval. If inventories are positive at the opening of the interval, that is, $H(t_1) = H(0) + Y(t_1) - S(t_1) > 0$, then we make $Y(t) = Y(t_1)$, scheduling a zero level of current production, until such time as the opening inventory is exhausted. Thereafter, the previous solution applies with current sales met out of current production. Of course, over any interval for which current production equals current sales requirements, that is, $\dot{Y}(t) = \dot{S}(t)$, the inventory part of the model disappears. The solutions for

$x_1{}^0(t)$, $X_2{}^0$, and $\lambda^0(t)$ are then obtained by simultaneously satisfying $\int_0^T (w_1 f_2/f_1)\, dt = W_2$, $\dot{S}(t) = f[x_1(t), X_2]$, and $\lambda(t) = w_1/f_1[x_1(t), X_2]$.

If the equality holds in (11.5.12) over some interval, the solutions $x_1{}^0(t)$, $X_2{}^0$, $\lambda^0(t)$, and $Y^0(t)$ are obtained by simultaneously satisfying (11.5.7)–(11.5.12). In obtaining these solutions, however, the latter conditions are separable in a most interesting way. Suppose, for simplicity, we assume the equality in (11.5.12) to hold over the entire planning horizon. By integrating (11.5.12), and evaluating the integration constant at $t = 0$ and $t = T$, we get $kt + \lambda(0) - \lambda(t) = k(t - T) + \lambda(T) - \lambda(t) = 0$, which defines marginal *production cost* as a (linear) function of time. Hence, insofar as the short-run marginal cost function depends upon time, this relationship is determined by the differential equation (11.5.12) *independently of sales requirements, $S(t)$, and the production function.* This is in sharp contrast to the no-inventory case in which $x_1{}^0(t)$ and $X_2{}^0$ are jointly determined by the dynamic marginal-rate-of-substitution condition $\int_0^T (w_1 f_2/f_1)\, dt = W_2$ and the technological constraint $\dot{Y}(t) = \dot{S}(t) = f[x_1(t), X_2]$. Only after $x_1{}^0(t)$ and $X_2{}^0$ are so determined do we obtain the equilibrium dynamic marginal cost function from $\lambda(t) = w_1/f_1[x_1(t), X_2]$. In the no-inventory case the dependence of marginal cost on time is obtained only after we know the optimal path of current input consumption, $x_1(t)$. But the moment we introduce inventories, fix sales requirements, and allow output to be a decision variable, the variation in marginal production costs with time is no longer due only to the marginal productivity conditions and the production function constraint. With inventories, production planning is constrained by the requirement that the marginal cost of producing a unit at any time be equal to the marginal cost of producing a unit at any earlier time and holding it to the given time. The consumption of current input over time, and therefore the marginal cost function over time, must conform to this condition. The structure of optimal production policy is altered thereby in a manner which may not be *prima facie* obvious.

Assuming the equality holds in (11.5.12), we can write the simultaneous conditions on $x_1(t)$, X_2, $\lambda(t)$, $Y(t)$, and $x_1(T)$, as follows:

$$k(t - T) + \frac{w_1}{f_1[x_1(T),X_2]} - \frac{w_1}{f_1[x_1(t),X_2]} = 0 \quad (11.5.14)$$

$$\int_0^T \frac{w_1 f_2[x_1(t),X_2]}{f_1[x_1(t),X_2]}\, dt = W_2 \quad (11.5.15)$$

$$Y(T) = \int_0^T f[x_1(t),X_2]\, dt = S(T) - H(0) \quad (11.5.16)$$

$$\lambda(t) = k(t - T) + \frac{w_1}{f_1[x_1(T),X_2]} \quad (11.5.17)$$

$$Y(t) = \int_0^t f[x_1(t),X_2]\, dt \quad (11.5.18)$$

Equations (11.5.14)–(11.5.16) determine jointly the variables $x_1^0(T)$ and X_2^0, and the extremal $x_1^0(t)$. Using the solutions X_2^0 and $x_1^0(T)$, we obtain $\lambda^0(t)$ as a function of t and all the parameters of (11.5.14)–(11.5.16), from (11.5.17). Finally, using $x_1^0(t)$ and X_2^0, we obtain $Y^0(t)$ from (11.5.18). The same procedure applies for any subinterval over which the equality holds in (11.5.12).

In comparing these results with those of the Modigliani-Hohn model the important thing to observe is the different role played by (11.5.12). In models of the Modigliani-Hohn type, the marginal cost function $\lambda = \lambda[\dot{Y}(t)]$ is a function of current output given *independently* of inventory and production planning considerations. Under such conditions (11.5.12) places a constraint on $\dot{Y}(t)$ only, whereas in our model, in which λ is dependent upon choice of technique, the inventory condition (11.5.12) places a constraint on both λ and $\dot{Y}(t)$.

PROFIT MAXIMIZATION UNDER DYNAMIC
DEMAND CONDITIONS

Any of the models of sections 2, 3, and 4 can be extended to cases in which a demand function over time is given instead of output requirements over time. The important new question to be considered in such models concerns the nature of price policy. Product price can be viewed as an extremal that is continuously variable over the planning interval. The problem then is to choose the capital input stock levels, the current input consumption paths, and the price path for the product.[21] Such a model assumes price policy, along with current input policy, is a short-run operating phenomenon. This extreme flexibility in price policy does not seem to be typical of most business practice. Apparently there is an implicit assumption on the part of price policymakers that attaches some "cost" to frequent price changes. In practice, price is therefore likely to be stable over considerable time periods. Much of the literature of oligopoly theory is concerned with rationalizing this phenomenon. In oligopolistic situations the cost of too-frequent price changes may appear in the form of expected price wars. Whatever may be the reason for such stable price phenomena, it is reasonable, within the framework of our analysis, to formulate the firm's pricing problem as that of choosing a price *level* over time rather than a price path. Price policy, like investment policy, becomes thereby a problem in "long-run" planning.

To illustrate these matters consider the two-input, finite-horizon case. We assume that demand at time t, $0 \leq t \leq T$, is a decreasing function of the price level P that is maintained over the T year planning interval. That is,

$$y = D(P,t). \qquad (11.5.19)$$

Total revenue at t is then

$$R = R(P,t) = PD(P,t). \qquad (11.5.20)$$

The expression for discounted annual profit over the interval

---

[21] See Miller, pp. 674–681, for an analysis of such a model and its comparison with the corresponding model in which output requirements are given. In view of Miller's fine discussion, we will not analyze the case of continuously variable price policy in detail.

is

$$\pi = \frac{r}{1 - e^{-rT}} \left\{ \int_0^T [R(P,t) - w_1 x_1(t)] e^{-rt} \, dt - W_2 X_2 \right\}.$$

$$(11.5.21)$$

Maximizing π with respect to the variables P and X_2, and using the technological condition $y(t) = f[x_1(t), X_2]$ gives

$$\int_0^T \left[\frac{\partial R(P,t)}{\partial P} - \frac{w_1}{f_1[x_1(t), X_2]} \frac{\partial D(P,t)}{\partial P} \right] e^{-rt} \, dt = 0, \quad (11.5.22)$$

$$\int_0^T \frac{w_1 f_2[x_1(t), X_2]}{f_1[x_1(t), X_2]} e^{-rt} \, dt - W_2 = 0. \quad (11.5.23)$$

The first term in equation (11.5.22), $\int_0^T (\partial R / \partial P) e^{-rt} \, dt$, is the present discounted value of the additional revenue stream resulting from an incremental decrease in the price level over the interval. In the second term of (11.5.22), w_1 / f_1 is the marginal cost of an additional increment in output at t, while $\partial D / \partial P$ is the additional output (sales) resulting from an incremental decrease in price. Therefore

$$\int_0^T (w_1 / f_1)(\partial D / \partial P) e^{-rt} \, dt$$

is the discounted present value of the additional operating cost stream resulting from an incremental decrease in price. Hence, equation (11.5.22) requires price to be lowered (or raised) until the last incremental decrease in price brings in an additional stream of revenue whose present value is just equal to the present value of the additional operating cost stream resulting from the increased sales. In contrast to the case where price policy is continuously variable, marginal revenue is not required to equal marginal operating cost at each instant over the planning interval. Equation (11.5.23) is, of course, the now familiar requirement that the last unit of physical capital installed produce discounted savings in current input just equal to the unit cost of capital.

It should be noted that the condition (11.5.23) is the same as condition (11.2.23) for optimal technique in the corresponding minimum cost model. Hence, cost minimization in such a model is separable from profit maximization. That is (11.5.23) or (11.2.23) together with the production function $y(t) = f[x_1(t), X_2]$, can be used to determine independently the optimum marginal operating cost function $\lambda = w_1/f_1$ appearing in the price policy condition (11.5.22).

6. Investment Demand and the "Acceleration Principle" [22]

One of the persistent interests of modern economic research has been the determinants of investment expenditure. It is therefore of some importance that we explore the investment implications of our theory. Specifically, it would be desirable if we could examine the received "marginal efficiency" and "accelerator" theories of investment from a microeconomic point of view. How and in what way do the interest rate and the rate of change in output requirements affect the investment behavior of the firm whose choice of production-investment technique over time is guided by cost minimization? Unfortunately, the discontinuous character of the investment process in the above models renders them somewhat unhandy for answering such questions. For example, in Fig. 11–3, investment in the first period is $I_1 = \Delta K_1 = W_2 X_{21}{}^0$, in the second is $I_2 = \Delta K_2 = W_2 X_{22}{}^0$, and in the kth is $I_k = \Delta K_k = W_2 X_{2k}{}^0$. All the parameters of (11.4.1) enter into the determination of $X_{2k}{}^0$ and therefore I_k.

To answer the above questions we will develop a continuous investment model that is somewhat simpler and more manageable than the previous models of this chapter. Our primary objective is to develop the Keynesian investment demand schedule and the acceleration principle from individual firm behavior under cost minimization.

Again we will consider a process requiring one current and one capital input. The capital input is assumed to require no upkeep and is replaced at fixed intervals every L years. Let $y(t)$ be the given output requirements at time t; $x_1(t)$, the rate of current input consumption at t; $X_2(t)$, the net stock

---

[22] See Smith, "Theory of Investment and Production," pp. 83–86.

of equipment at t; $P_2(t)$, the rate of equipment purchases at t; and $D_2(t) = P_2(t - L)$, the rate of equipment discards or replacements at t. If discarded equipment has no resale or salvage value, the expression for current account cost over an infinite horizon can be written

$$C = r \int_0^\infty \left[w_1 x_1(t) + W_2 P_2(t) \right] e^{-rt} \, dt. \qquad (11.6.1)$$

The objective is to minimize this cost function with respect to $x_1(t)$, $X_2(t)$, and $P_2(t)$, subject to an input-output constraint of the form

$$y(t) = f[x_1(t), X_2(t)] \qquad (11.6.2)$$

and the replacement identity

$$P_2(t) = \dot{X}_2(t) + P_2(t - L). \qquad (11.6.3)$$

It is assumed that $X_2(t)$ in (11.6.2) is continuously adjustable.[23] The identity states that total equipment purchases (gross investment) is equal to the net addition to the stock of capital (net investment, $\dot{X}_2 = dX_2/dt$) plus the quantity of discarded equipment (replacement investment). Since we must have $P_2(t) \geq 0$, it follows that $\dot{X}_2(t) \geq -P_2(t - L)$. Net disinvestment cannot proceed faster than the current stock is being discarded.

Substituting from (11.6.3) into (11.6.1), we obtain

$$C = r \int_0^\infty \left[w_1 x_1(t) + W_2 \dot{X}_2(t) + W_2 P_2(t - L) \right] e^{-rt} \, dt, \qquad (11.6.4)$$

which is to be minimized over $x_1(t)$ and $X_2(t)$ subject to (11.6.2). This problem is equivalent to the variational prob-

[23] This model has certain similarities to the Arrow, Beckman, and Karlin model. They assume constant operating cost up to "capacity," at which point cost becomes infinite. As stated before, I do not believe such a concept of output capacity is realistic. In the present model, as in the previous models, the form of the operating cost function grows out of technology and the decision process. The Arrow-Beckman-Karlin model further assumes that "capacity" creating capital can be expanded but never contracted. Our model introduces irreversibility in a weaker form by permitting disinvestment at a discard rate which is limited only by the purchase rate L years ago. I suppose assumptions are partly a matter of convenience and taste, and everyone is entitled to his own. Mine is a given equipment life. At the present writing I do not see how to solve the more general case.

lem of minimizing

$$\phi = r \int_0^\infty ([w_1 x_1(t) + W_2 \dot{X}_2(t) + W_2 P_2(t - L)]e^{-rt}$$
$$- \lambda \{f[x_1(t), X_2(t)] - y(t)\}) \, dt. \tag{11.6.5}$$

Necessary conditions for such a minimum are written [24]

$$\left. \begin{array}{l} w_1 e^{-rt} - \lambda f_1 = 0 \\ r W_2 e^{-rt} - \lambda f_2 \geq 0 \end{array} \right\} \quad \text{or} \quad \frac{w_1 e^{-rt}}{f_1} = \lambda \leq \frac{r W_2 e^{-rt}}{f_2}, \quad \begin{array}{l} (11.6.6) \\ (11.6.7) \end{array}$$

where λ is discounted marginal cost. In equation (11.6.7), if "$>$" holds in any interval $t_1 \leq t \leq t_2$, then in that interval $X_2(t)$ must be chosen as small as possible subject to the nonnegativity condition $P_2(t) = \dot{X}_2(t) + P_2(t - L) \geq 0$. Hence, in such an interval we will have

$$\dot{X}_2(t) = -P_2(t - L), \quad \text{or} \quad X_2(t) = X_2(t_1) - \int_{t_1}^t P_2(\tau - L) \, d\tau.$$

The expressions (11.6.2), (11.6.3), (11.6.6), and (11.6.7) provide four conditions on $x_1(t)$, $X_2(t)$, $P_2(t)$ and $\lambda(t)$. If a solution exists, it will be of the form

$$x_1(t) = h[y(t), w_1, r W_2] \tag{11.6.8}$$

$$X_2(t) = H[y(t), w_1, r W_2] \tag{11.6.9}$$

$$\lambda(t) = \lambda[y(t), e^{-rt}, w_1, r W_2] \tag{11.6.10}$$

$$P_2(t) \begin{cases} = H_y \dot{y} + P_2(t - L) & \text{if} \quad \lambda = \dfrac{r W_2 e^{-rt}}{f_2} \\[2ex] = \dot{X}_2(t) + P_2(t - L) = 0 & \text{if} \quad \lambda < \dfrac{r W_2 e^{-rt}}{f_2} \end{cases} \tag{11.6.11}$$

Figure 11–5 illustrates a possible solution path for $X_2(t)$. In the interval $t_1 \leq t \leq t_2$, the dotted segment representing $X_2(t_1) - \int_{t_1}^t P_2(\tau - L) \, d\tau$ replaces the lower hatched path,

---

[24] The problem is of the form $\min \int_{T_1}^{T_2} F(x, \dot{x}, y, \dot{y}, t) \, dt$, with solution

$$\partial F / \partial x - (d/dt)\left(\frac{\partial F}{\partial \dot{x}}\right) = 0 \quad \text{and} \quad \partial F / \partial y - (d/dt)\left(\frac{\partial F}{\partial \dot{y}}\right) = 0.$$

See C. Fox, *An Introduction to the Calculus of Variations*, pp. 62–63.

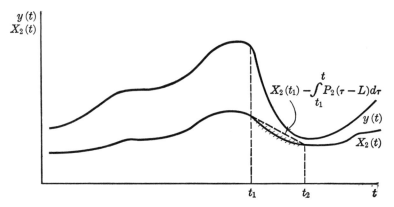

Fig. 11-5. The requirements path and an investment path.

the latter being in violation of the nonnegativity of total equipment purchases.

From (11.6.9), assuming an interior solution for $X_2(t)$, the Keynesian net investment demand function is

$$I_N(t) = W_2\dot{X}_2 = W_2H_y[y(t), w_1, rW_2]\dot{y}. \quad (11.6.12)$$

The level of net investment expenditures depends upon the prices of the current and capital inputs, the interest rate, and *both the level and the rate of change of output.* This result demonstrates the logical inseparability of "marginal efficiency" and "accelerator" determinants of investment expenditure. We must have $\dot{y} > 0$, that is, a rising rate of output requirements if net investment is to be positive. One interpretation that can be placed upon the aggregate investment demand schedule of Keynesian theory, $I = I(r)$, is that it assumes implicitly an underlying growth in output or an expectation of growth in output. Otherwise we have $I \leq 0$.

In solving for $P_2(t)$ and $P_2(t - L)$ from (11.6.11), note that the initial boundary conditions must be known. Specifically, we require knowledge of $P_2(t - L)$ for $0 \leq t \leq L$. For example, suppose $P_2(t - L) = 0$ for $0 \leq t < L$, with $P_2(t - L) = P_2{}^0$ when $t = L$. Now, letting gross investment at time t

be $I_G(t) = W_2P_2(t)$ and replacement investment be $I_R(t)$ $= W_2P_2(t - L)$, we can generate the firm's replacement and gross investment demand patterns as follows:

For

$$0 \leq t < L \quad , I_R(t) = W_2P_2(t - L) = 0, I_G(t) = I_N(t)$$
$$L \leq t < 2L \quad , I_R(t) = W_2P_2(t - L) = I_N(t - L),$$
$$I_G(t) = I_N(t) + I_N(t - L)$$

$$\cdot \qquad\qquad \cdot$$
$$\cdot \qquad\qquad \cdot$$
$$\cdot \qquad\qquad \cdot$$

$$kL \leq t < (k + 1)L, I_R(t) = W_2P_2(t - L) = I_N(t - L)$$
$$+ I_N(t - 2L) + \cdots + I_N(t - kL),$$
$$I_G(t) = I_N(t) + I_N(t - L) + I_N(t - 2L)$$
$$+ \cdots + I_N(t - kL).$$

To illustrate the above model and demonstrate the effect of returns to scale on the relationship between net investment and the level of output requirements, suppose the production function (11.6.2) has the Cobb-Douglas form

$$y(t) = A x_1{}^{\alpha}(t) X_2{}^{\beta}(t). \tag{11.6.13}$$

The marginal productivity conditions (11.6.6)–(11.6.7) are now

$$\frac{w_1 e^{-rt}}{\alpha A x_1{}^{\alpha-1}(t) X_2{}^{\beta}(t)} = \frac{r W_2 e^{-rt}}{\beta A x_1{}^{\alpha}(t) X_2{}^{\beta-1}(t)} = \lambda, \quad (11.6.14)$$

for an interior solution. From (11.6.13) and (11.6.14) we get the flow and stock input demand functions

$$x_1(t) = \left[\frac{w_1\beta}{rW_2\alpha}\right]^{-\frac{\beta}{\alpha+\beta}} \left[\frac{y(t)}{A}\right]^{\frac{1}{\alpha+\beta}}, \tag{11.6.15}$$

$$X_2(t) = \left[\frac{w_1\beta}{rW_2\alpha}\right]^{\frac{\alpha}{\alpha+\beta}} \left[\frac{y(t)}{A}\right]^{\frac{1}{\alpha+\beta}}. \tag{11.6.16}$$

These are the particular forms of h and H in (11.6.8) and (11.6.9) under the assumed technology. Marginal operating cost for this case is

$$\lambda(t) = \frac{w_1 e^{-rt}}{\alpha A} \left[\frac{rW_2\alpha}{w_1\beta} \right]^{\frac{\beta}{\alpha+\beta}} \left[\frac{y(t)}{A} \right]^{\frac{1}{\alpha+\beta} - 1}. \quad (11.6.17)$$

From (11.6.16) we can write the expression for net investment corresponding to (11.6.12) thus:

$$I_N(t) = \frac{W_2}{A(\alpha+\beta)} \left[\frac{w_1\beta}{rW_2\alpha} \right]^{\frac{\alpha}{\alpha+\beta}} \left[\frac{y(t)}{A} \right]^{\frac{1}{\alpha+\beta} - 1} \dot{y}(t). \quad (11.6.18)$$

Inspection of this equation reveals that optimal net investment is a decreasing function of the interest rate, an increasing or decreasing function of the output level, depending upon whether the process shows decreasing ($\alpha + \beta < 1$) or increasing ($\alpha + \beta > 1$) returns to scale, and an increasing (proportional) function of the rate of change in the level of output. Net investment expenditures are independent of the level of output only in the special case of constant returns to scale ($\alpha + \beta = 1$). If there is anything to the widely held view that most manufacturing processes exhibit increasing returns to scale, it could well mean that the aggregate investment demand function is a decreasing function of the level of output.

Appendix

Bibliography

Index

Appendix on the Kuhn-Tucker Conditions

This appendix is designed to supplement the text by providing an expository discussion of the Kuhn-Tucker generalization of classical marginalism.

1. Constrained Maximization

    a. Suppose a criterion variable such as profit, π, is a function of two "activity" or decision variables, that is, $\pi = F(x_1,x_2)$. Consider the problem of maximizing

$$\pi = F(x_1,x_2), \tag{A.1.1}$$

subject to the two functional constraints on our freedom to adjust x_1 and x_2

$$\left.\begin{array}{l} f_1(x_1,x_2) \leq 0, \\ f_2(x_1,x_2) \leq 0, \end{array}\right\} \tag{A.1.2}$$

where $x_1 \geq 0$, $x_2 \geq 0$.

  (i) The criterion function $\pi = F(x_1,x_2)$ might appear as indicated by the contours π_1, π_2, and π_3 in Fig. A–1.

 (ii) The function $f_1(x_1,x_2) = 0$, appearing in (A.1.2) above, defines a relation between x_1 and x_2 such as that indicated by the contour AB in Fig. A–1. For each x_1 there is a corresponding x_2 given by $f_1(x_1,x_2) = 0$. When the inequality sign is added to provide the condition $f_1(x_1,x_2) \leq 0$, this condition defines not only the set of points *on* the contour AB, but also all the points under this contour. Hence, the inequation $f_1(x_1,x_2) \leq 0$, together with the nonnegativity conditions, $x_1 \geq 0$, $x_2 \geq 0$, defines the *set* of points within and on the boundary of the region OAB in Fig. A–1.

 (iii) Similarly, the condition $f_2(x_1,x_2) \leq 0$ in (A.1.2) and the nonnegativity conditions define a point set bounded by OCD in Fig. A–1. Combining these conditions, $f_1(x_1,x_2)$

≤ 0, $f_2(x_1,x_2) \leq 0$, and $x_1 \geq 0$, $x_2 \geq 0$, defines the set of points in the shaded area of Fig. A–1. Any point such as P, Q, or R in this shaded area satisfies the conditions (A.1.2) above, and is said to be *feasible*, that is, it satisfies the constraints of the problem.

b. According to the Kuhn-Tucker theorem if a point such as (x_1^0, x_2^0) maximizes (A.1.1) subject to (A.1.2), then there

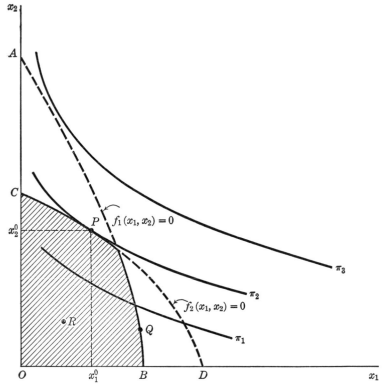

Fig. A–1. Illustration of Kuhn-Tucker Solution: Maximization, I.

must exist a set of two nonnegative numbers (one for each constraint) called *imputed values*, λ_1 and λ_2, such that the following necessary conditions are satisfied:

(i) The solution must be feasible, that is, it must be contained in the set of points defined by (A.1.2), or

$$f_1(x_1{}^0, x_2{}^0) \leqq 0,$$
$$f_2(x_1{}^0, x_2{}^0) \leqq 0,$$
$$x_1{}^0 \geqq 0,$$
$$x_2{}^0 \geqq 0.$$

Furthermore, if $f_1(x_1{}^0, x_2{}^0) < 0$, then $\lambda_1 = 0$, while

if $f_2(x_1{}^0, x_2{}^0) < 0$, then $\lambda_2 = 0$.

In words, if either constraint is satisfied with a surplus (the point is below the boundary AB or CD above), the associated imputed value is zero. [Note in Fig. A–1 that the point P satisfies the first constraint with a surplus, that is, $f_1(x_1{}^0, x_2{}^0) < 0$. Therefore $\lambda_1 = 0$. How about the point Q? The point R?]

(ii) We must have

$$\left.\begin{aligned} \frac{\partial F}{\partial x_1} - \lambda_1 \frac{\partial f_1}{\partial x_1} - \lambda_2 \frac{\partial f_2}{\partial x_1} &\leqq 0, \text{ if } < \text{ holds, } x_1 = 0 \\[2mm] \frac{\partial F}{\partial x_2} - \lambda_1 \frac{\partial f_1}{\partial x_2} - \lambda_2 \frac{\partial f_2}{\partial x_2} &\leqq 0, \text{ if } < \text{ holds, } x_2 = 0 \end{aligned}\right\} \quad \text{(A.1.3)}$$

How can we interpret the conditions (A.1.3)? The derivatives $\partial F/\partial x_1$ and $\partial F/\partial x_2$ are easy. They are just the marginal profitabilities of the activity levels x_1 and x_2. But how about $\lambda_1(\partial f_1/\partial x_1) + \lambda_2(\partial f_2/\partial x_1)$? This is called the *marginal imputed cost* of activity number 1. By way of explanation, consider the following: The constraint functions $f_1(x_1, x_2)$ and $f_2(x_1, x_2)$ provided a restraining or limiting influence on profit. In this sense they represent an implicit opportunity cost in terms of foregone profit. Now, what $\lambda_1(\partial f_1/\partial x_1)$ does is to measure the marginal (implicit or imputed or opportunity) cost of constraint number 1 in the performance of activity number 1. Similarly, $\lambda_2(\partial f_2/\partial x_1)$ measures the marginal imputed cost of constraint number 2. Think of it this way: You would be willing to pay, at most, λ_1 dollars per unit relaxation in constraint number 1, because of the increase in profits it would permit. Now it is clear why $\lambda_1 = 0$, if $f_1(x_1{}^0, x_2{}^0) < 0$. If a constraint is not binding, what would you pay to have it relaxed a bit? You would pay nothing. For example, if you have all the capital you can profitably employ and the bank offers to increase your ration of credit, you will refuse the added credit because it has zero marginal value to you.

Similarly, you would pay nothing to increase the "capacity" of a plant whose output could not be sold at a profit.

Since $\lambda_1(\partial f_1/\partial x_1) + \lambda_2(\partial f_2/\partial x_1)$ is the marginal imputed cost of activity number 1, the first condition in (A.1.3) requires, *in equilibrium*, the marginal profitability of activity number 1 to be no greater than the marginal imputed cost of that activity. If, for some x_1, the marginal profitability of activity number 1 exceeds its marginal imputed cost, that activity is expanded until the equality holds. If the marginal profitability of the activity is below its marginal imputed cost, it is contracted until the equality holds or until zero is reached, whichever occurs first. Hence, in equilibrium we must have either " $<$ " or " $=$ " holding in both conditions (A.1.3).

c. Illustrations:
(i) A possible solution is P shown in Fig. A–1. At this point we have $f_1(x_1^0,x_2^0) < 0$ and $f_2(x_1^0,x_2^0) = 0$. Hence, $\lambda_1 = 0$, $\lambda_2 > 0$, and the conditions (A.1.3) become

$$\frac{\partial F}{\partial x_1} - \lambda_2 \frac{\partial f_2}{\partial x_1} = 0, \ \frac{\partial F}{\partial x_2} - \lambda_2 \frac{\partial f_2}{\partial x_2} = 0,$$

or $\quad \lambda_2 = \dfrac{\partial F/\partial x_1}{\partial f_2/\partial x_1} = \dfrac{\partial F/\partial x_2}{\partial f_2/\partial x_2}.$

Note: You would pay nothing to have the constraint $f_1(x_1,x_2)$ removed because it is not binding. Hence, $\lambda_1 = 0$. However, maximization takes place on the constraint boundary $f_2(x_1,x_2) = 0$, and, therefore, you would pay $\lambda_2 > 0$ dollars per unit expansion in this restriction.

(ii) Another solution is illustrated by Q in Fig. A–2. Write the conditions!

(iii) Suppose the solution is at U in Fig. A–2. The corresponding conditions are

$$f_1(x_1,x_2) = 0, \quad \lambda_1 > 0$$
$$f_2(x_1,x_2) < 0, \quad \lambda_2 = 0$$

$$\frac{\partial F}{\partial x_1} - \lambda_1 \frac{\partial f_1}{\partial x_1} = 0, \quad x_1 > 0$$

$$\frac{\partial F}{\partial x_2} - \lambda_1 \frac{\partial f_1}{\partial x_2} \leq 0, \quad x_2 = 0$$

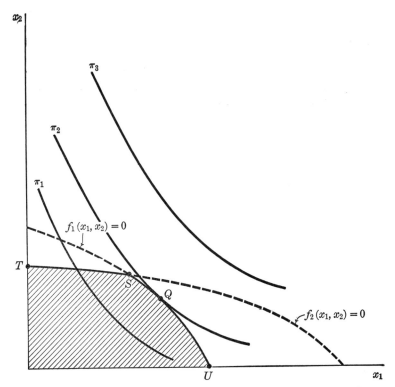

Fig. A-2. Illustration of Kuhn-Tucker Solution: Maximization, II.

The " = " sign in the last condition holds in the special case in which an isoprofit contour is just tangent to the constraint boundary at U. [Note that " < " here implies $x_2 = 0$, but the converse is false.] Write the conditions for a solution at T.

(iv) If the solution is at S, we have

$$f_1(x_1,x_2) = 0, \quad \lambda_1 \geq 0$$
$$f_2(x_1,x_2) = 0, \quad \lambda_2 \geq 0$$

$$\frac{\partial F}{\partial x_1} - \lambda_1 \frac{\partial f_1}{\partial x_1} - \lambda_2 \frac{\partial f_2}{\partial x_1} = 0, \quad x_1 > 0$$

$$\frac{\partial F}{\partial x_2} - \lambda_1 \frac{\partial f_1}{\partial x_2} - \lambda_2 \frac{\partial f_2}{\partial x_2} = 0, \quad x_2 > 0$$

giving four equations in x_1, x_2, λ_1, and λ_2. Both constraints may now carry a positive imputed cost.

d. In terms of the Lagrange formulation of the problem,

$$\phi = F(x_1,x_2) - \lambda_1[f_1(x_1,x_2)] - \lambda_2[f_2(x_1,x_2)]. \qquad \text{(A.1.4)}$$

Necessary conditions are obtained by setting the derivatives of this function equal to or less than 0. Thus,

$$\frac{\partial F}{\partial x_1} - \lambda_1 \frac{\partial f_1}{\partial x_1} - \lambda_2 \frac{\partial f_2}{\partial x_1} \leq 0, \quad \text{if} < \text{holds, } x_1 = 0,$$

$$\frac{\partial F}{\partial x_2} - \lambda_1 \frac{\partial f_1}{\partial x_2} - \lambda_2 \frac{\partial f_2}{\partial x_2} \leq 0, \quad \text{if} < \text{holds, } x_2 = 0,$$

$$f_1(x_1,x_2) \leq 0, \quad \text{if} < \text{holds, } \lambda_1 = 0,$$
$$f_2(x_1,x_2) \leq 0, \quad \text{if} < \text{holds, } \lambda_2 = 0.$$

2. Constrained Minimization

The corresponding minimum problem is

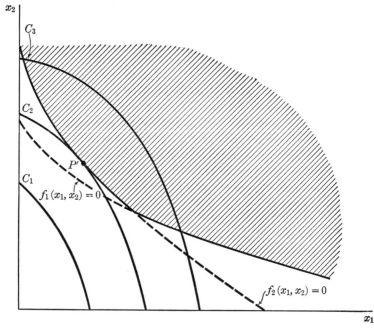

Fig. A-3. Illustration of Kuhn-Tucker Solution: Minimization, III.

minimize

$$C = F(x_1, x_2) \qquad \text{(A.2.1)}$$

subject to

$$\left.\begin{array}{l} f_1(x_1, x_2) \geq 0 \\ f_2(x_1, x_2) \geq 0 \end{array}\right\} \qquad \text{(A.2.2)}$$

where x_1, $x_2 \geq 0$.

If x_1^0, x_2^0 is a solution, there must exist λ_1, λ_2 such that

(i) $f_1(x_1^0, x_2^0) \geq 0$, if > holds, $\lambda_1 = 0$,

$f_2(x_1^0, x_2^0) \geq 0$, if > holds, $\lambda_2 = 0$,

$x_1^0 \geq 0$, $x_2^0 \geq 0$.

(ii) $\dfrac{\partial F}{\partial x_1} - \lambda_1 \dfrac{\partial f_1}{\partial x_1} - \lambda_2 \dfrac{\partial f_2}{\partial x_1} \geq 0$, if > holds, $x_1 = 0$,

$\dfrac{\partial F}{\partial x_2} - \lambda_1 \dfrac{\partial f_2}{\partial x_2} - \lambda_2 \dfrac{\partial f_2}{\partial x_2} \geq 0$, if > holds, $x_2 = 0$.

An illustrative solution is at P' in Fig. A–3.

BIBLIOGRAPHY

Alchian, Armen A., Economic Replacement Policy, R-224 (RAND Corporation), (Santa Monica, California: RAND Corporation, April 1952).

Alexander, K. J. W. and John Spraos, "Shift Working: An Application of the Theory of the Firm," *Quarterly Journal of Economics*, 70:603–612 (November 1956).

Alford, L. P., "Representative Policies and Methods for Purchasing New Equipment," *Manufacturing Industries*, 14:277–282 (October 1927).

——— "Can We Afford New Equipment?" *Manufacturing Industries*, 15:27–30 (January 1928).

——— "How Is Cost of New Manufacturing Equipment Charged to Product?" *Manufacturing Industries*, 15:107–110 (February 1928).

Allen, R. G. D., *Mathematical Economics* (London: Macmillan, 1956).

Arrow, Kenneth, Samuel Karlin, and Herbert Scarf, *Studies in the Mathematical Theory of Inventory and Production* (Stanford, California: Stanford University Press, 1958).

Baily, H. P., "Profitable Replacement in an 'Average Lot' Plant," *American Machinist*, 75:836–853 (December 1931).

Bellman, Richard, "Equipment Replacement Policy," *Journal of the Society for Industrial and Applied Mathematics*, 3:133–136 (September 1955).

Bonilla, Charles F., "Design of Multiple-Effect Evaporators for Minimum Area or Minimum Cost," *American Institute of Chemical Engineers — Transactions*, 41:529–537 (February 1945).

Bowman, Edward H. and Robert B. Fetter, *Analyses of Industrial Operations* (Homewood, Illinois: Richard D. Irwin, 1959).

Brems, Hans, *Output, Employment, Capital, and Growth* (New York: Harper, 1959).

Bullinger, Clarence E., *Engineering Economic Analysis* (New York: McGraw-Hill, 1942).

Carlson, Sune, *A Study on the Pure Theory of Production* (New York: Kelly and Millman, 1956).

Chenery, Hollis B., "Engineering Production Functions," *Quarterly Journal of Economics*, 63:507–531 (November 1949).

——— "Overcapacity and the Acceleration Principle," *Econometrica*, 20:1–28 (January 1952).

Churchman, C. West, Russell L. Ackoff, and E. Leonard Arnoff, *Introduction to Operations Research* (New York: Wiley, 1957).

Clower, R. W., "Business Investment and the Theory of Price," *Proceedings of the Twenty-Eighth Annual Conference of the Western Economic Association* (1953), pp. 22–24.

Clower, R. W., "An Investigation into the Dynamics of Investment," *American Economic Review*, 44:64–81 (March 1954).

―――― "Productivity, Thrift and the Rate of Interest," *Economic Journal*, 64:107–115 (March 1954).

Davidson, Ralph K., Vernon L. Smith, and Jay W. Wiley, *Economics: An Analytical Approach* (Homewood, Illinois: Richard D. Irwin, 1958).

Dorfman, Robert, Paul A. Samuelson, and Robert M. Solow, *Linear Programming and Economic Analysis* (New York: McGraw-Hill, 1958).

Dreyfus, Stuart E., A Generalized Equipment Replacement Study, P–1039 (RAND Corporation), (Santa Monica, California: RAND Corporation, March 1957).

Encyclopedia of Chemical Technology (New York: Interscience Publishers, 1957).

Fish, J. C. L., *Engineering Economics* (New York: McGraw-Hill, 1915).

Fox, Charles, *An Introduction to the Calculus of Variations* (London: Oxford University Press, 1950).

Funk, N. E., and F. C. Ralston, "Boiler-Plant Economics," *American Society of Mechanical Engineers — Transactions*, 45:607–641 (1923).

Gabor, André and I. F. Pearce, "The Place of Money Capital in the Theory of Production," *Quarterly Journal of Economics*, 72:537–557 (November 1958).

Gaylord, William W., "Don't Expect All New Equipment to Pay Out in Three Years," *Factory Management and Maintenance*, 98:52 (February 1940).

Getman, Frederick H. and Farrington Daniels, *Outlines of Physical Chemistry*, 7th ed. (New York: John Wiley, 1943).

Glasstone, Samuel, *The Elements of Physical Chemistry* (New York: D. Van Nostrand, 1946).

Grant, Eugene L., *Principles of Engineering Economy*, 3rd ed. (New York: Ronald Press, 1950).

Harbert, W. D., "Economic Process Operations," *Industrial and Engineering Chemistry*, 39:940–944 (August 1947).

―――― "Economic Distillation Design," *Petroleum Refiner*, 27:106–109 (April 1948).

Hart, Albert G., *Anticipations, Uncertainty, and Dynamic Planning, Studies in Business Administration*, 11:1–98 (October 1940), (Chicago: University of Chicago Press, 1940).

Heady, Earl O., "An Econometric Investigation of the Technology of Agricultural Production Functions," *Econometrica*, 25:249–268 (April 1957).

Hirshleifer, J., "On the Theory of Optimal Investment Decision," *Journal of Political Economy*, 66:329–352 (August 1958).

Holt, Charles C., Franco Modigliani, and John F. Muth, "Derivation of a Linear Decision Rule for Production and Employment," *Management Science*, 2:159–177 (January 1956).

Horwich, George, "Money, Prices and the Theory of Interest Determination," *Economic Journal*, 67:625–643 (December 1957).

——— "Open Market Operations, the Rate of Interest, and the Price Level," unpublished doctoral thesis, March 1954, University of Chicago.

Hotelling, Harold, "A General Mathematical Theory of Depreciation," *Journal of the American Statistical Association*, 20:340–353 (September 1925).

Johnson, H. H. and M. S. Umbenhauer, "Station Loading Slide Rule," *Power*, 82:62–64 (November 1938).

——— "An Effective Load Dividing Device," *Edison Electric Institute Bulletin*, 7:385–389 (August 1939).

Kalecki, Michal, "The Principle of Increasing Risk," *Essays in the Theory of Economic Fluctuations* (London: Allen and Unwin, 1939).

Kent, Robert T., *Kent's Mechanical Engineers' Handbook*, 11th ed. (New York: John Wiley, 1936).

Knowlton, Archer E., *Standard Handbook for Electrical Engineers*, 8th ed. (New York: McGraw-Hill, 1949).

Kuhn, H. W., and A. W. Tucker, "Nonlinear Programming," in U. Neyman (ed.), *Proceedings of the Second Berkeley Symposium on Mathematical Statistics and Probability* (Berkeley: University of California Press, 1951).

Lange, Oscar, "The Place of Interest in the Theory of Production," *Review of Economic Studies*, 3:159–192 (June 1936).

Lehn, H. C., "An Analysis of Gas Pipeline Economics," *American Society of Mechanical Engineers — Transactions*, 65:445–460 (July 1943).

Leontief, Wassily W., "Multiple-Plant Firms: Comment," *Quarterly Journal of Economics*, 61:650–651 (August 1947).

——— "Introduction to a Theory of the Internal Structure of Functional Relationships," *Econometrica*, 15:361–373 (October 1947).

——— *Studies in the Structure of the American Economy* (New York: Oxford University Press, 1953).

Levine, R. A. and R. B. Rainey, "Random Variations and Sampling Models in Production Economics," *Journal of Political Economy*, 68:219–231 (June 1960).

Leyes, Charles E. and Donald F. Othmer, "Continuous Esterification of Butanol and Acetic Acid, Kinetic and Distillation Considerations," *American Institute of Chemical Engineers — Transactions*, 41:157–196 (April 1945).

——— "Esterification of Butanol and Acetic Acid," *Industrial and Engineering Chemistry*, 37:968–977 (October 1945).

Linton, D. S., "Diversified Replacement in a Small Plant," *American Machinist*, 75:946–953 (December 1931).

Lovell, Alfred H., *Generating Stations* (New York: McGraw-Hill, 1951).

Lutz, Friedrich and Vera Lutz, *The Theory of Investment of the Firm* (Princeton: Princeton University Press, 1951).

McMillan, L. B., "Heat Transfer Through Insulation in the Moderate and High Temperature Fields: A Statement of Existing Data," *American Society of Mechanical Engineers — Transactions*, 48:1269–1317 (1926).

——— "Heat-Insulation Practice in the Modern Steam-Generating Plant," *Mechanical Engineering*, 51:349–354 (May 1929).

Makower, H. and William J. Baumol, "The Analogy Between Producer and Consumer Equilibrium Analysis," *Economica*, 17:63–80 (February 1950).

Manne, Alan S., *Scheduling of Petroleum Refinery Operations* (Cambridge: Harvard University Press, 1956).

MAPI Replacement Manual (Chicago: Machinery and Allied Products Institute, 1950).

Miller, Roger F., "A Note on the Theory of Investment and Production," *Quarterly Journal of Economics*, 73:672–681 (November 1959).

Modigliani, Franco and Franz E. Hohn, "Production Planning Over Time and the Nature of the Expectation and Planning Horizon," *Econometrica*, 23:46–66 (January 1955).

Morin, François, "Note on an Inventory Problem," *Econometrica*, 23:447–450 (October 1955).

Neyman, Jerzy (ed.), *Proceedings of the Second Berkeley Symposium on Mathematical Statistics and Probability* (Berkeley: University of California Press, 1951).

Patinkin, Don, "Multiple-Plant Firms, Cartels, and Imperfect Competition," *Quarterly Journal of Economics*, 61:173–205 (February 1947).

——— "Note on the Allocation of Output," *Quarterly Journal of Economics*, 61:651–657 (August 1947).

Preinreich, Gabriel A. D., "The Economic Life of Industrial Equipment," *Econometrica*, 8:12–44 (January 1940).

Richards, E. M., "To Buy or Not to Buy Equipment," *Factory Management and Maintenance*, 91:499–500 (December 1933).

Samuelson, Paul A., *Foundations of Economic Analysis* (Cambridge: Harvard University Press, 1948).

——— "Wages and Interest: A Modern Dissection of Marxian Economic Models," *American Economic Review*, 47[2]:884–912 (December 1957).

Schweyer, Herbert E., *Process Engineering Economics* (New York: McGraw-Hill, 1955).

Simons, Henry C., *Economics 201 Syllabus*, University of Chicago Book Store, 1944.

Smith, Vernon L., "Investment Theory and the Theory of Cost and Production: A Synthesis with Applications," multilithographed paper (Lafayette, Indiana: Purdue University, May 1956).

——— "Engineering Data and Statistical Techniques in the Analysis of Production and Technological Change: Fuel Requirements of the Trucking Industry," *Econometrica*, 25:281–301 (April 1957).

—— "Economic Equipment Policies; An Evaluation," *Management Science*, 4:20–37 (October 1957).

—— "The Theory of Investment and Production," *Quarterly Journal of Economics*, 73:61–87 (February 1959).

—— "Problems in Production-Investment Planning Over Time," *International Economic Review*, 1:198–216 (September 1960).

Steinberg, Max J. and Theodore H. Smith, *Economy Loading of Power Plants and Electric Systems* (New York: John Wiley, 1943).

Tarboux, J. G., "Most Economical Conductor," *Electrical World*, 93:591–594 (March, 1929).

Taylor, James S., "A Statistical Theory of Depreciation," *Journal of the American Statistical Association*, 18:1010–1023 (December 1923).

Terborgh, George, *Dynamic Equipment Policy* (New York: McGraw-Hill, 1949).

Thomson, William (Lord Kelvin), "On the Economy of Metal in Conductors of Electricity," *Report of the British Association for the Advancement of Science*, pp. 526–528 (London: John Murray, 1882).

—— "On the Sources of Energy in Nature Available to Man for the Production of Mechanical Effect," *Report of the British Association for the Advancement of Science*, pp. 513–518 (London: John Murray, 1882).

Thornton, Brian M., "A Method of Loading Boilers for Maximum Fuel Economy," *Engineering*, 128:796–797 (December 1929).

Tyler, Chaplin, *Chemical Engineering Economics*, 3rd ed. (New York: McGraw-Hill, 1948).

Waddell, John A. L., *Economics of Bridgework* (New York: John Wiley, 1921).

Walker, William H., Warren K. Lewis, William H. McAdams, and Edwin R. Gilliland, *Principles of Chemical Engineering*, 3rd ed. (New York: McGraw-Hill, 1937).

Walras, Leon, *Elements of Pure Economics*, trans. William Jaffe (Homewood, Illinois: Richard D. Irwin, 1954).

Weaver, J. R., "Determining the When and Why of Machine Tool Replacement," *American Machinist*, 72:1013–1015 (June 1930).

Wellington, A. M., *The Economic Theory of the Location of Railways* (New York: John Wiley, 1887).

Westfield, Fred M., "Marginal Analysis, Multi-Plant Firms, and Business Practice: An Example," *Quarterly Journal of Economics*, 69:253–268 (May 1955).

Whitin, T. M. and M. H. Peston, "Random Variations, Risk, and Returns to Scale," *Quarterly Journal of Economics*, 68:603–612 (November 1954).

Wicksell, Knut, *Lectures on Political Economy*, Vol. I (London: Routledge and Kegan Paul, 1934).

Wicksteed, Philip H., *An Essay on the Co-ordination of the Laws of Distribution* (London: Macmillan, 1894).

Name Index

Subject Index